Palgrave Macmillan Studies in Banking and Financial Institutions

Series Editor: **Professor Philip Molyneux**

The Palgrave Macmillan Studies in Banking and Financial Institutions are international in orientation and include studies of banking within particular countries or regions, and studies of particular themes such as Corporate Banking, Risk Management, Mergers and Acquisitions, etc. The books' focus is on research and practice, and they include up-to-date and innovative studies on contemporary topics in banking that will have global impact and influence.

Titles include:

Steffen E. Andersen
THE EVOLUTION OF NORDIC FINANCE

Seth Apati
THE NIGERIAN BANKING SECTOR REFORMS
Power and Politics

Roberto Bottiglia, Elisabetta Gualandri and Gian Nereo Mazzocco (*editors*)
CONSOLIDATION IN THE EUROPEAN FINANCIAL INDUSTRY

Dimitris N. Chorafas
BASEL III, THE DEVIL AND GLOBAL BANKING

Dimitris N. Chorafas
CAPITALISM WITHOUT CAPITAL

Dimitris N. Chorafas
SOVEREIGN DEBT CRISIS
The New Normal and the Newly Poor

Violaine Cousin
BANKING IN CHINA

Vincenzo D'Apice and Giovanni Ferri
FINANCIAL INSTABILITY
Toolkit for Interpreting Boom and Bust Cycles

Peter Falush and Robert L. Carter OBE
THE BRITISH INSURANCE INDUSTRY SINCE 1900
The Era of Transformation

Franco Fiordelisi and Ornella Ricci (*editors*)
BANCASSURANCE IN EUROPE
Past, Present and Future

Franco Fiordelisi, Philip Molyneux and Daniele Previati (*editors*)
NEW ISSUES IN FINANCIAL AND CREDIT MARKETS

Franco Fiordelisi, Philip Molyneux and Daniele Previati (*editors*)
NEW ISSUES IN FINANCIAL INSTITUTIONS MANAGEMENT

Kim Hawtrey
AFFORDABLE HOUSING FINANCE

Jill M. Hendrickson
REGULATION AND INSTABILITY IN U.S. COMMERCIAL BANKING
A History of Crises

Alexandros-Andreas Kyrtsis (*editor*)
FINANCIAL MARKETS AND ORGANIZATIONAL TECHNOLOGIES
System Architectures, Practices and Risks in the Era of Deregulation

Paola Leone and Gianfranco A. Vento (*editors*)
CREDIT GUARANTEE INSTITUTIONS AND SME FINANCE

Caterina Lucarelli and Gianni Brighetti (*editors*)
RISK TOLERANCE IN FINANCIAL DECISION MAKING

Roman Matousek (*editor*)
MONEY, BANKING AND FINANCIAL MARKETS IN CENTRAL AND EASTERN EUROPE
20 Years of Transition

Philip Molyneux (*editor*)
BANK PERFORMANCE, RISK AND FIRM FINANCING

Philip Molyneux (*editor*)
BANK STRATEGY, GOVERNANCE AND RATINGS

Imad A. Moosa
THE MYTH OF TOO BIG TO FAIL

Simon Mouatt and Carl Adams (*editors*)
CORPORATE AND SOCIAL TRANSFORMATION OF MONEY AND BANKING
Breaking the Serfdom

Victor Murinde (*editor*)
BANK REGULATORY REFORMS IN AFRICA

Anders Ögren (*editor*)
THE SWEDISH FINANCIAL REVOLUTION

Özlem Olgu
EUROPEAN BANKING
Enlargement, Structural Changes and Recent Developments

Daniela Pîrvu
CORPORATE INCOME TAX HARMONIZATION IN THE EUROPEAN UNION

Ramkishen S. Rajan
EMERGING ASIA
Essays on Crises, Capital Flows, FDI and Exchange Rate

Allesandro Roselli
FINANCIAL STRUCTURES AND REGULATION: A COMPARISON OF CRISES IN THE UK, USA AND ITALY

Yasushi Suzuki
JAPAN'S FINANCIAL SLUMP
Collapse of the Monitoring System under Institutional and Transition Failures

Ruth Wandhöfer
EU PAYMENTS INTEGRATION
The Tale of SEPA, PSD and Other Milestones Along the Road

The full list of titles available is on the website:
www.palgrave.com/finance/sbfi.asp

Palgrave Macmillan Studies in Banking and Financial Institutions
Series Standing Order ISBN 978–1–403–94872–4
(*outside North America only*)

You can receive future titles in this series as they are published by placing a standing order. Please contact your bookseller or, in case of difficulty, write to us at the address below with your name and address, the title of the series and the ISBN quoted above.

Customer Services Department, Macmillan Distribution Ltd, Houndmills, Basingstoke, Hampshire RG21 6XS, England

---

Corporate Income Tax Harmonization in the European Union

Daniela Pîrvu
Dean of the Faculty of Economics, University of Pitesti, Romania

palgrave
macmillan

First published 2012 by
PALGRAVE MACMILLAN

Palgrave Macmillan in the UK is an imprint of Macmillan Publishers Limited, registered in England, company number 785998, of Houndmills, Basingstoke, Hampshire RG21 6XS.

Palgrave Macmillan in the US is a division of St Martin's Press LLC, 175 Fifth Avenue, New York, NY 10010.

Palgrave Macmillan is the global academic imprint of the above companies and has companies and representatives throughout the world.

Palgrave® and Macmillan® are registered trademarks in the United States, the United Kingdom, Europe and other countries.

ISBN 978–1–137–00090–3

This book is printed on paper suitable for recycling and made from fully managed and sustained forest sources. Logging, pulping and manufacturing processes are expected to conform to the environmental regulations of the country of origin.

A catalogue record for this book is available from the British Library.

A catalog record for this book is available from the Library of Congress.

10 9 8 7 6 5 4 3 2 1
21 20 19 18 17 16 15 14 13 12

Printed and bound in Great Britain by
CPI Antony Rowe, Chippenham and Eastbourne

Contents

Figures

Tables

Appendices

Acknowledgements

Thanks to the following individuals without whose contributions and support this book would not have been written: Professor Gheorghe Matei, my husband Cristi, and the staff of Palgrave Macmillan.

Introduction

The elaboration of the fiscal policy of a state is a complex procedure that should take account of many issues. In this sense, fiscal policy may seek to consolidate public finances, to achieve and maintain macroeconomic balance, to stimulate economic development and so on. Taxes and other fiscal levies can influence phases of social reproduction, depending on specific public interests. Fiscal policy is an important component of economic policy, and European Union (EU) member governments' fiscal decisions can generate effects not only at national level but also at community level. The existence of a coherent network of multilateral tax agreements, designed to mitigate the differences between the tax systems of different member states, can eliminate the risk of distortions in intra-trade flows. However, within the context of removing barriers to capital flows, this form of tax coordination cannot meet the need of ensuring a fair and efficient allocation of resources at EU level.

The mobility of some factors of production creates the conditions for using taxes as leverage to attract mobile tax bases. In this context, public authorities in different regions or countries are encouraged to reduce the level of taxation on certain mobile factors of production, thereby becoming involved in a "tax competition". Since there is a market within the EU that ensures the free movement of goods, services, capital and labour, tax competition can occur in the case of taxes on goods and services, and on corporate and personal income taxes. To eliminate distortions generated by taxes on goods and services, EU member states have adopted a number of measures to harmonize these taxes since the early 1970s. Currently, the progress made towards indirect tax harmonization is significant, but for other categories of taxes the issues around tax trim are considerably diversified. The manifestation of the phenomenon of tax competition (particularly in terms of capital and corporate income taxes) was the starting point of the debate on corporate income tax harmonization. Economists are very interested in the issue of tax harmonization within the EU. Research has focused on indirect tax harmonization, since the application of common rules in the field of indirect tax and sustained efforts by the European Commission to improve the legislative framework have provided a favourable environment for study.

In the field of direct taxation, harmonization has proved to be a difficult process, punctuated by lengthy negotiations between the European Commission and EU member states. Important progress has been made regarding the taxation of companies engaged in cross-border activities, but the existing legislative rules are insufficient to solve the many potential problems related to the proper and efficient functioning of the Single Market.

In this context, several models for harmonizing corporate income taxes in the EU were proposed. The effects of these models were estimated using quantitative and qualitative analyses.

Since the European Commission published "Proposal for a Directive on the Common Consolidated Corporate Tax Base" (CCCTB) on 16 March 2011 (with a delay of three years from the programme undertaken in 2004), one can say that we are facing a key moment in the future evolution of taxation in the EU member states, which will have a direct impact on European citizens. The acceptance or rejection of the proposal will mean either the triumph of the European Commission's political will to promote a European identity on the international scene or, on the contrary, the increase of euroscepticism within the EU.

In point form, the objectives of this proposal are to:

- define the concepts of tax harmonization and coordination, since in many cases a clear conceptual distinction is not made and sometimes the two notions are used incorrectly;
- reveal the arguments for tax harmonization in the EU in order to preface European Commission initiatives in the field of tax harmonization and describe the current stage of this process, in terms of direct and indirect taxation;
- expose the main items of tax harmonization within the EU and subject them to critical examination in terms of how they respond to the Single Market's current and long-term needs in general, and in particular to the needs of the individual member states;
- identify the main objectives of the harmonization of corporate income tax and assess their feasibility based on an analysis of the

evolution of corporate income tax rates and differences among the corporate tax bases of the 27 EU member states;
- analyse the most important stages of corporate income tax harmonization in the EU from an economic and political perspective;
- expose the models of corporate income tax harmonization proposed by the European Commission and subject them to examination in terms of their opportunities and limitations;
- investigate the positions of some politicians and representatives of the business environment regarding corporate tax harmonization, in order to identify those models that are likely to be implemented in the future in the EU;
- expose the methodological and technical issues involved in the consolidation of the tax base of corporate groups operating within the EU and apportioning their tax base between different tax jurisdictions;
- achieve an incursion into the literature to identify the key research directions on the effects of corporate income tax harmonization/coordination;
- expose and analyse the results of simulations regarding the introduction of harmonized rules in corporate taxation.

Tax harmonization within the EU does not mean a common policy in the field of taxation, but the adjustment of national fiscal policies as necessary for the proper functioning of the Single Market. Tax harmonization can be achieved spontaneously (through market forces), by the actions of European institutions (coordination of tax policies, harmonization of tax laws, etc.) or by the actions of the European Court of Justice (prohibiting certain national tax rules that violate EU rules).

Even if tax harmonization through the actions of European institutions generates a limitation on national sovereignty in terms of taxes for EU member states, these actions are a necessary condition for the creation of an effectively functioning Single Market. According to the official position of EU bodies, full harmonization of the member states' tax systems is not necessary, in order to achieve common goals of economic and social policy. Different levels of economic development within member states and EU citizens' varying preferences for particular social measures require the existence of various tax structures. However, these structures should not create obstacles to the free movement of goods, services and factors of production across the Single Market or distort the competition. In this context, EU member states accepted and implemented a common law in the field of indirect taxes. Although member states have, in principle, the freedom to create their own tax systems, this freedom is conditioned by the priorities of the founding treaties of the EU. Thus, member states cannot introduce tax provisions that restrict free movement within the Single Market or discriminatory tax provisions that may generate less favourable treatment of persons, property or investments from other member states. Sometimes, restrictions regarding the freedom of movement within the Single Market may occur due to differences in national tax systems. Therefore, some rules to harmonize member states' tax legislations, including the corporate tax field, are absolutely necessary.

Currently, the approach regarding corporate income tax harmonization is an important subject of debate on the agenda of the European Commission and among experts. The extreme diversity of approaches is a telling indicator of the complexity of the problems that prevent the formulation – even in theory and independent of political considerations – of some widely shared solutions. It is interesting to note that, until the late 1980s, the European Commission used the term "harmonization" to define the process of approximating national regulations in the field of corporate income tax. Currently, the European Commission uses more careful language; often, the term "tax coordination" is used.

The coordination of tax systems for companies engaged in cross-border activities in the EU recorded significant progress in the early 1990s by adopting the following directivies: "Cross-border mergers directive", "Parent/subsidiary directive", "Arbitration convention", "Directive on taxation of savings income in the form of interest payments" and "Directive on a common system of taxation applicable to interest and royalty payments between associated companies of different Member States". However, these directives have not been able to properly regulate corporate taxation and to solve all the problems faced by both member states and companies operating in several countries.

Recent guidelines towards a common corporate tax policy start from a general goal – to simplify and streamline tax systems to ensure a better functioning of the Single Market – and go on to include specific and operational objectives such as: reducing compliance/administrative costs, facilitating expansion of cross-border activities in the EU and minimizing the distortions caused by national differences in terms of investment and tax bases.

According to the EU Treaty, member states have full autonomy in the field of direct taxation. This autonomy can be limited only if national taxes are not compatible with EU law. In principle, national tax legislation should not create obstacles to cross-border transactions. In reality, the existence of 27 national corporate income tax systems is an obstacle to the proper functioning of the Single Market. The main difficulties caused by the absence of some common corporate taxation rules include: costs incurred by having to know about the tax legislation in each member state, monitoring the transfer pricing, the risk of double taxation, the general inability to offset losses against profits, and the possibility of transferring the tax base from high tax countries to low tax countries.

On the other hand, tax competition in the EU could in the near future grow to become a phenomenon with far more important implications, because the movement of the factors of production – especially the movement of capital – will become much easier on the global market. The most competitive countries will have an advantage expressed in total revenues and a higher growth rate. Under these conditions, divergences between member states will intensify, increasing the controversies about the limits of national sovereignty in the field of direct taxation, and especially in the field of corporate income tax.

Even if the tax regime is not the only factor that determines the decisions of foreign capital relocation, reducing corporate tax rates in some new member states has increased the attractiveness of these countries for foreign investors. Under these conditions, other member states have announced and implemented significant reductions in their tax rates, accusing the new States that they have initiated competition in the area of tax with long-term adverse consequences. Also, tax rates are not an indicator of the corporate tax burden. All aspects regarding the ways of determining taxable income (deductions, reductions, tax credits and exemptions) must be considered.

To remove the obstacles arising from the existence of 27 different tax systems in the EU, two systems of corporate income tax harmonization were confirmed to have advantages: Home State Taxation and Common Consolidated Corporate Tax Base (CCCTB). These two projects were promoted by the European Commission and were supported by some EU member states, the European Parliament, the Economic and Social Committee and some representatives of the European business community.

The CCCTB is an ambitious European Commission project. The technical discussions for this project were launched in September 2004, when a working group was formed in order to assist the European Commission to prepare a legislative proposal in this regard. The common base involves establishing a single tax base for companies with cross-border activities, and consolidation means that the establishment of taxable profit should be made in one state (the country of the parent company).

In order to assess the effects of the introduction of corporate income tax harmonization/coordination measures in the EU, numerous studies were conducted by independent experts or specialized services of the European Commission (or at the request of the European Commission). The attention of the experts was mainly focused on an estimation of the economic impact of corporate income tax harmonization/coordination. For this purpose, the CETAX model, CORTAX model and the "European Tax Analyzer" model were used. The most important concern of specialists in this field was aimed at the localization of changes in gross domestic product (GDP), welfare and tax revenues. All the results of the simulations showed a reduction in tax revenues in the EU as a whole. The reduction is not uniform for all member states: while some countries will achieve gains in GDP, welfare or tax revenues, others will suffer losses. On the other hand, a reduction in tax revenues is usually accompanied by an increase in welfare due to the effects of increased investment as a result of improvements in the tax environment (the simplification of operations for the determination of taxable corporate income, the possibility of comparing the corporate tax burden in different member states, etc.). These divergent effects generated among experts a current of ideas, according to which, at least in a first step, enhanced cooperation between groups of member states in the field of corporate taxation would be appropriate. Given the good results of the simulation of enhanced cooperation, and the opposition of some member states to the adoption of a directive on the CCCTB, it seems that the harmonization of the tax base will be initially done by this method.

In the current economic and political context, differences and incompatibilities between corporate income tax systems in the EU distort investment decisions and give rise to disputes between taxpayers and tax authorities, so that corporate income tax coordination is a fair and appropriate approach for the EU to take. The proposal for a directive on the introduction of a CCCTB is a first step towards solving the problems caused by the existence of 27 different tax systems (which are often incompatible), but the final form of this proposal should be improved to limit the negative impact of some distribution factors (payroll and sales at destination) on tax revenues in the less economically developed member states.

Chapter 1 of this book examines particular tax harmonization issues within the EU. Thus, the distinction between the concepts of tax harmonization and tax coordination is made, the legal basis of tax harmonization is presented and the main reasons for tax harmonization in the EU are described, taking into consideration the fundamental problem of dealing with up to 27 different tax systems.

Chapter 2 starts by looking at the status of indirect tax harmonization in the EU. The most important part is dedicated to the presentation and investigation of the comprehensive approach and achievements in the field of direct tax harmonization within the EU. Finally, some suggestions as to the future evolution of tax harmonization within the EU are made.

Chapter 3 argues the need for tax harmonization within the EU through facts and statistics. More specific elements of corporate income tax (statutory tax rates, effective tax rates and rules for calculating the tax base) and the complex mechanisms used by groups of companies with cross-border activities in order to redirect taxable income are analysed.

Chapter 4 presents the objectives of corporate tax income coordination within the EU, considering the strategic framework for Europe's economy made via communications from the European Commission to the European Parliament and the European Council.

Chapter 5 examines the possibilities of corporate income tax harmonization within the EU. The advantages and disadvantages that could result from the practical application of a European tax system based on a CCCTB are highlighted. The main provisions of the European Commission's proposal for a CCCTB are reviewed.

Chapter 6 looks at effects of corporate income tax harmonization/coordination within the EU. A series of research studies by independent experts and by the European Commission's specialized services are presented and analysed.

Chapter 7 discusses selected theoretical and empirical studies regarding impact assessments of the CCCTB in EU member states. It covers all the impact assessments published on the European Commission's website and those conducted by independent experts.

Chapter 8 provides some background information about supporters and opponents of the corporate income tax coordination within the EU. A highly topical aspect refers to the views on the CCCTB draft political directive.

1
The Tax Harmonization in the European Union

1.1 Introduction

This chapter highlights the delicate aspects of tax harmonization in the European Union (EU) from a conceptual, legal and rational perspective. Tax harmonization in the EU is not a common policy in the tax field, but the adjustment of national fiscal policies are necessary for proper functioning of the single market. Tax harmonization can be achieved spontaneously (through market forces), by the actions of European institutions (fiscal policy coordination, the harmonization of tax laws, etc.), or by action of the European Court of Justice (prohibiting certain national tax rules that violate EU rules). It is a prerequisite for the creation and effective functioning of the Single Market. Although member states have, in principle, the freedom to set their own rules regarding national tax systems, this freedom is conditioned by observance of priority objectives of the EU's founding treaties. Member states should avoid discriminatory tax measures (which can lead to disadvantageous treatment of people, goods, services or capital from other member states).

1.2 Conceptual delimitations

At the international level, there is a rich literature on the issue of tax harmonization and coordination because, in recent years, many authors have tried to crystallize the two concepts into more comprehensive definitions.

Tax harmonization is understood by George Kopits as a process of adjusting the tax systems of different jurisdictions so as to achieve some common fiscal policy objectives (Kopits, 1992, p. 3). Taryn Rounds suggests that tax harmonization refers to any situation in which differences between the tax systems of states (provinces) are reduced, either by actions of cooperation between public authorities or by the implementation of government policy measures (Rounds, 1992, p. 24). Angelo Faria believes that tax harmonization implies a high level of intergovernmental cooperation that may materialize through regional economic agreements based on factors other than economic development that are common to the signatory states. One such factor might be geographical proximity (Faria, 1995, p. 228).

In light of the conceptual approaches described above, one can appreciate that tax harmonization should be seen as a process of organizing the tax systems of different countries along similar lines – that is, the adjustment of national taxation systems according to a common set of economic rules.

Like tax harmonization, tax coordination implies the adjustment of national fiscal policies, but using another method. Angelo Faria considers that tax coordination includes measures through which the taxation system of a state adapts to the taxation system of another state, but the respective measures do not intend to and will not lead to uniformity of taxes applied by public authorities (1995, p. 229). Because tax coordination does not concern a single level of adaptation, Simon James conceptualized it as a gradual process, with the lower limit as the complete absence of measures to approximate the tax systems of different countries, and with the upper limit as complete tax harmonization (James, 2000, p. 263).

Considering the causes of this process, Anthony Infanti distinguished between the notions of "concerted" tax coordination and "spontaneous" tax coordination. "Concerted" tax coordination implies negotiation and, accordingly, the governments agree to adopt a fiscal behaviour different from that which would have been practised without the agreement (Infanti, 2002, p. 1128). Bi- or multilateral taxation treaties (which are generally the result of a long process of negotiation between authorities of several states) may be considered as defining elements for "concerted" tax coordination. Thus, the determinants of "concerted" fiscal coordination can include: the appearance of international double taxation cases; the existence of some tax discrimination cases; or the assertion of some needs to stimulate investment by providing identical taxation measures for investors operating in several countries. "Spontaneous" tax coordination is the result of the action of competitive market mechanisms, which can lead to the adoption by the competent authorities of a state those fiscal policy measures that have proved effective in another state. Considering the multiple and complex effects that are generated by fiscal instruments, it is possible to conclude that the situation of "spontaneous" tax coordination can only occur in the case of states that have similarities in terms of structure and level of socioeconomic development. An example of "spontaneous" tax coordination is described by Anthony Infanti, who showed that, between the mid-1980s and the early 1990s, decreases in marginal income tax rates and expansion of the corporate income tax base were registered in all states of the USA. It was caused by competition between these states to attract capital (Infanti, 2002, p. 1133).

A short incursion into the specialized literature led me to conclude that the concepts of tax harmonization and tax coordination were not associated with uniformization of taxation (which could mean the duplication of national tax systems), but with the elimination of asymmetries in some tax systems' components in order to achieve some economic policy objectives.

The Neumark Report, prepared by the Fiscal and Financial Committee in 1962, demonstrated the need to establish specific tax conditions for an economically unified framework. Underlining the difficulty of achieving this goal due to differences between the tax laws of member states, the authors of the report showed that it was not necessary to create a community-wide tax system, rather, it was necessary to resort to harmonization, thus allowing for the existence of national particularities that did not endanger the community's objectives (International Bureau of Fiscal Documentation, 1963).

The Werner Report, carried out by the same committee in 1970, suggested that in the case of indirect taxes it was necessary to approximate national laws and abolish border controls for individuals. However, in the case of direct taxes, the report recommended only the harmonization of those taxes that influenced capital movements. More specifically, the report targeted taxes on securities and, in a more general way, the structure of corporate income tax (Council/Commission of the European Communities, 1970).

According to the glossary of tax terms developed by the Organization for Economic Co-operation and Development (OECD), tax harmonization is the process of eliminating the tax barriers and discrepancies between the tax systems of member states.[1] The Maastricht Treaty of 1992 ensured the removal of tax barriers (this principle guaranteed the movement of goods and services within the European Community free from discriminatory taxation) and the elimination of disparities between the various tax systems.

According to Constantin Tulai and Simona Serbu, tax harmonization is not an optimal system with a single objective, but a search for the best possible compromise between economic imperatives dictated by market integration and free movement, on the one hand, and the requirements of member states' autonomy in terms of tax options, on the other hand (Tulai and Serbu, 2005, p. 133). Thus, a first requirement for tax harmonization is a clear statement of political will by the community authorities, which must then be adopted by all member states through their representatives in the European Council.

Tax harmonization in the EU can be defined as the approximation of member states' tax systems in order to achieve common objectives stated in EU treaties, a process which may lead to the same national tax systems in the short or medium term. In this context, tax coordination in the EU is an expression of tax harmonization. It is reflected in the action of "compatibility" of national tax systems, in order to prevent any national tax measures that could have a negative effect on the Single Market, namely the free movement of goods, services and capital.

The coordination of different legal rules within the member states results in a tendency to eliminate the contrasts that exist between them. The harmonization of legislation is a more evolved system, because the substance of regulations can be altered during attempts to eliminate those elements that are not in line with application in different EU member states. In principle, harmonization allows the existence of a diversity in the origin, structure and drafting of national regulations.

Dragos Negrescu and Anton Comanescu believe that in terms of tax parameters, tax harmonization refers to four factors: the type of tax (e.g. value added tax has widespread application in the EU), tax rates, tax bases and the administration of taxes. Generally, it is considered that harmonization measures regarding tax bases have a clear priority compared to harmonization measures for tax rates. In fact, in terms of tax rates, some harmonization measures have been adopted only in relation to indirect taxes; an "*acquis communautaire*" on direct tax rates has not been included. The justification for this reticence is related to the fact that a harmonization of these rates is considered inadequate in circumstances where member states have specific characteristics (demographic situations, social programmes, different sources of competitive advantage), so it is necessary for leverage tax to be used in different ways and in different dosages in order to achieve specific economic and social objectives (Negrescu and Comanescu, 2007, p. 46).

1.3 The legal basis of tax harmonization

The analysis of tax harmonization in the EU should start from its legal basis, respectively from the tax provisions of the Treaty of Lisbon, signed in 2007,[2] which assumed the fundamental tax rules stipulated in the

Treaty of Rome, by which the European Economic Community was created in 1957 (Articles 90–96):

- no Member State shall impose, directly or indirectly, on the products of other Member States any internal taxation of any kind in excess of that imposed directly or indirectly on similar domestic products. Furthermore, no Member State shall impose on the products of other Member States any internal taxation of such a nature as to afford indirect protection to other products (Article 110);
- where products are exported to the territory of any Member State, any repayment of internal taxation shall not exceed the internal taxation imposed on them whether directly or indirectly (Article 111);
- in the case of charges other than turnover taxes, excise duties and other forms of indirect taxation, remissions and repayments in respect of exports to other Member States may not be granted and countervailing charges in respect of imports from Member States may not be imposed unless the measures contemplated have been previously approved for a limited period by the Council on a proposal from the Commission (Article 112);
- the Council shall, acting unanimously in accordance with a special legislative procedure and after consulting the European Parliament and the Economic and Social Committee, adopt provisions for the harmonization of legislation concerning turnover taxes, excise duties and other forms of indirect taxation to the extent that such harmonization is necessary to ensure the establishment and the functioning of the internal market and to avoid distortion of competition (Article 113);
- the European Parliament and the Council shall, acting in accordance with the ordinary legislative procedure and after consulting the Economic and Social Committee, adopt the measures for the approximation of the provisions laid down by law, regulation or administrative action in Member States which have as their object the establishment and functioning of the internal market. The above paragraph shall not apply to fiscal provisions, to those relating to the free movement of persons nor to those relating to the rights and interests of employed persons (Article 114);
- without prejudice to Article 114, the Council shall, acting unanimously in accordance with a special legislative procedure and after consulting the European Parliament and the Economic and Social Committee, issue directives for the approximation of such laws,

regulations or administrative provisions of the Member States as directly affect the establishment or functioning of the internal market (Article 115);

- where the Commission finds that a difference between the provisions laid down by law, regulation or administrative action in Member States is distorting the conditions of competition in the internal market and that the resultant distortion needs to be eliminated, it shall consult the Member States concerned. If such consultation does not result in an agreement eliminating the distortion in question, European Parliament and the Council, acting in accordance with the ordinary legislative procedure, shall issue the necessary directives. Any other appropriate measures provided for in the Treaties may be adopted (Article 116).

It is noticeable that EU institutions have certain powers in the development of tax legislation and tax harmonization, but only in the field of indirect taxes, because this may affect the free movement of goods and services and may distort the competition within the Single Market. Direct taxation is not expressly stipulated in the EU treaties, since the potential influence on the Single Market is lower, and the majority of member states wished to retain sovereignty in the area of direct tax, commonly used as an instrument of economic policy. Interpreting Article 116 of the Treaty of Lisbon, it becomes apparent that within the EU, national tax regimes (including provisions for direct taxes) can implement corrective measures as long as they do not interfere with the principle of free movement of goods, persons, services and capital.

It can thus be stated that a coordinated fiscal policy in the EU is necessary and that this must take into account the different nature of taxes as follows:

- indirect taxes require a higher degree of harmonization because they are related to the free movement of goods and services;
- direct taxes requires certain harmonization rules, especially in the field of corporate income, but also for individuals who receive incomes in many countries, because cases of double taxation may arise.

The effect of EU treaties on the powers of European institutions is to limit fiscal policy, so that the EU's objectives regarding the functioning of the Single Market without borders is not restricted by the autonomy of national public authorities in tax matters. The tax harmonization process recorded a significant advance as a result of decisions taken by the European Court of Justice which, based on the principle of the four freedoms, the free movement of people, goods, services and capital, forced national public authorities to eliminate those tax law provisions that favoured discriminatory treatment or restricted the movement of goods, services, capital and persons within the Single Market.

The European Court of Justice's activity in the tax field caused many observers to question whether this institution is limited to the role of interpreter of the Treaty, or whether it in fact promotes its own agenda directed towards "implicit" tax harmonization. Dragos Negrescu and Anton Comanescu have claimed that, in this context, the quality of some of the rules obtained in this way may not be optimal because the internal coherence of national tax systems may be affected by punctual decisions, and because there is no guarantee against preventing situations such as decisions of the European Court of Justice generating asymmetric effects on individual member states (Negrescu and Comanescu, 2007, p. 14).

1.4 Reasons for tax harmonization in the EU

1.4.1 Stimulating effective functioning of the Single Market

The single market idea was based on a principle formulated by representatives of liberal economic doctrines over two centuries ago: removing barriers to trade between countries generates increased competition among firms and thereby reduces costs and eliminates inefficient business practices. The effects of the economic impact of the Single Market in the European Community were quantified at the request of the European Commission, by a team of specialists led by Professor Paolo Cecchini. Thus, in 1988, a study entitled "The cost of non-Europe" was published. This study, known as the "Cecchini Report", outlined the advantages and disadvantages of the Single Market. The "Cecchini Report" predicted the economic growth and strengthened competition of the European Community in the global market by achieving savings of around 200 billion ECU, by reducing consumer prices by about 6 per cent, by the creation of about two million new jobs in member states by the end of 1992, and by removing obstacles to economic exchanges, such as border controls, technical barriers and fiscal barriers (European Commission, 1988, p. 9). As Kitty Ussher says, although some experts criticized the simplistic assumptions that led to the conclusions of the "Cecchini Report" – considered to be altogether too optimistic – the document succeeded in popularizing among policy-makers the concept according to which the efficient functioning of the Single Market would generate increased general welfare within the European Community (Ussher, 2000, pp. 9–10).

Thus, an argument in favour of tax harmonization was the stimulation of efficient functioning within the Single Market because eliminating tax barriers generated an improvement in the capacity of investors, businesses and consumers to make decisions based on resource allocation efficiency, unaltered by different levels of taxation in the various member states. However, the stimulatory effect of tax harmonization should be analysed in relation to the mobility of elements covered by these decisions. Since the trade in goods and services and portfolio investment are characterized by very high mobility, harmonization of taxation with regard to these processes should focus on achieving the maximum effect of stimulating efficient operation within the Single Market. It is important to note that the stimulatory effect of tax harmonization would be reduced in the case of less mobile factors of production (such as labour and land).

1.4.2 Preventing revenue erosion

With growing economic globalization, the existence of different tax systems favours the phenomenon of tax export that involves moving the tax burden from taxpayers residing in high tax states to taxpayers residing in low tax states. Economic globalization – through increased interdependence between individuals and national economies, through the interconnection and integration of financial markets and trade, and through the internationalization of production by multinational corporations – has important implications in terms of tax, because the tax source can be moved more easily in jurisdictions with lower taxation.

As Simon James and Lynne Oats have stated, the revenues erosion issue started from the competition between different tax jurisdictions, which aimed to encourage individuals and businesses to establish residency in their area (James and Oats, 1998, p. 9). The concept of "tax competition" was introduced by Charles Tiebout and was based on the idea of the existence of an equivalent of private goods markets for public goods. Because the law of supply and demand acts on the public goods market, taxpayers should opt for those residences that provide the optimal combination of public goods and taxes (viewed as prices paid for public goods). In turn, tax authorities will try to attract taxpayers into their jurisdictions by offering the tax–public goods combination desired by them, until it reaches the tax base reaches an optimal size – that is, one that minimizes the cost of the public goods provided (Tiebout, 1956, pp. 416–424).

Using the Rohác Dalibor approach, tax competition is the phenomenon by which mobile tax bases are attracted to jurisdictions with low taxation (Dalibor, 2006, p. 88). Thus, the tax competition can be compared to a kind of "poaching", whereby a country, using certain types of tax incentives, causes the transfer of tax bases from abroad to come under its jurisdiction.

Ioan Talpos and Alexandru Crasneac consider that, in the broad sense, tax competition is any fiscal context in which various independent governments do not coordinate their fiscal policies. In a narrower sense, tax competition can be defined as any fiscal context in which various independent governments do not coordinate their fiscal policies, and the fiscal policy of each government affects the allocation of tax revenue between these countries. Usually, the phenomenon of tax competition is associated with actions of governments to attract foreign direct investment, portfolio investment, foreign buyers, labour (especially the highly skilled) and tax bases (Talpos and Crasneac, 2010, pp. 39–40).

Tax competition could lead to a reduction in tax revenue up to a level at which public authorities could no longer meet the demand for services and public goods. The Zodrow–Mieszkowski model, known in the literature as the "basic tax competition model", demonstrates, under restrictive conditions, that diminishing tax rates on capital income will lead to a decrease in the supply of public goods to a suboptimal level. Thus, the introduction of certain supranational rules by means of which one should at least state the minimum tax rates would ensure the provision of services and public goods under proper conditions. This idea has been expressed by George Zodrow and Peter Mieszkowski, who firmly supported the need for common tax rules that ensure the collection of sufficient revenue to guarantee the continuity of finance for the welfare state (Zodrow and Mieszkowski, 1986, pp. 356–370).

This view was also shared by John Douglas Wilson, who believed that, under the increased mobility of capital, tax competition may generate the erosion of tax bases (especially in developing countries), affecting the amount of disposable income available for investments in the social field or infrastructure (Wilson, 1999, pp. 289–291). Wallace Oates believed that reducing taxes so as to attract mobile capital would lead to a reduction in public spending to the point where marginal benefits would be equal to marginal costs. As the financing of actions and objectives not proving sufficiently attractive to small businesses would be reduced in particular, the author concluded that this phenomenon would lead to a reduction in social welfare (Oates, 1993, pp. 237–243). According to Dragos Negrescu and Anton Comanescu, privileged investors tend to be residents in countries that offer a high level of public services, but they do not contribute equally to finance them through taxes. So the lost revenue from reducing taxes on the mobile taxpayer's income will eventually be made up by a rise in taxes on the less mobile taxpayer's income, leading to a deeply unfair situation (Negrescu and Comanescu, 2007, p. 73).

Tax competition within the EU, facilitated by the integration of national markets, began to be studied as an economic phenomenon with the enlargement of the EU. In the context of EU accession, new member states were obliged to ensure equal treatment for foreign and local investors, thereby abandoning effective tools for the stimulation of economic activity: tax advantages. To keep their economies attractive, the practice of reducing the corporate income tax rate was generalized across these states. This was contested by the governments of those member states, who relied on a high rate of taxation to ensure resources to finance the "general welfare state". A reduction in the corporate income tax rate would generate the movement of foreign direct investment (FDI) to areas with low taxation, so the measures for fiscal relaxation adopted by new member states generated similar reactions from other member states.

At a certain volume of goods and services provided by the government, reducing corporate income tax revenues or capital tax revenues should be compensated for by increasing the tax burden on other tax revenues. If the relaxation of corporate income taxation does not generate a stimulation of investment in the economy and other positive implications (the creation of new jobs, the improvement of the balance of trade, an increase in revenue from the rise in personal income, etc.), the whole mechanism described above will bring about the erosion of public income.

In the EU, the notion of tax competition was analysed in particular in connection with the possibility of capital migrating from one country to another, in the search for better tax conditions. Because tax competition is reflected in decreased capital taxation, this decrease is often compensated by the government by increasing the tax on labour. Therefore, tax competition can be regarded as a "game". The "winners" are the owners of mobile factors (in this case, capital) and the "losers" are the holders of immobile factors (such as the less skilled workforce), because they face many more difficulties when trying to migrate (legislative, social, psychological, barriers, etc.). Peter Grau and Molina Herrera believe that taxes will move from corporate income to personal income, from capital to labour, and generally, from income and welfare taxation to consumption taxation, so tax competition may lead to a substantial change in the tax structure, and thus to the erosion of certain categories of income (Grau and Herrera, 2003, p. 30).

Tax competition was analysed using descriptive methods (based on the evolution of tax rates), regression methods (highlighting the impact of capital mobility on tax rates) and methods based on game theory (emphasizing the strategy of the fiscal game).

In recent years, the results of many studies demonstrate the hypothesis of the EU member states' engagement in a "race to the minimum" because:

- governments react by lowering their own tax rates in the case of reduced tax rates in neighbouring countries;
- in recent years, tax rates on mobile factors of production have declined significantly in all EU member countries.

Although so far, no evidence has been provided to prove a direct correlation between tax competition and the erosion of public services in EU member states, increasing tax competition following the accession of the new member states has generated criticism of the lax fiscal policies of these states. Thus, Murilo Portugal (2007), Deputy Director of the International Monetary Fund, expressed in 2007 the concern that, in the future, tax competition would reduce the capacity of governments to maintain the current amount of tax revenue.

Some experts showed that the high rate of tax on corporate income in some member states discourages FDI inflows, even though other factors – including the volume and quality of public goods and services – would be favourable to attracting FDI. Thus, the analysis of FDI flows between seven home countries for multinational companies (Austria, Germany, France, Italy, Netherlands, UK and USA) and eight host countries (Bulgaria, Croatia, Czech Republic, Hungary, Poland, Slovakia, Slovenia and Romania) made by Christian Bellak and Markus Leibrecht during 1995–2002 shows that corporate income tax is a factor in the foreign company's location investment decision. The deduced tax-rate elasticity was about –2.93 (Bellak and Leibrecht, 2005, p. 21).

Following the analysis of Ruud de Mooij and Sjef Ederveen on the impact of taxation on capital flows, an elasticity of –2.4 per cent was determined. Consequently, the reduction by one percentage point of the capital tax rate will lead to an increase of capital flows by 2.4 per cent (de Mooij and Ederveen, 2003, p. 23).

Agnès Bénassy-Quéré, Lionel Fontagné and Amina Lahrèche-Révil (2003, p. 18) studied the sensitivity of FDI to taxes in 11 OECD countries during 1984–2000, revealing that the corporate income tax rate played a significant role in the FDI location. Thus, while the low tax rate contributes significantly to attracting FDI, a high tax rate discourages FDI inflows. On the other hand, the positive impact of tax differences is not the same in all countries choosing to reduce tax rates in order to attract foreign capital. FDI flows are directly related to the tax differences between different countries.

Disputes about the importance of corporate income tax for FDI location are ongoing, given that many studies regarding the elasticity of FDI with respect to corporate income tax have focused exclusively on the tax rates issue.

A step forward in researching the effects of taxation on FDI location decisions has been made by Salvador Barrios, Harry Huizinga, Luc Laeven and Gaetan Nicodème. These researchers have studied a sample of companies from 33 European countries and have achieved more detailed results. These authors have shown that the sensitivity of FDI to corporate income tax varies greatly according to the size of the study group. So, for a small study group, sensitivity appears to be very high (Barrios et al., 2008, p. 26). These results suggest that estimates regarding the impact of taxation on FDI location decisions will become significant only if the database includes more countries and sampled companies are heterogeneous in terms of investment. Currently, the aggregation of the two conditions is difficult in the absence of a very large and complete international database.

Although studies attempting to measure the intensity of the relationship between taxation and FDI location decisions do not provide significant results, it is clear that corporate income tax is a strong determinant of the financial structure of FDI. Thus, the econometric modelling carried out by Padraig Moore and Frances Ruane based on observations of over 300,000 companies in the AMADEUS database during 1994–2002 showed that an increase of 10 percentage points in the level of taxation in one country would generate growth of the debt by 3.4 percentage points of the financial structure of subsidiaries based in that country (Moore and Ruane, 2005, p. 7). Harry Huizinga, Luc Laeven and Gaetan Nicodème obtained similar results in 2007, showing that through intra-group loans, an increase of 10 percentage points in the level of taxation in one country would generate an increase of the debt by 2.44 percentage points in the financial structure of subsidiaries in that country (2007, p. 4).

By reducing fiscal pressure differences between EU member countries, tax harmonization creates prerequisites for setting a minimum level of income tax under which governments can provide a certain amount of public goods and services. On the other hand, there are views according to which tax competition motivates the government to promote a responsible fiscal policy. The reduced tax burden on companies creates a fertile ground for economic growth. In the absence of tax competition, governments can levy excessive taxes, and the higher rate of income tax discourages economic activity, leading to a reduction in public revenues (Mitchell, 2001, p. 2). Therefore, tax competition is beneficial because it reduces the waste of public financial resources, it disciplines the politicians, and it can lead to an increase in welfare provision (Janeba and Schjelerup, 2002, p. 9). Tax competition forces nations to compete with one another so as to attract "customers" (taxpayers), offering a better quality of "tax services". So the practice of favourable tax regimes in some countries should not give rise to "winner" and "loser" positions (Christensen and Kapoor, 2004, p. 9). Behind this reason is the idea that both individual taxpayers and companies are able to migrate between different tax jurisdictions according to their preferences. In reality, the full mobility of tax bases is blocked by the existence of some relocation costs, political and cultural barriers, etc., so that tax competition in effect generates a number of economic distortions.

1.4.3 Avoiding harmful tax competition

If the tax competition between states is accompanied by a lack of fiscal transparency, the absence of an exchange of information between tax authorities and an advantageous tax regime for non-residents, it is possible to make an argument for tax competition being harmful.

OECD Reports from 1998 and 2000 revealed the existence of some harmful tax practices. These included: certain tax incentive measures that can be considered as irrelevant for the specifics of the national economy and tax benefits granted in the absence of effective economic activities in that country and associated in particular with tax havens (OECD, 1998 and 2000). The fiscal and banking policies of tax havens generate numerous disadvantages for onshore states: losing tax revenues, reducing the possibilities of financing the national economy, the licit and illicit migration of capital, etc.

The existence of some very low tax jurisdictions encourages transnational corporations to use tax avoidance strategies involving the transfer pricing mechanism, intra-group loans, thin capitalization, using organizational structures without a significant economic activity in order to operate abroad, etc. John Christensen and Sony Kapoor (2004, pp. 6–8) noted that the ability of corporations to use these strategies gave them a significant tax advantage over national competitors, so the tax competition favoured large businesses, developed at an international level, over small businesses, developed at a local level. Also, companies with experience in using tax avoidance strategies are advantaged over start-up companies. Since the most start-up companies are recorded in developing countries, extrapolating from this fact, one can say that tax competition encourages the businesses of multinational companies in developed countries as opposed to their competitors in developing countries.

Debates on the issue of harmful tax competition in the EU began after the publication, in 1999, of the first Primarolo Group Report, which identified 66 "harmful tax measures", of which 40 were measures in force in member states (Council of the EU, 1999).

The Primarolo Group used the following criteria to identify potentially harmful tax measures:

- an effective level of taxation that is significantly lower than the overall level of taxation in that country;
- non-residents can enjoy tax benefits;
- tax incentives for activities that are isolated from the domestic economy;
- tax exemptions are offered even in the absence of a real economic activity;
- a lack of transparency in the fiscal environment.

The conclusions of the Primarolo Group Report motivated the European Commission to initiate a series of actions in order to eliminated those tax measures considered to be harmful (according to state aid rules), actions supported by the European Court of Justice based on their interpretation of the free movement principles of the EU treaty.

Currently, the tax practices of some EU member states stimulate the transfer of benefits and the development of commercial activities on their territory. Thus, in the Netherlands, Luxembourg, Belgium and Cyprus there is favourable legislation for the development of holding companies,[3] which results in an increased attractiveness of these countries to foreign investors and encourages foreign capital accumulation.

Shipping companies or companies with maritime interests enjoy specific tax advantages in Cyprus and the Netherlands. In addition to fiscal benefits, Luxembourg is a recognized jurisdiction that guarantees confidentiality and financial secrecy. In 2009, Luxembourg and Belgium both belonged to a list of countries that did not fully implement the international tax cooperation standards according to the requirements of the OECD (OECD, 2009). Even if the favourable fiscal and financial environments existing in some EU member states cannot be defined as harmful tax competition, the advantages these countries have are evident, and considerable movement of certain economic structures across the EU will continue to be possible in the future.

In the absence of common corporate tax rules, the emergence of examples of harmful tax competition within the EU is inevitable. The settlement of the European Court of Justice of the issues generated by the adoption of national tax provisions that harm the interests of some states and distort competition within the Single Market is a difficult and costly mechanism, and could possibly be avoided through tax harmonization.

1.4.4 Preventing distortions regarding resource allocation

In the event that governments are required to achieve reductions in tax rates, grant deductions, tax credits and exemptions to attract capital or to prevent its migration to more favourable tax jurisdictions, the resulting tax competition may lead to the misallocation of resources in the world economy. Thus, production activities can be targeted at countries where input costs are high, but taxes are low. Dennis Coates asserts that, in this context, tax competition generates a cumulative reinforcement of potential fiscal inequalities (Coates, 1993, p. 177).

According to Charles Edwards and Veronique Rugy, tax competition is harmful because it distorts the effective allocation of capital and services at the international level. Input of services, capital and skilled labour will increase in countries which choose low tax rates (especially developing countries), while neighbouring countries will be confronted with the reverse situation (Edwards and Rugy, 2002, pp. 21–22). According to Reuven Avi-Yonah, the advantages to be gained by developing countries from tax competition are, however, questionable. Thus, tax incentives granted by the governments of China, Brazil, Mexico and India, in the early 2000s, following the suggestions of some business consulting firms, did not generate a substantial increase in the volume of FDI (Avi-Yonah, 2001, p. 61).

Since there are certain significant differences between countries involved in the competition to attract international capital, from the economic, social and political point of view, the influence of taxation on capital location cannot be easily calculated. Thus, a multi-criteria analysis which takes into account infrastructure development, taxation, legislative and political stability, workforce costs, workplace training, size of the domestic market, proximity to raw material sources, etc. underlies global investment decisions. Also, generalizations about the localization behaviour of capital is not possible because there are differences in the perceptions of decision makers about the many investment options and differences in their attitudes towards risk.

A neutral tax system, generated through tax harmonization within the EU, would provide the advantage of eliminating distortions in economic decisions and would allow the proper allocation of resources within the Single Market. In the event that goods produced in any member state should be taxed identically, producers would allow the manufacturing of those goods where input costs are lower.

According to Taryn Rounds, tax competition is a phenomenon that occurs naturally in the context of globalization, so it is not necessary or opportune to combat it. Thus, in most cases, attractive tax systems are ways to counter exogenous disadvantages (such as lower levels of development within the new EU member states) and to determine a more uniform allocation of resources within a certain area. Tax competition and tax harmonization do not have a conflict of objectives. Thus, tax competition should encourage governments to adopt fiscal policy measures like those promoted in countries that succeed in attracting capital using favourable tax regimes. In time, these practices could lead to a certain degree of uniformity of tax systems in some areas (Rounds, 1992, p. 22).

1.5 Conclusion

The evolution of the tax harmonization process in the EU is closely linked to the challenges of integration and economic globalization needed to allow the Single Market to function under optimal conditions. Tax harmonization in the EU should not be confused with tax uniformity. From a *legal point* of *view,* the EU treaties substantiate tax harmonization measures in the EU. Tax competition, the risk of double taxation, the loss of opportunities for increasing economic competitiveness within the EU are just a few of the issues generated by the peculiarities of the member states' tax systems. To avoid improper operation of the Single Market, national tax systems must be designed to ensure a high degree of neutrality. In this context, the relevant institutions of the EU have prioritized the harmonization of indirect taxes and the harmonization of some matters affecting corporate taxation.

2
The Evolution of Tax Harmonization in the European Union

2.1 Introduction

Tax harmonization helps to implement the four freedoms of the Single Market. Indirect taxation within the European Union (EU) requires a high level of harmonization, due to its influence on the free movement of goods and services. This idea was underlined in Article 99 of the Treaty of Rome in 1957 and repeated in Articles 90 and 93 of the Treaty of Maastricht in 1992. The main efforts of indirect tax harmonization (harmonization does not mean the uniformization of taxes) were focused on value added tax (VAT) and excise duties. According to the EU treaties, there are no express provisions requiring the harmonization of direct taxes, as there are in the case of indirect taxes. Common European legislation does not expressly specify the alignment of direct taxes, and by virtue of the subsidiarity principle member states are free to adopt those regulations regarded as necessary for their own economies.

2.2 The status of indirect tax harmonization in the EU

2.2.1 The evolution of the legal system of VAT in the EU

In the European Economic Community (EEC) countries, two systems of indirect taxation were applied in 1960. France was the only state that used the VAT system, while the other countries applied a tax system based on cumulative turnover tax (under this system, indirect tax was levied at each stage of production and circulation of goods). The latter of these two systems was not able to ensure fiscal neutrality, since the tax burden may be influenced by the vertical and horizontal integration of production, thus creating competition distortions within the European Community. Under these circumstances, the European Commission considered it necessary to extend the VAT system, taking into account two possible principles of taxation:

1. *The principle of destination*, according to which goods and services are taxed in the countries where they are consumed. This system requires economic cooperation between countries in order to avoid double taxation (when goods are supplied by traders from a state that practises the origin principle, these goods would be the subject of indirect tax twice, in the home and the destination state) or competitiveness alteration (where EEC countries apply different tax rates for imported and indigenous goods).
2. *The principle of origin*, under which goods and services are taxed in the country where they are produced. This principle means that tax rates need to be unified across different countries, since differences between these rates may otherwise distort market competition.

Indirect tax harmonization actions were initiated at the beginning of the European economic integration process and resulted in the following provisions.

- The replacement of the existing tax system on the movement of goods with a system of VAT. Thus, according to Directive 67/227/EEC, known as the "First Directive", EEC countries were obliged to levy a tax on all goods and services as a percentage of their sales price, regardless of the number of production and distribution process links. Tax rates and possible tax exemptions remained within the competencies of the member states. The due date proposed for the common system of VAT to come into effect was 1 January 1970.
- A clear definition of the items and services to which VAT was to be applied and the method of taxation. Thus, Directive 67/228/EEC, known as the "Second Directive", specifies that the right to charge VAT is for those member states in which goods are sold and services are provided, regardless of their origin. Member states retained the right to adopt special regulations that exempt from VAT the sale of certain goods/services according to their need to stimulate specific economic sectors.
- Directive 69/463/EEC, known as the "Third Directive", replaced the original deadline for the introduction of the common system of VAT of 1 January 1970 with 1 January 1972.

- Directives 71/401/CEE and 72/250/CEE, known as the "Fourth Directive" and "Fifth Directive", focused on the introduction of VAT in Italy.

The VAT system had the advantage – compared with the tax systems on the movement of goods used previously in most EEC countries – of making visible the tax content of a product at each stage of production or distribution chain. This tax was chosen as a method of indirect taxation to avoid the cumulative effect of cascading taxes, and to ensure the neutrality of taxation in the case of trade between member states. The "Five Directives", adopted by the early 1970s, paved the way for VAT harmonization in the EEC.

Directive 77/388/EEC, known as the "Sixth Directive", founded VAT harmonization in the EEC by establishing the tax base, the rules of assessment and exemptions, and by defining constraints, the liquidation of tax liabilities and payment. Therefore, this directive established a common tax trim for the entire European Community and constituted a veritable legislative instrument at community level. In addition, it helped to establish a work programme aimed at a target already addressed by the "First Directive": the suspension of tax borders.

Directive 79/1072/EEC (the "Eighth Directive") regulated the system of VAT refunds to taxable persons established outside the territory of the country that charged the tax. Article 8 of the directive provided that in the case of taxable persons not established within the territory of the European Community, member states may refuse refunds or may impose special conditions. Directive 86/560/EEC (the "Thirteenth Directive") clarified the right of member states to refund the VAT in exchange for the granting by third states of comparable advantages in business taxation.

Since the presence of control administrative formalities was an obstacle to freedom of trade, Directive 91/860/EEC was adopted in 1991. One of the purposes of this directive is the elimination of fiscal frontiers between member states. This measure significantly influenced the VAT system used in the EU. Thus, for intra-community trade, VAT is not payable when goods pass through customs, but upon reception of goods in the destination country. Private consumers could make purchases in any member state without being subject to border controls, paying VAT according to the rate of that country, with some exceptions (the purchase of new vehicles from another member state and mail-order sales of a company established in another member state).

Differences between VAT rates in the member states were likely to encourage supplies from countries that had the lowest rates, so they all agreed on rate harmonization. With effect from 1993, Directive 92/77/EEC fixed the minimum limits for VAT rates: 15 per cent for the normal rate and 5 per cent for the reduced rate. Reduced rates may apply for products listed in Annex H of the "Sixth Directive" (live animals, cereals, plants, food – excluding alcoholic beverages – pharmaceuticals, medical equipment, supplies of books, drinking water supply, passenger transport, etc.). Directive 2004/15/EC extended the facility for member states to apply the reduced VAT rate to certain services based on intensive use of labour (hospitality, certain types of restaurants).

In the absence of intra-community border controls, the use of the destination principle in the taxation regime governing intra-community trade generated administrative difficulties, therefore, the VAT directives of 1991 and 1992 established a so-called transitional regime, combining the rules of the origin principle with the destination principle.

The traditional VAT system provided a number of economic advantages, including:

- an invoicing system applied to each stage of the production and circulation circuit of goods and services, thus avoiding the cascade effect of indirect taxes (which is characteristic of gross turnover taxes) and the discrimination against specialized firms as opposed to vertically integrated companies;
- the possibility of VAT recovery, allowing the settlement of the tax burden only at the point of the final consumer, regardless of the VAT rates applicable to intermediate stages in the production and circulation circuit;
- the levy of VAT only in destination countries, ensuring the taxation of goods and services sold to final consumers in the destination country according to the same rules, regardless of whether they were produced in that country or abroad.

Applying the VAT system according to the 1967 directives generated smaller administrative and economic costs for public authorities and allowed EEC governments to obtain an increase in tax revenues (Cnossen and Shoup, 1987, pp. 59–84). However, the common VAT legislation diminished the fiscal autonomy of member states when it was implemented in national laws.

In 1996, the European Commission revealed in a report to the European Council and European Parliament[1] that the differences in the transposition and implementation by member states of the provisions of the VAT directives, and the complexity of these provisions, could generate, on the one hand, difficulties both for tax administrations and economic operators, and provided an opportunity for the exploitation of these differences, in terms of tax evasion, on the other hand. In this context, the European Commission proposed as a medium- and long-term goal the full revision of common VAT legislation, and in the short term the creation of tools to improve administrative cooperation between member states in order to overcome these difficulties.

A strategy to improve the common VAT system was proposed by the European Commission in 2000 (European Commission, 2000), its main objectives being to:

- simplify existing legislation;
- standardize rules for implementing the provisions of VAT directives;
- improve cooperation between national administrations in order to combat tax evasion.

This strategy was revised and updated in 2003 when the Commission announced its intention to promote a system that allowed any trader to fulfil all VAT obligations in a single member state for activities across all EU member states (European Commission, 2003a).

In principle, most VAT directives adopted after 1995 focused on amending and supplementing the "Sixth Directive". Thus, the VAT arrangements applicable to special goods such as second-hand goods, antiques and certain collectable items were regulated by Directive 94/5/EC. Directive 98/80/EC established rules regarding the sale of gold used for investment purposes. VAT arrangements applicable to radio and television broadcasting services and certain electronically supplied services were adopted through Directive 99/59/EC and Directive 2002/38/EC. Directive 2001/115/EC harmonized requirements within the EU, creating a common legal and technical framework for electronic invoicing. In order to limit possible tax evasion and distortions of the Single Market (the tax competition surrounding electricity and natural gas provision was overcome by shifting the tax base from the place of supply to the place of consumption), Directive 2003/92/EC amended Directive 77/388/EEC regarding the terms of rules on place of origin.

On 17 October 2005, the European Council adopted Regulation No. 1777/2005, which guaranteed the uniform application of common rules regarding VAT in the EU. It provided methods to align certain

VAT legislated items, such as electronically supplied services, place of taxable transactions and the scope of VAT exemptions, thus ensuring greater transparency and higher security for both trading partners and national administrations.

From 1 January 2007, the "Sixth Directive" was replaced by Directive 2006/112/EC on the common VAT system (amended later), which became the legal basis currently available in the EU. Because it was intended to present VAT legislative provisions in a clear and logical form (given the many substantial changes of Directive 77/388/EEC), the adoption of Directive 2006/112/EC generated only a small number of changes in the existing legislation.

In the current (complex and constantly changing) economic environment, the good functioning of the common VAT system requires continuous improvement actions. European Commission objectives regarding the simplification, modernization and more uniform application of the common VAT system are justified and will lead to approximation of EU member states' tax systems.

2.2.2 European regulations on excise duty

As in the case of VAT, excise duties can also affect the proper functioning of the Single Market, since harmonized measures eliminate the potential competitive advantage of businesses exempted by the authorities to pay all or part of such taxes.

The harmonization of excise duties in EU member states was a complementary measure to the introduction of the common VAT system. In compliance with the principle of fiscal neutrality, European excise duty rules provide (as in the case of VAT) the use of the destination principle (excisable goods are taxed in the country of the consumer) and establish (in contrast to the case of VAT) a general and final regime on the holding, movement and surveillance of excisable products. The European Community excise duty system was introduced on 1 January 1993. It was applied to the following categories of products: tobacco, alcoholic beverages and mineral oils.

The harmonization of excise duties in the EU is based on the following directives:

- Directive 92/12/EEC regulated in general the production, storage and transport of excisable products: mineral oils, alcoholic beverages and alcohol and tobacco products.
- Directive 92/81/EEC on the harmonization of the structures of excise duties on mineral oils and Directive 92/82/EEC on the approximation

of the rates of excise duty on mineral oils. Directive 2003/96/EC extended the system for the taxation of mineral oils to all energy products, in particular, to products that are direct or indirect substitutes for mineral oils, for example, coke, lignite, natural gas, electricity. This directive fixed the minimum levels of excise duty on mineral oils (used as fuel or for industrial and commercial purposes).

- Directive 92/83/EEC established categories of excisable alcoholic beverages: beer, wine and other beverages produced by fermentation, intermediate products and alcohol.
- Directive 92/84/EEC established minimum levels of excise duties on beer and products fabricated by mixing beer and other alcoholic beverages (with an alcohol content of more than 0.5 per cent), intermediate products (containing alcohol levels between 1.2 and 22 per cent) and alcoholic beverages with an alcohol content of more than 22 per cent.
- Directive 92/79/EEC established European Community legislation on excise duties for cigarettes. This directive was amended in 1999, 2002 and 2010 by introducing provisions regarding the structures and minimum levels of excise duties on tobacco products.

European Community legislation provides harmonized rules regarding structures of excise duties (definition, product units, exemptions), the movement between member states of excise products and minimum tax rates for each product group. Under this legislation, goods are subject to excise duty if they are produced in the EU or imported from a third country, and the duty is payable only to the member state in which the goods are released for consumption, according to the rates applicable in that state.

According to Directive 2008/118/EC on the general arrangements for excise duties, which replaced Directive 92/12/EEC, member states have the option for introducing or maintaining excise duties on other products, as long as these taxes do not generate the need for cross-border tax compliance formalities in trade between member states.

The justification for the intervention of European Community institutions on excise duties to harmonize them across the EU is the fact that these taxes can influence Single Market mechanisms. Since tax harmonization does not mean the same thing as standardization, measures adopted at EU level in the excise duties field are designed to create an economic framework in which national tax systems are compatible and in line with EU goals.

2.3 Initiatives and achievements in the field of direct taxation in the EU

2.3.1 Initiatives in the field of direct tax harmonization within the EU: from the conclusions of the Neumark report (1962) to the adoption of the tax package to avoid harmful tax competition in the Single Market (2003)

If direct taxation affects the free movement of goods, services, persons and capital, any given member state must ensure the functioning of a national tax system that respects the right of establishment of individuals and firms, under Articles 94 and 308 of the Treaty of Maastricht. The Acquis communautaire in the field of direct taxation mainly concerns the corporate income tax and tax on capital income and less the personal income tax.

Viewpoints on concrete ways to harmonize direct taxes within the EU are different, depending on the preferences of member states to maintain a degree of fiscal sovereignty and the need to coordinate certain tax issues to avoid loss of revenues as a result of tax competition. The European Commission believes that member states must act vigorously to eliminate tax obstacles in the Single Market. If European Commission proposals for tax harmonization mainly aim to improve the functioning of the Single Market, perspectives on erosion of tax revenue in the member states increased their availability to adopt certain direct taxation harmonization measures.

The first harmonization initiatives were very radical, and were aimed at equalizing tax rates and bases. In this context, the following findings and actions are significant.

- The conclusions of the Neumark Report (1962) showed that the differences registered in terms of tax structures and tax bases distort competition within the EEC, requiring the harmonization of corporate income taxes. The report concluded that the "normalization" of competition conditions within the EEC did not require action on tax rates. Instead, the need for uniformity of corporate income tax bases was emphasized (to this end, a common system of taxation was recommended, with two tax rates depending on the destination of profits) and also the need to improve cooperation between national tax authorities.[2]
- Based on the conclusions of the Neumark Report, in 1967, the European Commission presented the "Program for the harmonization of direct taxes" that provided a series of measures for

the approximation of personal and corporate income tax systems, including the following: introducing a single tax on the global income of individuals, taxation of investment income earned by financial intermediaries, avoiding double taxation, combating international tax evasion, the elimination of tax obstacles to cross-border mergers and economic operations between a parent company and its subsidiaries, and removing the practice of withholding tax on payments of interest or dividends.[3]

- The European Commission Memorandum on the coordination of economic policies and monetary cooperation within the European Community in 1969 underlined the need to remove all barriers to the free movement of capital and to create conditions of fair competition for investments, by aligning tax incentives and methods for determining the tax liabilities of companies (European Commission, 1969).
- The van den Tempel Report (1970) identified the non-harmonized tax treatment of cross-border payments of dividends as a major problem within the Single Market. The use of different dividend taxation systems in EEC countries created advantages and disadvantages for investments. Thus, the fair allocation of financial resources within the Single Market was distorted. For example, non-resident investors were disadvantaged by the imputation dividend taxation system in the home state of the company owned by shareholders if the classical dividend taxation system was used in the state of residence. A situation of this kind could lead to the attenuation of the investor's interest for companies that conducted activities in other member states, representing a barrier to the free movement of capital. In order to correct this deficiency, Professor A. J. van den Tempel recommended the introduction of the classical income taxation system (easier to use than other systems) for legal entities in all EEC countries. This allowed a clear distinction between the sphere and scope of corporate income tax and personal income tax (1970, pp. 11–30).
- In 1975, the European Commission presented an action programme in the field of taxation (in order to harmonize corporate income tax and dividend tax) that specified the alignment of corporate income tax rates in the range of 45–55 per cent and the use of a partial imputation system (tax credit) to prevent the double taxation of dividends. Granting tax credits for non-resident recipients of dividends requires a budgetary compensation mechanism that would have functioned only if national tax systems had been similar

(European Commission, 1975). The European Council did not discuss this proposal because the European Parliament (which had to be consulted in accordance with EC treaty rules) had not given its opinion. In 1979, the European Parliament refused to give a final opinion on the European Commission's proposal, arguing that it would be wrong to attempt the harmonization of corporate tax rates in the absence of certain rules for tax base harmonization, instead recommending a more comprehensive approach to the problem. In 1990, the proposal was withdrawn by the European Commission (Patterson and Martinez, 2000, p. 4).
- In 1980, the European Commission published a proposal for a European Council directive on a common system of taxation applicable to mergers, divisions and contributions of assets occurring between companies from different member states. The main purpose of this proposal was to defer the taxation that would otherwise occur when two companies from different member states engaged in a merger or similar operation. The proposal would have had to remove some of the tax obstacles to cooperation across frontiers between companies wishing to concentrate or disperse their activities (European Commission, 1980).
- In 1988, the European Commission presented a draft proposal to harmonize the rules for determining taxable income, in connection with depreciation, the taxation of capital gains and losses, the provisions for risks and expenses, the assessment of inventory items, the measurement of other assets and the deductibility of fees and expenses. The harmonization of provisions relating to carrying forward tax losses and prohibiting the granting of tax incentives could generate improvements in a company's competitive ability. In 1991, the earlier proposal was withdrawn (Patterson and Martinez, 2000, p. 5).

After rejection of these proposals by member states, the European Commission followed a "policy of small steps" that was founded on two principles: (1) the perfection of the Single Market by removing "residual" obstacles, and (2) subsidiarity.

In 1990, the European Commission formed a committee of independent tax experts (Ruding Committee), in order to study the possibility of approximating income tax systems and rates within the EU. The starting point was provided by three questions needing answers:

1. Do the differences in the EU corporate tax systems generate significant economic distortions, incompatible with the functioning of the Single Market?

2. Can one expect that these differences might disappear by means of tax competition and market forces, or should one consider a community action?
3. Is a minimum of regulations imposed at EU level necessary?

Experts meeting at the Ruding Committee carried out a comprehensive analysis (an objective analysis and a subjective analysis).

The objective analysis aimed at comparing (using a simulation model) the tax situation of the same firm operating in each member state in terms of the profit before and after tax and the tax treatment of domestic and foreign investment. It was found that the disparities between member states were important, but they were not only related to tax differences. They were also determined by differences between interest rates and inflation rates in different EU member states.

The subjective analysis was based on a survey of companies from different member states. It aimed to provide information about the role of differences in tax regimes on investment location decisions. The investigation revealed that the majority (58 per cent of companies) of these decisions were influenced by tax considerations. Furthermore, 75 per cent of surveyed companies' representatives did not believe in the capacity of the Single Market to generate the convergence of tax systems, and they pronounced in favour of an EU common legislation. Finally, the analysis revealed that significant differences between pre-tax profits and after tax profits were much reduced in the late 1980s to early 1980s, even in the absence of any concerted action by member states (European Commission, 1992).

Considering these results, the Ruding Committee proposed an action programme which provided, inter alia:

- the abolition of discriminations and distortions (in terms of investment and cross-holdings) generated by the different tax systems existing within the EU;
- the avoidance of excessive tax competition between member states through the introduction of minimum rules on tax rates and the tax base.

Thus, the committee of experts proposed the extension of the abolition of withholding tax on dividends in member states for all types of companies and a reduction of the participation threshold. The Ruding Committee also insisted on the necessity of setting harmonized rules in the field of transfer prices (the price at which an item is transferred internally between two subsidiaries of the same corporate group).

Without these measures, situations may occur where costs are located in countries with high corporate income tax rates and profits are located in countries with low corporate income tax rates. In order to reduce competition distortions which may result from differences in national tax regimes, the adoption of a minimum corporate income tax rate of 30 per cent and a maximum corporate income tax rate of 40 per cent was recommended. It was also recommended that the income corporate tax base should be harmonized at a minimum level (minimum standards for determining the main parameters of the income corporate tax base to cover: depreciation, provisions, reporting losses).

The most important conclusion of the Ruding Report refers to the effects of corporate income tax harmonization in member states. It was found that harmonization could lead to an increase in the efficiency of the Single Market, because in the absence of distortions caused by the differences between corporate tax systems, capital would be allocated to those countries where it could be invested more productively. In the event of harmonization of tax rates at the lowest level, member states had an additional gain generated by the attraction of capital from non-community countries.

According to Dragos Negrescu and Anton Comanescu, the non-uniformity of progress on the two coordinates (type of tax and tax parameters) reflects the relative opportunity considerations, but also the willingness shown by some member states for tax harmonization measures. This willingness was higher from countries that had large tax bases or a less important financial sector. Thus, representatives from Germany and France usually expressed opinions in favour of tax harmonization, while representatives from Luxembourg and Ireland consistently objected to such initiatives. The particularities of countries such as the Netherlands (which has a relatively narrow tax base) and the UK (which has an important financial sector) determined nuanced manifestations to certain tax harmonization proposals (2007, p. 46).

In April 1996, a "High Level Group" on taxation under the Economic and Financial Affairs (ECOFIN) Council was established. Its chairman was the tax commissioner, Mario Monti. The European Commission's initial conclusions, formulated after this group's meetings, were published in October 1996 under the title "Taxation in the EU: Report on the development of tax systems".

The Monti Report revealed a number of challenges facing taxation in the EU (European Commission, 1996):

- Single Market failures, especially with regard to cross-border payments of interest and dividends and the taxation of international business activities;
- changes in the tax revenue structures (increasing the share of social contributions and personal income taxes), representing in part the effects of the excessive tax competition between member states;
- the need to adopt certain fiscal measures to encourage cross-border economic activities, together with measures to protect member states from tax revenues losses due to the tax arbitrage actions of corporations or tax evasion.

In order to meet these challenges, representatives from the "High Level Group" indicated that cooperation and coordination actions were needed. They did not recommend the introduction of a minimum tax rate or common rules on the corporate income tax base. The report showed very clearly that any proposal for a community action in the field of taxation had to take full account of the principles of subsidiarity and proportionality. The European Commission should refrain from introducing proposals for directives in the field of direct taxation in order to achieve tax harmonization if it was not necessary.

The content of the Monti Report (which was written in a very generalized way) did not include any concrete proposals for economic policy measures, but rather recommendations for future tax initiatives in the member states:

- to achieve wide-ranging agreement on the definition of tax measures harmful to the Single Market;
- to strengthen cooperation between tax authorities in the fight against tax fraud and tax evasion;
- to introduce fiscal coordination measures, in order to avoid excessive tax competition within the Single Market, discriminatory tax treatment and cases of double taxation.

In October 1997, the European Commission submitted to the European Council and European Parliament a communication entitled "Towards tax co-ordination in the European Union – A package to tackle harmful tax competition", which included some recommendations made by the Monti Report. This communication showed that the benefits arising from the removal of barriers on capital flows were accompanied by the increased possibility of taxpayers avoiding taxes, such that taxation had become a key factor influencing the economic decisions made in the EU. Due to the introduction of the single currency, the differences between national tax systems had become more visible and had generated a greater influence on resource allocation decisions, and therefore on the effectiveness of economic activity. The impact of taxation on business decision making may also have increased due to the development of electronic commerce and the increased mobility of some economic activities (European Commission, 1997).

In this changing environment, the European Commission predicted the development of harmful tax competition and the potential resulting emergence of some sources of conflict between member states. Because a high degree of administrative cooperation and tax coordination within EU member states already allowed for the avoidance of such problems, the European Commission proposed a package of fiscal measures known as the "Tax Package". The suggested components of this package were as follows:

- a Code of Conduct for business taxation and, in parallel, a European Commission communication concerning state aid;
- measures to eliminate distortions from capital gains taxes;
- measures to avoid taxation of cross-border interest and royalty payments between associated companies.

The Code of Conduct for business taxation was considered to be a key element of the package, being developed as a non-binding political instrument, whereby member states were committed to the principles of fair competition and refrained from introducing any harmful tax measures.

On 1 December 1997, after the ECOFIN Council meeting on tax policy, some of its conclusions were published. As a result, the resolution on the Code of Conduct for business taxation was adopted, and a proposal to develop certain directives on a common system of taxation applicable to savings, interest and royalty payments made between associated companies was approved.[4] Potentially harmful tax measures introduced by member states were regulated by the Code of Conduct for business taxation. The Code of Conduct aimed to tackle the following:

- tax benefits reserved for non-residents or transactions conducted by non-residents;
- tax benefits granted to some companies without any real economic activity and/or a substantial economic presence within the territory of the member state;

- legislative rules for determining the profits of multinational groups of companies that have departed from internationally accepted principles, in particular, the rules approved by the OECD;
- the lack of transparency with regard to tax measures.

At the ECOFIN Council meeting on 9 March 1998, it was established that compliance with this code would be monitored by a body delegated by the Finance Ministries of the member states. This is known as the "Primarolo Group" after its chairwoman Dawn Primarolo. In 1999, the group presented a report on harmful tax measures identified in countries such as the Netherlands, Belgium, Ireland, Luxembourg and others, which had a significant influence on the location of economic activities within the EU. These were legislative or administrative measures to set up a lower net effective tax rate than the net effective tax rate usually practised within the member state, taking into account tax rates and tax bases.

Most of these measures were aimed at financial services, offshore companies and multinational groups. Tax incentives in the shipping sector were not sanctioned because it was believed that in the context of a globalized world market, these fiscal measures were necessary to maintain the competitiveness of EU countries compared to other countries. According to Stephen Bond, Lucy Chennells, Michael P. Devereux, Malcolm Gammie and Edward Troup, this aspect suggested that the main concern of the working group was to incriminate those actions that could generate the erosion of member states' tax revenues and not to prevent the distortion of the location of real economic activities (2000, p. 58).

In 2000, the "Primarolo Group" proposed a series of deadlines by which the member states listed in the report had to eliminate the harmful tax measures identified. In June 2003, the 15 EU member states approved the final form of the package of fiscal measures to avoid harmful tax competition within the Single Market. Approving the Code of Conduct for business taxation, member states committed themselves to the following:

- to refrain from introducing any new tax measures harmful to the competitive environment within the Single Market;
- to review the existing tax provisions and to eliminate any harmful tax measures, taking into account the ECOFIN recommendations made after completion of the evaluation procedures;

- to mutually inform each other about any tax measures that may fall within the scope of the Code of Conduct for business taxation;
- to promote principles regarding the elimination of harmful tax measures in third countries and territories in which the treaty was not applied.

The Code of Conduct for business taxation consecrated the open method of coordination[5] in the field of direct taxation. In a first step, all the member states (including the UK, Ireland, Luxembourg and the Netherlands who had criticized the idea of using European governance for limiting international tax competition) agreed on specific criteria for the definition of harmful tax competition. It was very clear that the European Commission's main argument in favour of the tax package against harmful tax competition – tax regimes with the aim of only attracting foreign tax bases are incompatible with the functioning of the Single Market – could not be combated.

The negotiation of the provisions of the Code of Conduct for business taxation was carried out within an intergovernmental framework, and the activities of the "Primarolo Group" were done in the same way. As a second step, the group published a report on harmful tax measures, measures that were identified and incriminated.

Because the Code of Conduct for business taxation is not binding for member states, its contribution to the coordination of some corporate tax policy issues in the EU depends on how this initiative is translated into legislative changes in each state.

2.3.2 The European Commission's strategic objectives for 2001–2007

In 2000, the European Council meeting in Lisbon set as the strategic goal for the EU economy "to become the most competitive and dynamic knowledge-based economy in the world".[6] Achieving this objective requires the creation of a general framework for stimulating economic activities within the EU, in which corporate taxation can play an important role. A strategy for corporate taxation was developed, which would recognize the following changes in the general economic context in which companies had been operating from 1990 onwards:

- the growing number of international mergers and acquisitions;
- the appearance of electronic commerce and the increased mobility of factors of production, which generated serious difficulties in defining and protecting tax bases;

- the economic (but non-tax), technological and institutional barriers which continued to hinder cross-border trade;
- large companies had begun to approach the entire EU as a "home market" and they had started to establish pan-European business structures;
- taxpayers (individuals or corporate) had begun to request the removal of preferential tax regimes that operated within the Single Market.

Since many of these developments were likely to be accelerated as a result of EU enlargement, the European Commission identified clearly the need to adapt EU corporate taxation to this changing environment. The assessment of the overall importance of such issues and the goal of finding settlement solutions started with the concept of economic efficiency. In terms of economic activities, EU corporate taxation had to meet the following requirements:

- to help to increase international competitiveness of EU companies in accordance with the strategic objectives set out by the European Council in Lisbon;
- to ensure the neutrality of taxation, fiscal considerations should affect the economic decision-making process as little as possible;
- to avoid unnecessary or unreasonably high compliance costs and tax barriers to cross-border economic activity;
- not to prevent tax competition in general, but to eliminate "harmful tax competition" effects.

In this context, the 2001 communication from the European Commission to the European Council, the European Parliament and the Economic and Social Committee entitled "Towards an Internal Market without tax obstacles. Considering the complex relationship between tax revenue and the efficiency of social-economic or administrative activities, a strategy for providing companies with a consolidated corporate tax base for their EU-wide activities" highlighted the need to reform member states' corporate tax systems. It also presented the results of a study on the impact of taxation on the location decisions of companies in EU countries, and it formulated some general directions for actions to adopt a strategy for the reform of corporate taxation.

The Companies Tax Survey was conducted by specialized departments of the European Commission and it presented estimates of effective corporate tax rates (marginal and average) on domestic and transnational investments in 15 EU countries, taking into account the different forms of investment in the production sectors and various funding sources. Given that the effective tax rate for a particular member state depends on the specific characteristics of investment projects, the study was not intended to provide "universally valid values" in order to illustrate the level of tax burden in different countries, but rather to illustrate the interrelation between taxation and investment in a number of relevant cases. The survey's conclusions explained the mechanism by which member states' tax regimes created incentives to allocate resources.

Since the quantitative results depend heavily on the assumptions that underlie the applied methodologies, the analysis did not provide empirical evidence of the effective tax impact on economic decisions, but permitted the observation that differences in tax levels across the member states could have an important influence on the international competitiveness of EU companies, and could provide incentives for companies when choosing locations for their investments (which were not necessarily the most efficient locations in the absence of fiscal stimulus). The survey did not attempt to quantify the size of efficiency losses or the costs of welfare that could be associated with differences in corporate taxation, but it did show that the differences between the effective corporate income tax levels may involve an inefficient allocation of resources. The results of the survey explained the significant gap between the various nominal rates of corporate income tax (more than 30 percentage points): it was determined, firstly, by the necessity of compensating differences in the size of the corporate income tax base, and, secondly, by political and economic choices related to attracting FDI. It was noted that the relative share of corporate income tax rates in determining the effective tax burden increased when the return on investment increased. Accordingly, any compensatory effect of a lower tax base on effective tax rates tends to disappear when profitability increases (European Commission, 2001a).

The Companies Tax Survey identified a number of areas where current systems of corporate income taxation generated or could generate barriers in cross-border trade or in investment location. Essentially, the European Commission made the following observations:

- There are high compliance costs and tax costs – potentially double – when profit is transferred between subsidiaries located in different countries.
- There are major limitations on cross-border offsetting of losses, which may generate double taxation.

- Cross-border restructuring operations generate substantial tax costs. Merger Directive 90/434/EEC provides for the delay in the payment of income tax for such operations, but its scope is too narrow and the implementation of this directive in various member states differs, thus reducing the effectiveness of this measure. Taxes on capital gains from cross-border restructuring operations were often prohibitively high, so that companies were forced to leave those structures that did not fit the optimal economic parameters.
- As a result of conflicts surrounding taxation rights, the existence of different tax regimes for corporate income has the considerable potential for double taxation.

In order to remove these obstacles, the European Commission identified two sets of solutions:

1. Specific measures were designed to solve the most urgent problems. These included: the mediation of double taxation agreements between member states and actions to facilitate cross-border restructuring operations.
2. A complete solution to solve the tax problems faced by companies with business activities on the territory of two or more member states. This solution was to materialize as a series of concrete proposals at a later date, and it focused on the creation of the necessary framework for companies to determine the taxable income of the group under a common set of rules and to allow the settlement of consolidated accounts for tax purposes, thereby eliminating potentially adverse tax effects of intra-group transactions. Such an approach does not violate the right of member states to establish corporate income tax rates, because corporate income tax is calculated by applying national tax rates on the tax base calculated by an allocation mechanism that was to be set up in the future.

A consolidated tax base for companies involved in cross-border activities within the EU should result in the following benefits:

- *A reduction in administrative costs* for both the companies and tax administrations who must monitor the transfer pricing process, because according to the existing fiscal regulations, companies (members of the group) operating in multiple EU tax jurisdictions are treated as independent units in terms of tax.

- *A reduction in compliance costs* incurred by corporations who are required to know the tax-accounting laws of all the countries in which they operate, in order to determine the tax base or to calculate any tax refunds.
- *Tax consolidation* (which allows a group of companies to offset profits and losses arising from its various component entities).
- *Simplification of some cross-border restructuring operations.*
- *Avoidance of double taxation.* In the absence of any unifying or harmonizing measures at community level, member states have the power to establish the tax criteria needed to eliminate double taxation. This means that a member state does not need to consider, when applying its tax law, any unfavourable outcomes resulting from a particular regulation of another member state, applicable to a permanent establishment situated on its territory and belonging to a company whose headquarters are located in the other state.
- *The elimination of many discriminatory situations and restrictions* on companies.

Therefore, a consolidated tax base for companies involved in cross-border activities within the EU could lead to increased efficiency, effectiveness and transparency of national taxation systems and, by extension, to increased competitiveness within the EU. This context could provide a relevant basis for achieving the objectives set out by the European Council in Lisbon.

The Companies Tax Survey (2001) identified the following technical solutions, in order to remove barriers caused by the existence of different tax regimes for companies operating within the member states:

- Home State Taxation;
- Common Consolidated Corporate Tax Base (CCCTB);
- European Corporate Income Tax;
- Single Harmonized Tax Base in the EU.

These approaches mainly exhibited features related to the degree of harmonization of the tax base, the speed of introduction of these measures and the political reforms needed for their application. These approaches had a common element: the principle of corporate income consolidation for EU companies. The European Commission did not consider promoting just one of the above technical solutions, but rather the creation of a complex system to meet the particular requirements of all companies involved in cross-border activities within the EU.

The quantitative analysis of the Companies Tax Survey provided a comprehensive picture of corporate income tax rates in member states, but it did not present any evidence in support of the harmful tax competition generated by differences between tax regimes in those countries. In this context, the European Commission did not recommend specific actions on the approximation of national income tax rates or the establishment of a minimum corporate tax rate. The European Commission also recognized that tax neutrality should not be the sole goal of the fiscal policy. The level of taxation in a state is a political choice, requiring a compromise between ensuring economic efficiency and other objectives of economic and social policy.

The schedule established in 2001 to identify the optimal for harmonizing corporate tax systems included the following targets:

- organizing a conference entitled "European business taxation" in 2002, with very broad participation: member states' representatives, business representatives, academics and others, in order to debate the main approaches to harmonizing corporate income taxes in the EU;
- listing companies able to register their income in consolidated accounts in accordance with International Accounting Standards, starting in 2005;
- creating a new form of business organization to provide the status of "European companies" up until 2004. The European Commission has mainly taken into account the application in all member countries of Directive 90/435/EEC on the common system of taxation applicable in the case of parent companies and subsidiaries in different member states;
- initiating a "pilot project" for assessment of the impact of the introduction of a CCCTB.

The idea of creating a CCCTB in the EU affirmed by the European Commission was quickly accepted by most representatives of the business community and welcomed by many specialists. Policy responses to the fiscal strategy proposed in 2001 were numerous, most member states showing more scepticism towards the practical application of the strategy for a number of technical and political reasons (the chances of ensuring unanimity in approving the legislative proposal by the member states were reduced).

In response to these reactions, the European Commission recognized in 2003 that the proposed approaches had a high degree of difficulty, but it informed that it remained convinced that the CCCTB was a measure designed to improve the Single Market. For this reason, the European Commission maintained its determination to continue the "Common Consolidated Corporate Tax Base" project, initiating an evaluation of its impact. The European Commission considered that a systematic approach to the problem of corporate taxation in the EU would protect the financial interests of member states and would potentiate the growth of their ability to collect income (European Commission, 2003b).

In 2003, a model of corporate income tax harmonization based on the mutual recognition of a home country's tax laws was recognized as a possible solution for difficulties faced by small and medium enterprises (SMEs) involved in cross-border activities within the EU. In order to assess the impact of adopting measures based on the principles of this model, the European Commission proposed the launching of a pilot project. This initiative received considerable support from academics and employers' organizations. The workshop and public consultation on these issues provided many ideas, considered technical "inputs" for the project initiation, and they showed a broad convergence regarding basic motivation and the need to run the project.

Analysing the role of SMEs in the economic development of the EU, the European Commission noted that the participation of this category of firms in the Single Market was considerably lower than the participation of large companies for various reasons, including those of a fiscal nature. This situation leads to a loss of potential growth and jobs, which could compromise the Lisbon objectives.

According to a survey accomplished by interviewing a representative sample of SMEs' representatives, compliance costs for different tax regimes in various member states were found to be the primary obstacle to expanding business across national borders. Secondly, the difficulties in offsetting profits and losses between members of corporate groups were a particular problem for SMEs because, usually, a company suffers losses at the inception of business in a foreign state, and these losses are more difficult to bear by companies with low capitalization (European Commission, 2005a). In the case of SMEs, Duanjie Chen, Frank Lee and Jack Mintz identified another barrier to expanding across borders: they were disadvantaged because they could not access some incentives or fiscal facilities offered by public authorities in certain countries to encourage SMEs with domestic capital (Chen et al., 2002, p. 4).

In this context, the European Commission recommended eliminating the tax barriers that prevented the proper functioning of the Single Market through better coordination of the corporate income tax systems of the member states.

The basic principles of corporate tax coordination in the EU were as follows:

- to eliminate discrimination and double taxation;
- to prevent abuses and non-taxation due to negligence;
- to diminish compliance costs resulting from the application of several tax systems.

The goal of coordination of non-harmonized corporate tax systems in EU countries was to ensure their compatibility with one another and with European Community law. In this respect, in a communication dated December 2006, the European Commission specified that an adequate level of coordination and cooperation between member states would enable them to achieve their fiscal policy objectives and to protect their tax bases, while ensuring elimination of fiscal discrimination and certain situations of double taxation, also reducing compliance costs. In this way, tax systems could contribute to the success of the Single Market and to an increased competitiveness of EU enterprises within a globally competitive market, in accordance with the revised Lisbon strategy. The European Commission showed its willingness to assist member states in developing coordinated solutions based on the principles stipulated in the communication and in improving practical arrangements for administrative cooperation (European Commission, 2006a).

The European Commission communication dated May 2007 – "Implementing the Community Program for improved growth and employment and the enhanced competitiveness of EU business: Further Progress during 2006 and the next steps towards a proposal on the Common Consolidated Corporate Tax Base (CCCTB)" – reiterated its conviction that, while better tax coordination between member states could contribute to the elimination of certain tax barriers to cross-European companies' development, a comprehensive approach (by introducing the CCCTB) might offer the greatest benefits in terms of general taxation of profits (European Commission, 2007a).

The implementation of the CCCTB rules could contribute significantly to the success of the Single Market and to the achievement of a higher rate of economic growth and employment because, globally, the EU could become more attractive for investment. The creation of a CCCTB involves the appearance of some differences between the new base and the current national tax bases. Member states would have to accept that the CCCTB cannot replicate the characteristics of all existing tax bases. In general, the new base should rather be "extended" than "restricted", because most economists argue that a broad tax base with a low tax rate is the most efficient one, because the potential distortion effects are minimal in number and importance. Practical implications of this approach translate into a smaller number of facilities and exceptions. Thus, specific exemptions and incentives should be limited in number, properly targeted and justified (tax incentives for research and development deserve particular analysis because these can influence economic competitiveness).

Key principles for building the new corporate income tax system in the EU are as follows:

- the common corporate tax base must be accompanied by consolidation;
- the common corporate tax base should be optional (companies must be able to retain existing rules if they are similar to the CCCTB rules, or to opt for these rules, provided that the state aid rules are respected).

In this way, the problem of the absence of an EU mechanism available to offset cross-border losses would be solved. In a document issued by the European Parliament, it is specified that, currently, member states apply different rules for granting fiscal incentives for losses incurred in branches, subsidiaries and entities of corporate groups that distort business decisions and investment policies in the Single Market, with consequences for their economic strategies and tax revenues (European Parliament, 2008). The European Commission communication "Tax Treatment of Losses in Cross-Border Situations", dated December 2006, presented the following options for the introduction of cross-border offset of losses (European Commission, 2006b):

- *Definitive transfer of losses ("intra-group loss relief")*. Here, the losses of a company (or more companies) are fully absorbed by profits incurred by other companies in the group. One way to neutralize the negative impact of applying this system to tax revenues of member states (where "absorbed" companies are resident) could be to introduce a compensation mechanism between member states.
- *Temporary loss transfer ("deduction/reintegration method")*. Here, a loss incurred by a subsidiary located in a member state, which was

deducted from the positive fiscal result of the parent company or other subsidiaries, will be recovered, in terms of taxes, when that subsidiary returns to profitability. Therefore, the loss transfer is temporary.

- *Current taxation of a subsidiary's results ("system of consolidated profits")*. Here, the profits and losses of the subsidiary/subsidiaries will be recorded in the consolidated financial statement of the parent company. The income tax paid by the subsidiary/subsidiaries in the state/states of residence will be deducted from the income tax paid by the parent company, in order to avoid double taxation. The application of such a system is not related or limited to the existence of tax losses.

Using a cross-border mechanism to offset cross-border losses will allow corporate groups in the EU to make substantial tax savings, thereby creating the conditions for increased attractiveness of the European business environment and obtaining associated advantages such as: attracting FDI, new jobs and so on.

2.3.3 The main legal regulations relating to direct taxation within the EU

The most important progress in the coordination of direct taxation has targeted international double taxation and cross-border economic activities.

On 23 July 1990, the European Council adopted Directive 90/434/EEC on a common system of taxation applicable to mergers, divisions, transfers of assets and exchanges of shares concerning companies from different member states ("the Merger Directive").[7] This directive has been amended by Directive 2005/19/EC.[8] The Merger Directive provides for deferral of the taxes that could be charged on the difference between the real value of such assets and liabilities and their value for tax purposes. It therefore seeks to avoid the occurrence of tax liability solely as a result of cross-border corporate restructuring. The deferral is granted provided that the receiving company continues with its tax values and effectively connects them to its own permanent establishment in the member state of the transferring company. These rules apply to transfer of assets where the assets transferred form a branch of activity. The Merger Directive also covers triangular cases where the transaction includes a permanent establishment of the transferring company situated in a different member state.

Operations covered by this directive are as follows:

1. Merger shall mean an operation whereby:

   - one or more companies, on being dissolved without going into liquidation, transfer all their assets and liabilities to another existing company in exchange for the issue to their shareholders of securities representing the capital of that other company, and, if applicable, a cash payment not exceeding 10 per cent of the nominal value, or, in the absence of a nominal value, of the accounting par value of those securities;
   - two or more companies, on being dissolved without going into liquidation, transfer all their assets and liabilities to a company that they form, in exchange for the issue to their shareholders of securities representing the capital of that new company, and, if applicable, a cash payment not exceeding 10 per cent of the nominal value, or in the absence of a nominal value, of the accounting par value of those securities;
   - a company, on being dissolved without going into liquidation, transfers all its assets and liabilities to the company holding all the securities representing its capital.

2. Division shall mean an operation whereby a company, on being dissolved without going into liquidation, transfers all its assets and liabilities to two or more existing or new companies, in exchange for the pro rata issue to its shareholders of securities representing the capital of the companies receiving the assets and liabilities, and, if applicable, a cash payment not exceeding 10 per cent of the nominal value or, in the absence of a nominal value, of the accounting par value of those securities.
3. Transfer of assets shall mean an operation whereby a company transfers without being dissolved all or one or more branches of its activity to another company in exchange for the transfer of securities representing the capital of the company receiving the transfer.
4. Exchange of shares shall mean an operation whereby a company acquires a holding in the capital of another company such that it obtains a majority of the voting rights in that company in exchange for the issue to the shareholders of the latter company, in exchange for their securities, of securities representing the capital of the former company, and, if applicable, a cash payment not exceeding

10 per cent of the nominal value or, in the absence of a nominal value, of the accounting par value of the securities issued in exchange.

A member state may refuse to apply or withdraw the benefit of all or any part of the directive where it appears that the merger, division, transfer of assets or exchange of shares:

- has as its principal objective or as one of its principal objectives tax evasion or tax avoidance; the fact that one of the operations referred to in Article 1 is not carried out for valid commercial reasons, such as the restructuring or rationalization of the activities of the companies participating in the operation, may constitute a presumption that the operation has tax evasion or tax avoidance as its principal objective or as one of its principal objectives;
- results in a company, whether participating in the operation or not, no longer fulfilling the necessary conditions for the representation of employees on company organs according to the arrangements which were in force prior to that operation.

On 17 February 2005, the European Council adopted Directive 2005/19/EC (amending the Merger Directive). The main amendments introduced by Directive 2005/19/EC are as follows:

- The benefits of the Merger Directive are extended to a greater number of legal entities, including European companies.
- The coverage of a new type of transaction: a special division known as a "split off", named in the directive as partial division. The splitting company is not dissolved and continues to exist. It transfers part of its assets and liabilities, constituting one or more branches of activity, to another company. In exchange, the receiving company issues securities representing its capital. These securities are transferred to the shareholders of the transferring company.
- The directive provides for capital gains exemption when the receiving company holds shares in the transferring company. The holding threshold required to enjoy this exemption has been modified by Directive 2005/19/EC to align it with that of the Parent-Subsidiary Directive. This threshold will be lowered in stages from 25 per cent to 10 per cent, in line with the amendments to the Parent-Subsidiary Directive introduced by European Council Directive 2003/123/EC.

A survey on the implementation of the directive, carried out by Ernst and Young during 2007–2008, reveals the following issues:

- Because the content of the directive does not provide definitions of terms such as: branch of activity, real value, provisions and reserves, comparable circumstances, etc., in several member states the local interpretation of these terms is inconsistent with the directive.
- The purpose of the Merger Directive is to establish what happens to taxable assets after corporate reorganization, however, the representatives of tax authorities believe that its purpose is to determine the taxation competences of the member states.
- In some countries, tax incentives for mergers, divisions, transfers of assets and exchanges of shares concerning companies of different member states are granted on terms more restrictive than those defined in the Merger Directive.
- In many cases, member states abused the option to refuse or withdraw the benefits provided by the directive in cases of tax evasion or tax fraud. (2009, pp. 14–17)

Because many of the provisions of the Merger Directive continue to be controversial, some companies in cross-border reorganizations fail to benefit from fiscal facilities under the directive.

On 17 February 2005, the European Council adopted Directive 90/435/EEC on the common system of taxation applicable in the case of parent companies and subsidiaries in different member states ("the Parent-Subsidiary Directive").[9] This legislative regulation (amended by Directive 2003/123/EEC[10]) applies to the following situations:

- distributing profits received by companies of that state which come from their subsidiaries in other member states;
- distributing profits by companies of that state to companies of other member states in which they are subsidiaries.

If a parent company (the parent company had to hold at least 10 per cent as from 1 January 2009) receives distributed profits, by virtue of its association with its subsidiary, the state of the parent company must:

- either refrain from taxing such profits;
- or tax such profits while authorizing the parent company to deduct from the amount of tax due that fraction of the corporation tax paid by the subsidiary which relates to those profits.

The directive was designed to eliminate tax obstacles in the area of profit distribution between groups of companies in the EU by:

- abolishing withholding taxes on payments of dividends between associated companies of different member states; and
- preventing double taxation of parent companies on the profits of their subsidiaries.

The amending directive contained three main elements:

1. an updated list of companies covered by the directive;
2. a relaxation of the conditions for exempting dividends from withholding tax (reduction of the participation threshold); and
3. the elimination of double taxation for subsidiaries of subsidiary companies.

The amending directive deals with imputing tax paid by subsidiaries of these direct subsidiary companies. Member states must impute against the tax payable by the parent company any tax on profits paid by successive subsidiaries downstream of the direct subsidiary. This ensures that the objective of eliminating double taxation is better achieved.

The inter-governmental Convention on the elimination of double taxation in connection with the adjustment of profits of associated enterprises 90/436/EEC[11] ("the Arbitration Convention") came in addition to the above directives, and addressed the issue of transfer pricing. This agreement stipulates the compulsory arbitration in cases where tax authorities fail to solve, within a maximum of two years, a situation of double taxation, generated by the different approaches of tax authorities involved in the transfer pricing.

Here, in the absence of a double taxation agreement between tax authorities and companies, a case will be presented to an advisory committee (composed of a chairman, two representatives from each tax jurisdiction involved and an even number of independent persons appointed by common agreement on a predefined list). The committee suggests a method to solve the problem.

The Arbitration Convention was signed in 1990 by all 15 member states. The protocol of the convention stipulated an automatic extension of a period of five years unless a contracting state opposes. The signing of the Arbitration Convention by all the member states was a clear recognition of the importance of eliminating international double taxation situations in the EU.

Initially, the European Commission proposed a draft directive in this area, however, the member states preferred a multilateral convention. Joseph Ghislain considered that this was a signal of the refusal by member states to give up their tax sovereignty on transfer pricing policy (Ghislain, 2002, p. 47).

As stated in the preamble of the Arbitration Convention, the legal basis for its signature is Article 220 of the Treaty of Rome, which states that, if necessary, member states may enter into negotiations in order to eliminate double taxation within the European Community, in the interest of their citizens.

In order to address the issue of double taxation in terms of tax coordination within the EU, it is possible to identify some deficiencies in the Arbitration Convention:

- Unlike the directive, the Convention is to be ratified at regular intervals.
- The interpretation of the Convention is the responsibility of national courts, and it is outside the jurisdiction of the European Court of Justice (for example, in the uniform interpretation of regulations).

The Merger Directive, the Parent-Subsidiary Directive and the Arbitration Convention played an important role in eliminating some tax obstacles for corporate groups in the EU. However, these legal instruments proved to be insufficient to keep pace with the trend of increasing integration in the Single Market. In the future, their scope should be extended to cover a wide range of companies, taxes and economic operations.

On 3 June 2003, the European Council adopted Directive 2003/48/EC[12] on taxation of savings income in the form of interest payments, and Directive 2003/49/EC[13] on a common system of taxation applicable to interest and royalty payments made between associated companies of different member states.

These regulations are part of the package of fiscal measures to avoid harmful tax competition within the Single Market proposed by the European Commission.

According to the European Commission communication "Towards tax coordination in the EU: A package of measures to tackle harmful tax competition" published in October 1997, residents of member states could avoid any form of taxation in the state of residence on interest earned in another member state, due to the free movement of capital and the lack of any coordination of national systems for the taxation of savings income in the form of interest payments. Distortions affecting the movement of capital between member states were incompatible with the Single Market, and the existing situation encouraged tax evasion in the case of savings income and increased the tax burden on less mobile sources of revenue, such as wages, with direct negative effects on the costs of labour and, indirectly, on the creation of jobs.

In this context, the European Council adopted Directive 2003/48/EC on taxation of savings income in the form of interest payments ("Savings Directive"). The Savings Directive seeks to allow taxation of savings income (paid in a member state in favour of some beneficiaries – individuals – who have their residence in another member state) under the laws of the state of residence. The tool that facilitates the taxation of these payments is the automatic exchange of information between member states.

The general regime applicable to the automatic exchange of information between member states includes the following:

- *Authorizing the paying agent to report information:* if the beneficial owner is resident in a member state other that in which the paying agent is established, the directive provides that the paying agent must report to the competent authority of its member state a minimum amount of information such as: the identity and residence of the beneficial owner, the name and address of the paying agent, the account number of the beneficial owner or, where there is none, identification of the debt claim giving rise to the interest and information concerning the interest payment. Member states may restrict the minimum amount of information concerning interest payment to be reported by the paying agent to the total amount of interest or income, and to the total amount of the proceeds from sale, redemption or refund.
- *The automatic exchange of information:* the competent authority of the member state of the paying agent shall communicate – at least once a year, within six months following the end of the tax year of the member state of the paying agent – the minimum amount of information to the competent authority of the member state of residence of the beneficial owner.

The directive provisions have been implemented in national laws and applied from 1 July 2005 in all member states except Austria, Belgium and Luxembourg, who opted to retain bank secrecy. These countries were not obliged to immediately introduce the system for providing information. They could receive information from other member states and were to introduce a system for providing information after a transitional period during which they were to charge a withholding tax at a rate of 15 per cent for the first three years, 20 per cent for the next three years and thereafter at a rate of 35 per cent. A part of tax revenues (75 per cent) could be transferred to the member state of residence of the individual – subject to tax on savings income in the form of interest payments. The transition periods were to finish with agreements on the exchange of information on request between the EU and the USA, Switzerland, Liechtenstein, San Marino, Monaco and Andorra, only if the last five countries listed simultaneously applied the withholding tax.

The European Commission issued its first report on the effects of Directive 2003/48/EC on 15 September 2008. The main conclusions of this evaluation were as follows:

- The introduction of the directive does not appear to have led to major changes in the composition of savings incomes.
- For deposits by non-bank depositors, there has been an observable shift from countries within the scope of the directive towards third countries.
- The data on information exchange from EU member states and other jurisdictions show that reported interest payments increased significantly between the second half of 2005 and 2006. Unsurprisingly, the largest payments can be found in the largest economies. The data on withholding tax countries show that Switzerland and Luxembourg are the main sources of withholding tax revenue, while Germany, Italy and the UK receive the largest share of tax revenue.
- Regression analysis does not show a statistically significant and robust effect of the Savings Directive on the level and share of interest in the total property income received by households. (European Commission, 2008)

Another impact assessment of the introduction of Directive 2003/48/EC on the taxation of savings income in the form of interest payments was made in 2009 by Thomas Hemmelgarn and Gaetan Nicodème. It showed that the volume of exchanges of information between member states increased significantly during the period of analysis (2005–2007). Switzerland and Luxembourg were the main sources of income tax withholdings, while Germany, Italy and Britain were the main destinations of these tax revenues (Hemmelgarn and Nicodème, 2009, p. 26).

Another problem solved by the fiscal package adopted in 2003 was the elimination of double taxation in the case of taxation applicable to interest and royalty payments made between associated companies of different member states. Since the application of national legislation on taxation of interest and royalty payments made between associated companies from different member states often lead to difficult administrative formalities, to cash costs for the companies and to the risk of double taxation, the European Commission proposed a directive which would ensure that payments of interest and royalties were taxed only once in a member state.

On 3 June 2003 the Council adopted Directive 2003/49/EC on a common system of taxation applicable to interest and royalty payments made between associated companies from different member states based on a proposal from the European Commission (COM (1998) 67).

According to this regulation, interest and royalty payments between affiliated companies arising in a member state shall be exempt from any taxes imposed on those payments in that state, whether by deduction at source or by assessment, provided that the beneficial owner of the interest or royalties is a company from another member state or has a permanent establishment situated in another member state of a company of a member state.

A company is an "associated company" of a second company if, at least:

- the first company has a direct minimum holding of 25 per cent in the capital of the second company; or
- the second company has a direct minimum holding of 25 per cent in the capital of the first company; or
- a third company has a direct minimum holding of 25 per cent both in the capital of the first company and in the capital of the second company.

Member states have the option of replacing the criterion of a minimum holding in the capital with that of a minimum holding of voting rights. Also, member states have the option of not applying this directive to a company from another member state or to a permanent establishment of a company from another member state in circumstances where the conditions on the status of associated companies have not been maintained for an uninterrupted period of at least two years.

A payment made by a company from a member state or with a permanent establishment situated in another member state is considered to have been generated in that state, known as the "source state".

If the paying company or permanent establishment withheld tax at source to be exempted under the provisions of Directive 2003/49/EC, it may make a request for reimbursement for withholding.

Member states may request an attestation, valid for at least one year, which proves the following:

- the company's residence for tax purposes and, where necessary, the existence of a permanent establishment certified by the tax authority of the member state in which the receiving company is resident for tax purposes or in which the permanent establishment is situated;
- the status of beneficial ownership by the receiving company;
- the payment of one of the following taxes without being exempt, or to a tax which is identical or substantially similar and which is imposed after the date of entry into force of this directive in addition to, or in place of, those existing taxes;
- a minimum holding or the criterion of a minimum holding of voting rights;
- the period for which the holding of voting rights has existed.

The source state shall repay the excess tax withheld at source within one year following due receipt of the application and such supporting information as it may reasonably ask for. If the tax withheld at source has not been refunded within that period, the receiving company or permanent establishment shall be entitled on expiry of the year in question to interest on the tax which is refunded at a rate corresponding to the national interest rate to be applied in comparable cases under the domestic law of the source state.

The source state is not obliged to ensure the benefits of this directive in the following cases:

- payments which are treated as a distribution of profits or as a repayment of capital under the law of the source state;
- payments from debt-claims which carry a right to participate in the debtor's profits;
- payments from debt-claims which entitle the creditor to exchange his right to interest for a right to participate in the debtor's profits;

- payments from debt-claims which contain no provision for repayment of the principal amount or where the repayment is due more than 50 years after the date of issue.

The directive's provisions were applied as from 1 July 2005, but transitional measures were implemented for a number of countries (Czech Republic, Greece, Spain, Latvia, Lithuania, Poland, Portugal and Slovakia).

In a report to the European Council in 2009, the European Commission considered to be satisfactory the method for implementing Directive 2003/49/EC on the taxation of interest and royalty payments between affiliated companies of different member states. Since in some cases, the interpretation and transposition into national law of certain notions (tax residence of the beneficial owner, holding threshold, reclassification of hidden profits, etc.) did not comply with the directive, the European Commission recommended the continuation of guidance on the key concepts necessary to ensure the uniformity of interpretation and to reduce the legal uncertainty (European Commission, 2009).

2.4 Perspectives on the evolution of tax harmonization in the EU

With a view to limit the interference of taxation on the optimal functioning of the Single Market, the European Commission promoted in a sustained manner the idea of tax harmonization and coordination of member states' tax systems. Despite these efforts, tax harmonization within the EU did not reach a satisfactory level. This was due to the following factors:

- The member states' fiscal sovereignty (especially in direct taxes) was maintained by the EU treaties.
- EU institutions have insufficient legal instruments to achieve a true Single Market due to the resistance of the member states to retain national tax sovereignty and the unanimity rule in tax matters.
- Although the EU has an effective judicial instrument – the European Court of Justice – able to eliminate restrictions on the four fundamental freedoms, generated by national legislative measures, fiscal coordination between member states requires "harsh governance", i.e. normative acts that are binding for all member states.

- In recent years, due to the political hesitation of member states towards "harsh governance", EU institutions with attributions in tax matters opted for "light governance", based on communications, recommendations and resolutions, with poor results in terms of the progress of tax harmonization.

When analysing the issue of the progress of tax harmonization within the EU, one cannot ignore the fact that the various social preferences in each state require the independence of fiscal policy. The EU's objective of improving the economic competitiveness of the Single Market should be pursued not only through measures of tax harmonization because, in some cases, they are not necessary. In the field of direct taxation, a certain degree of tax competition is not only inevitable but also desirable, if taken as a fair tax competition. This stimulates governments to provide the best possible conditions for business at a certain level of taxation. Member states' efforts should focus on the combating of harmful tax competition that generates the attraction of tax bases and the diversion of the capital flows. Clearly, an economic union and a Single Market require a harmonized tax system. It is also preferable that the allocation of resources in this market should be based on competitive economic advantages rather than on the level of taxation.

One can note that the development of EU tax system is not only an economic process, but also a political one. The creation of the supranational fiscal institutional infrastructure is a complex and difficult *démarche,* marked by numerous clashes of interest between member states regarding political and economic integration. In recent years, the movement of factors of production, especially capital, has become much easier in the global marketplace, and this could lead to important implications for the structural balance of the economies of member states, where migration flows of mobile factors of production will be strongly influenced by tax benefits. Therefore, the most competitive countries in terms of taxes will benefit from higher growth rates, and divergences between member states will intensify, increasing controversies about the limits of national tax sovereignty.

Coordination and cooperation in tax matters are essential elements of a common strategy that will enable the EU to achieve economic efficiency and member states to protect against the erosion of tax bases. Given the increasing financial instability facing the global economy, it will be necessary for the tax systems of member states to be reformed in order to simplify them and increase transparency.

Uncontrolled tax competition in an area characterized by high mobility of factors of production (such as the EU) may reduce public revenues and may affect the redistributive role of public finances. In this context, intensifying efforts are expected to increase the degree of harmonization within EU member states, in particular, in order to achieve tax harmonization in the case of taxable incomes generated by mobile factors of production. The harmonization of these taxes is inevitable, but it will probably be a medium- or long-term process. The harmonization of direct taxes is currently at an early stage of development, because there are discrepancies in the economic development levels of various member states, and differences in the ideological approaches of the national authorities in the field of taxation.

A review of the main initiatives in the field of corporate income tax harmonization shows that efforts of the European Commission to harmonize this tax have not resulted in a comprehensive regulatory framework that is able to solve all the problems facing both the member states and corporate groups, because there is no unanimity on the harmonization of direct taxes within the EU.

The main objections regarding the trends in the harmonization of direct taxes in the EU are related to the following issues:

- There is a lack of appreciation for the positive valences of tax competition.
- The promotion of some measures designed to ensure a relaxed tax environment for taxpayers (including companies) is justified by the need to compensate for location disadvantages in the case of certain member states.
- Diminishing the "tax sovereignty" of the member states is understood to be a restriction of the freedom of public authorities to administer fiscal instruments dependent on their specific needs.

In this context, the European Commission is forced to promote a prudent policy in harmonizing direct taxation and to find those tools that meet the needs of member states' fiscal sovereignty and the need for Single Market' equity and fiscal neutrality.

2.5 Conclusion

The evolution of EU rules regarding tax harmonization is closely related to the challenges of the Single Market generated by economic integration and globalization. Tax competition, the risk of double taxation, the loss of opportunities for increasing the economic competitiveness of the EU are only a few of the problems caused by particularities of the member states' tax systems. In order not to disturb the functioning of the Single Market, national tax systems need to be designed so as to ensure a greater degree of neutrality. Therefore, the competent institutions of the EU prioritized the harmonization of indirect taxes and addressed some issues affecting corporate taxation. There have been relatively few political actions related to the coordination of corporate income taxes within the EU and these have focused on the issue of cooperation between member states' tax authorities. Currently, there is a trend towards tax harmonization in the EU because it should facilitate and support economic and trade liberalization.

3
The Need for European Union Coordination of Corporate Income Taxes: Facts and Statistics

3.1 Introduction

The need for coordination of corporate income taxes within the European Union (EU) must be demonstrated by facts and statistics. The absence of common corporate income tax rules within the EU can encourage member states to operate reductions in tax rates in order to stimulate foreign direct investment (FDI) and generate the possibility of transferring the tax base from high tax countries to low tax countries. Because the mechanisms by which corporate groups transfer the tax base from one country to another reduce tax receipts, public authorities act so as to avoid tax revenue losses by investigating financial and commercial intra-group operations.

3.2 Corporate income tax in the EU and tax competition

3.2.1 The trend to reduce corporate income tax rates

The removal of barriers to the free movement of capital and labour encourages governments to reduce tax burdens in order to attract FDI, financial investment or to achieve other economic policy objectives. Annex 1 presents both nominal rates of tax on profits (set at national level) and rates of local corporate income tax and surcharges that are practised in some countries.

Reducing the corporate income tax rates is a common practice in new member states. They have used this measure to keep their economies attractive after the elimination of some tax advantages granted to foreign investors in the pre-accession period.

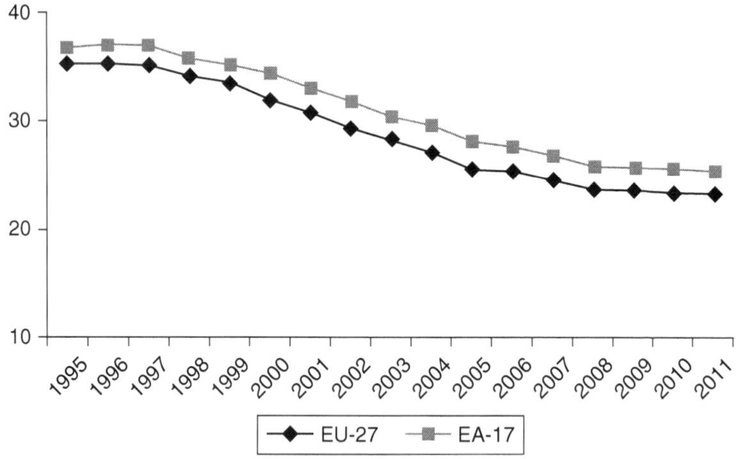

Figure 3.1 Development of adjusted statutory tax rate on corporate income
Source: European Commission – Taxation and Customs Union (2011), p. 130.

Thus, in Poland the adjusted statutory tax rate on corporate income fell from 27 per cent in 2003 to 19 per cent in 2010, in Romania from 25 per cent in 2003 to 16 per cent in 2010, in Bulgaria from 23.5 per cent in 2003 to 10 per cent in 2010.

These fiscal policy measures have not remained unanswered by the older member states. The average adjusted statutory tax rates on corporate income fell from 35.3 per cent in 1995 to 23.2 per cent in 2010 in the EU, and from 37.5 per cent in 1995 to 25.7 per cent in 2010 in the Euro Area (EA) (Figure 3.1).

In recent years, the most significant reductions were made in Germany (8.9 percentage points in 2008 compared to 2007), Italy (5.9 percentage points in 2008 compared to 2007) and the Netherlands (4.1 percentage points in 2007 compared to 2006).

However, the average corporate income tax receipts in the EU (expressed as a percentage of GDP), for the period 1999–2008, showed an upward trend (Figure 3.2).

According to John Becker, Clemens Fuest and Thomas Hemmelgarn, the expansion of corporate tax bases in member states (by eliminating tax deductions and provisions, on the one hand, and by increasing the profitability of companies, on the other hand) determined this development (Becker et al., 2006, pp. 9–32). Rachel Griffith and Alexander Klemm found that reducing the tax burden in the EU stimulated economic activity by broadening the tax base (Griffith and Klemm,

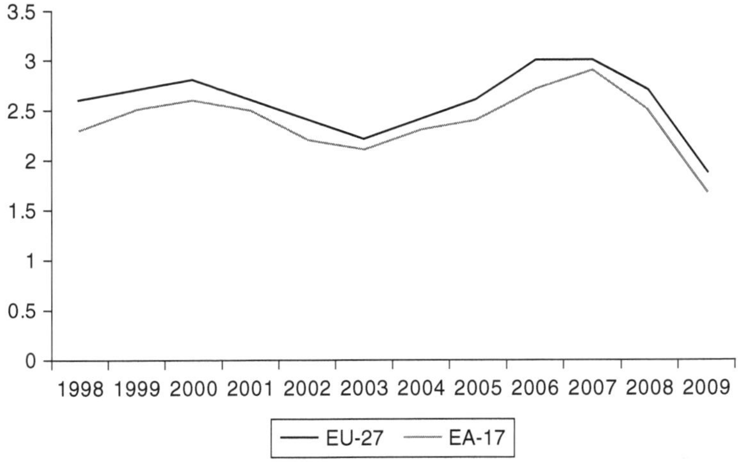

Figure 3.2 Development of the average corporate income tax receipts in the EU (as a percentage of GDP)
Source: European Commission – Taxation and Customs Union (2011), p. 300.

2004, p. 14). Peter Birch Sørenson introduced a new idea by explaining the phenomenon of increasing corporate income tax receipts: the decline of certain sectors such as agriculture was compensated for by the growth of other sectors (industry and financial intermediaries), which enhanced the corporatization of member states' economies (Sørenson, 2006, pp. 3–11). Globalization also generated an increase in gross profit rate by intensifying investment.

In the 27 EU countries, the reduction of the statutory tax rates on corporate income was accompanied by a reduction in corporate income tax receipts (expressed as a percentage of GDP) during the period 2001–2004, followed by a revival due to the high rates of economic growth recorded during the period 2005–2007 and a further decline in the context of the global economic crisis. The same trend can be observed in the development of the average corporate tax receipts, expressed as a percentage of total taxation (Figure 3.3).

Statutory tax rates are not a complete indicator of the tax burden. European Commission reports on issues of taxation use the notion of implicit tax rate. The implicit tax rate measures the effective tax burden of different types of economical activities. The implicit tax rate is the percentage ratio between aggregate taxes and the potential tax base. According to the methodology presented by the European Commission,

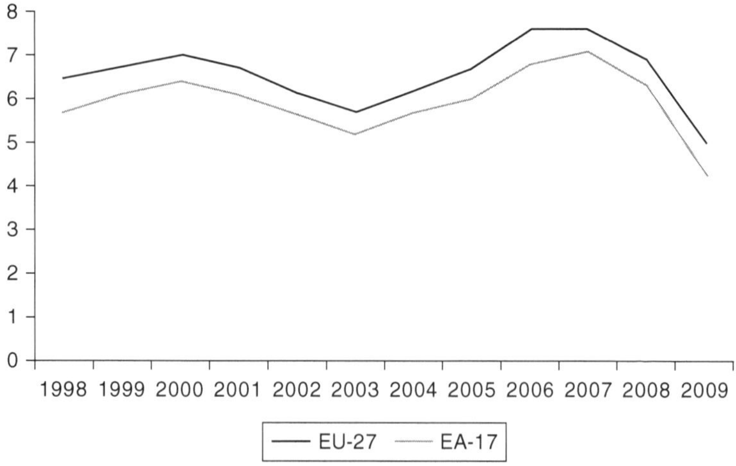

Figure 3.3 Development of the average corporate income tax receipts in the EU (as a percentage of total taxation)
Source: European Commission – Taxation and Customs Union (2011), p. 301.

the implicit tax rate on corporate income is determined by the following formula:

> The implicit tax rate on corporate income = taxes on corporate income/(net operating surplus of non-financial and financial corporations + interest received by non-financial and financial corporations – interest paid by non-financial and financial corporations + rents on land received by non-financial and financial corporations – rents on land paid by non-financial and financial corporations + dividends received by non-financial and financial corporations – dividends paid by non-financial and financial corporations + dividends received by general government + dividends received by rest of world + dividends received by households, self-employed and non-profit institutions + insurance property income attributed to policy-holders received by non-financial and financial corporations) × 100.
> (European Commission – Taxation and Customs Union, 2011)

Figure 3.4 shows the differences between statutory tax rates and implicit tax rates in some EU member states for the year 2009.

In most of the countries examined, the implicit tax rate is lower than the statutory tax rate. Differences between the two rates are very high for countries such as Belgium, France and the Netherlands.

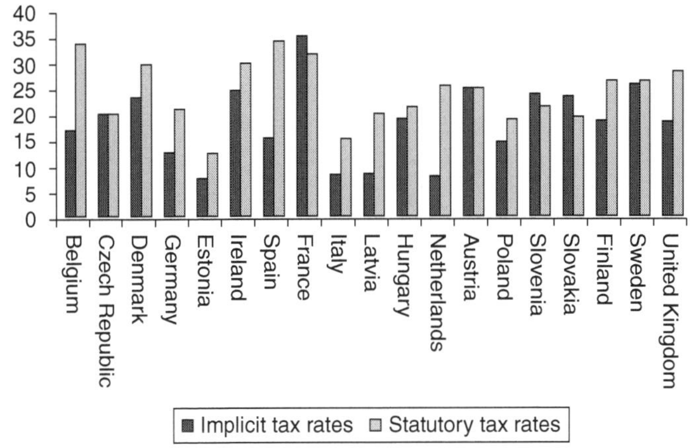

Figure 3.4 Implicit and statutory tax rates on corporate income in some member states (2009)
Source: European Commission – Taxation and Customs Union (2011), pp. 130 and 362.

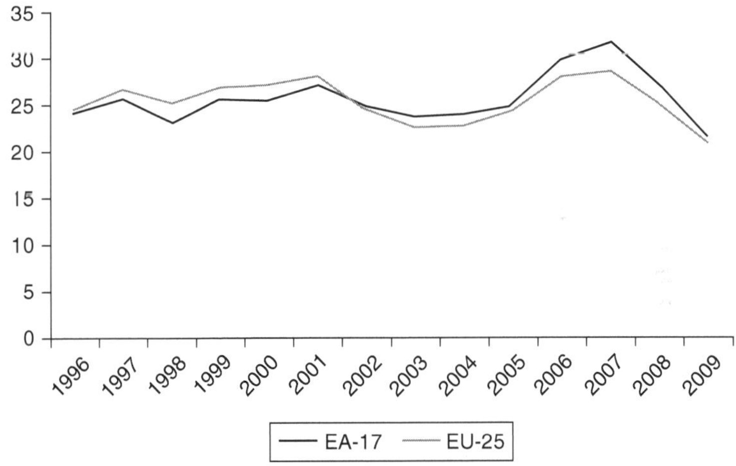

Figure 3.5 Development of the average implicit tax rate in the EU
Source: European Commission – Taxation and Customs Union (2011), p. 362.

Over time, the average implicit tax rate in the EU had a fluctuating evolution, with a strong reduction occurring since 2008 (Figure 3.5).

Since 2002, the average implicit tax rate was higher in the Euro Area countries compared to the EU-25.

3.2.2 Differences in determining the taxable income of companies in EU countries

The assessment of differences between national taxation systems is a difficult endeavour, especially since companies are subject to the common tax law or the privileged tax law (because they operate in certain areas or specific activities) that applies in a state. The provisions governing these regimes are numerous, and a simple comparison of national tax rates alone is not sufficient to give us the differences in the tax burden between countries. Thus, one must consider the method of determining the tax base. The description of the main factors that determine the taxable income of companies (see Annex 2) demonstrates the heterogeneity of the member states' tax systems. For example, practices regarding the depreciation of fixed assets vary widely from state to state, both in terms of methods and rates of depreciation, generating competitive advantages for certain tax jurisdictions.

From the corporate perspective, the most important differences between corporate income tax systems of member states are determined by the following:

- the tax losses regime;
- the possibility of consolidated tax returns;
- the nature and number of corporate tax incentives.

Tax losses may be carried forward and set off against the taxable income of subsequent years without any time limit in 15 member states. Under certain conditions, the carry back of losses is permitted in Germany, Ireland and the UK. In other states, tax losses may be carried forward for a certain period (a minimum of four years in Portugal and a maximum of 15 years in Spain).

Member states apply different rules on consolidated tax returns, which distort business decisions and investment policies in the Single Market. In some member states, corporate groups may be taxed on the basis of a consolidated balance sheet. To qualify as corporate groups, parent companies must own at least 75 per cent of their local subsidiaries in Spain. In Italy, parent companies must hold more than 50 per cent of the share capital of another resident company and must be entitled to more than 50 per cent of the profits of that company. In Portugal, the dominant company must hold more than 50 per cent of voting rights in its subsidiaries, for consolidated tax returns. Also, all members of the corporate group must exercise management activities in Portugal. In Luxembourg, tax consolidation is allowed for domestic companies or permanent establishments of foreign companies that are subject to tax corresponding to the Luxembourg corporate income tax rate and own at least 95 per cent of their local subsidiaries. The Netherlands allows the offset of losses of one company against the profits of another company if these companies form a group and the parent company owns at least 95 per cent of its subsidiaries. A similar regulation also exists in Poland.

In some member states, even if legislation does not permit tax consolidation for corporate groups, losses or profits can be transferred between members of a corporate group (this situation is found in Cyprus, Ireland and the UK, respectively in Sweden and Finland).

Corporate tax incentives granted by public authorities in member states aim to encourage technological research and development, environmental protection, development of professional training programmes for employees, increasing investment in intangible assets (patents, trademarks, know-how, etc.) and business development in certain regions or sectors. The analysis of corporate tax regimes in member states allows us to observe a variety of corporate tax incentives. Tax credit is a tool used in order to achieve economic policy objectives. Also, in many member states, small businesses are subject to a more advantageous tax regime, usually by charging a reduced rate of tax on profit.

It is clear that when assessing a future location for investment location, representatives of multinational companies will consider the many facets of taxation systems. As a factor of attractiveness, a state's low corporate tax rate may be placed ahead of other issues: the possibility of carrying forward tax losses for a long period, the offsetting of losses against profits within the group of companies, a large number of incentives tax, etc. Thus, one can explain situations where some countries receive a significant amount of FDI (per GDP), despite imposing a relatively high rate of corporate income tax.

For multinational companies, the tax regime of dividends, interest and royalties is particularly important because there are channels by which benefits obtained by subsidiaries are transferred to the home country of ownership. Also, the corporate group, by applying different rates on dividend remittances, can reduce the total amount of corporate tax payable. Thus, the corporate group will try to transfer funds from those subsidiaries with the lowest transfer costs.

Directive 90/435/EEC on the common system of taxation applicable in the case of parent companies and subsidiaries was implemented in all member states, so that dividends paid by a company resident in a member state to a company resident in another member state are exempt from taxation, when trustees hold a 10 per cent minimum stake in the ordinary share capital. In most member states, dividends received by a resident company from its subsidiaries are not taxable (in whole or in part) if a number of conditions (different from state to state) are met: the minimum participation of the parent company in the capital of subsidiaries, the period of this participation and the residence of paying companies in the EU or European Economic Area (EEA).

Thus, in some member states the taxation of dividends is more advantageous than in other member states. In Cyprus, Hungary, Ireland, Slovakia, Slovenia, Spain and the UK, dividends received by resident companies from resident or non-resident companies (regardless of their location – except for companies located in tax havens – or the participation of the parent company in the capital of subsidiaries) are not taxed.

Directive 2003/49/EC on a common system of taxation applicable to interest and royalty payments made between associated companies of different member states has been implemented in most member states, so that interest and royalty payments between affiliated companies arising in a member state shall be exempt from any taxes imposed on those payments, in that member state, if the owner (beneficiary of the interest or royalties) is a company of another member state or is a permanent establishment of a company from another member state. Bulgaria has been authorized to delay the application of Directive 2003/49/EC until 31 December 2014, and Latvia, Poland and Portugal until 30 June 2013. For interest and royalties paid by companies resident in EU member states that are not subject to the provisions of Directive 2003/49/EC, the withholding tax rates vary from state to state. In Bulgaria, the interest withholding tax rate is 5 per cent; and in Greece, the withholding tax rates on royalty payments vary from 5 per cent in Cyprus to 28 per cent in Finland.

Therefore, the defining elements for determining the taxable income of companies in EU member states have distinctive particularities from one state to another and determine the different tax conditions for multinational companies, acting as incentives or barriers for FDI. However, the differences between corporate income tax regimes can cause considerable difficulties for corporate groups in the interpretation and understanding of legal provisions regarding the determination and distribution of profits.

As a general conclusion, it can be said that the tax burden in the EU is a major factor in the location of investments, and their sensitivity to tax rates and the size of the tax base is growing. The tendency to reduce corporate income tax rates in the EU has accelerated in recent years, and national taxation systems have specific elements designed to attract companies with a high degree of mobility. Decreasing the corporate income tax burden in various member states, however, can be seen as an act of alignment with the trend shown internationally. It is the result of deliberate actions of governments only to a lesser extent.

Since the fiscal policies promoted by public authorities in EU member states can influence corporate location decisions, corporate income tax harmonization will contribute to reducing distortions on competition in the Single Market. However, corporate income tax harmonization will remove tax barriers related to the offset of losses of one company against the profits of another company. The absence of the possibility of transferring losses within groups of companies is currently a barrier to entry into certain markets for many companies. This encourages the location of investment in large member states, where the national market is large enough to absorb possible losses.

3.3 Corporate tax arbitrage opportunities

3.3.1 Transfer pricing mechanism

The transfer pricing mechanism is a tool often used by corporate groups to avoid high taxation in certain countries. This can be illustrated by a simple example: the subsidiary of a multinational company builds a car with a final cost of €30,000 and the sale price of the car is €50,000. A high rate of tax on profit (let's suppose 30 per cent) will generate a tax liability of payment representing €6000 (€20,000 × 30 per cent). To avoid paying taxes in the producing country, the subsidiary sells the car for €40,000 to another subsidiary (located in a more low tax country) that will put the product on the market. Let's suppose that in this country the rate of tax on profit is 10 per cent. The corporate group would have paid €4000 (€10,000 × 30 per cent + €10,000 × 10 per cent), representing profit tax. So, the corporate group will make a significant saving on resources. For the car-producing country, however, this situation creates a significant loss in tax revenues.

Transfer pricing is a term used to describe inter-company pricing arrangements relating to transactions between related business entities (sale and purchase of tangible and intangible assets, provision/procurement of some services, including administrative, financial, leasing, etc.). Transfer pricings are set by the corporate group decision-making structures, and they can be involved in the following functions:

- decreasing payments on profit tax or duties;
- transferring income from countries where there are bans or limitations on profit repatriation.

The corporate group policy regarding transfer pricing is based on many factors, such as:

- fiscal aspects of countries involved in the cross-border activity of corporate group members;
- currency legislation;
- political and economic risks (for example, legislative changes, currency devaluation, etc.);
- price levels in the host country, etc.

Repeated transfer pricing practices of corporate groups have generated efforts to define the phenomenon and its regulation. The Organization for Economic Cooperation and Development (OECD) realized in 1979 a report on transfer pricing used by transnational companies, and in 1995 published a transfer pricing guide addressed at both corporate groups and tax administrators.

The issue of transfer pricing is becoming increasingly important in the globalized economy, as more companies expand their business beyond the borders of the country of origin, making transactions of goods and services within the corporate group. In principle, transfer pricing rules recommended by the OECD provide the following conditions:

- the existence of cross-border transactions;
- the transaction takes place between two affiliated entities;
- the transaction will be the subject of a good, service or any other thing with economic value.

Since transfer pricing may also have other purposes than tax avoidance, fiscal authorities should not automatically assume that companies with cross-border activities are trying to manipulate profits, especially as, in some cases, it is very difficult to determine with accuracy the price market. The OECD Committee on Fiscal Affairs has created a set of rules to reduce the risk of misinterpretation or abuse regarding the taxation on some operations of corporate groups, implementing the so-called "arm's length principle". The OECD Model Tax Convention explains the essence of this principle: "[When] conditions are made or imposed between... two [associated] enterprises in their commercial or financial relations which differ from those which would be made between independent enterprises, then any profits which would, but for those conditions, have accrued to one of the enterprises, but, by reason of those conditions, have not so accrued, may be included in the profits of that enterprise and taxed accordingly" (OECD, 2008, p. 47). So, it tries the adjustment of corporate profits by reporting intra-group transactions to the conditions that should have governed the relations between independent companies in comparable transactions and in a similar context. The principle of "arm's length" seeks to avoid the appearance of advantages and disadvantages for associated companies and independent companies, and implicitly the distortion of the competitive position of each entity. The application of the principle has proved efficient in situations where one can make comparisons with other similar transactions carried out between independent entities. There are many situations where the application of this principle is difficult (for example, if corporate groups are active in the production of highly specialized goods).

According to the transfer pricing guide developed by the OECD, there are five methods for determining transfer pricing, divided into two main groups: traditional methods based on analysis of price ("Traditional Transactional Methods") and methods based on analysis of profit ("Transactional Profit Methods"). Traditional transaction methods are regarded as the most direct means of establishing whether conditions in the commercial and financial relations between associated enterprises are arm's length. This is because any difference between the price of a controlled transaction and the price in a comparable uncontrolled transaction can normally be traced directly to the commercial and financial relations made or imposed between the enterprises, and the arm's length conditions can be established by directly substituting the price in the comparable uncontrolled transaction for the price of the controlled transaction. A traditional transaction method and a transactional profit method can be applied in an equally reliable manner, but the traditional transaction method is preferable to the transactional profit method. Conversely, there are situations where transactional profit methods are found to be more appropriate than traditional transaction methods. For example, where there is no or limited publicly available reliable gross margin information on third parties, traditional transaction methods might be difficult to apply in cases other than those where there are internal comparables, and a transactional profit method might be the most appropriate method in view of the availability of information (OECD, 2010a, pp. 59–105).

Traditional transaction methods that are used to apply the arm's length principle are as follows:

1. **The comparable uncontrolled price (CUP) method** compares the price charged for property or services transferred in a controlled transaction to the price charged for property or services transferred in a comparable uncontrolled transaction in comparable circumstances. If there is any difference between the two prices, this may indicate that the conditions of the commercial and financial relations of the associated enterprises are not arm's length, and that the price in the uncontrolled transaction may need to be substituted for the price in the controlled transaction. An uncontrolled transaction is comparable to a controlled transaction for purposes of the CUP method if one of two following conditions is met:
   - none of the differences (if any) between the transactions being compared or between the enterprises undertaking those transactions could materially affect the price in the open market;
   - reasonably accurate adjustments can be made to eliminate the material effects of such differences.
2. **The resale price (RP) method** begins with the price at which a product that has been purchased from an associated enterprise is resold to an independent enterprise. This price (the "resale price") is then reduced by an appropriate gross margin on this price (the "resale price margin"), representing the amount from which the reseller would seek to cover his selling and other operating expenses and, in the light of the functions performed (taking into account assets used and risks assumed), make an appropriate profit. What is left after subtracting the gross margin can be regarded, after adjustment for other costs associated with the purchase of the product (e.g. customs duties), as an arm's length price for the original transfer of property between the associated enterprises. An uncontrolled transaction is comparable to a controlled transaction (i.e. it is a comparable uncontrolled transaction) for purposes of the RP method if one of the two following conditions is met:

- none of the differences (if any) between the transactions being compared or between the enterprises undertaking those transactions could materially affect the RP margin in the open market;
- reasonably accurate adjustments can be made to eliminate the material effects of such differences. In making comparisons for purposes of the RP method, fewer adjustments are normally needed to account for product differences than under the CUP method, because minor product differences are less likely to have as material an effect on profit margins as they do on price.

3. **The cost plus (CP) method** begins with the costs incurred by the supplier of property (or services) in a controlled transaction for property transferred or services provided to an associated purchaser. An appropriate CP mark up is then added to this cost, to make an appropriate profit in light of the functions performed and the market conditions. What is arrived at after adding the CP mark up to the above costs may be regarded as an arm's length price of the original controlled transaction. This method probably is most useful where semi finished goods are sold between associated parties, where associated parties have concluded joint facility agreements or long-term buy-and-supply arrangements, or where the controlled transaction is the provision of services. An uncontrolled transaction is comparable to a controlled transaction (i.e. it is a comparable uncontrolled transaction) for purposes of the CP method if one of the following two conditions is met:

   - none of the differences (if any) between the transactions being compared or between the enterprises undertaking those transactions materially affect the CP mark up in the open market;
   - reasonably accurate adjustments can be made to eliminate the material effects of such differences.

   The transactional profit methods are as follows:
4. **The transactional profit split (TPS) method** seeks to eliminate the effect on profits of special conditions made or imposed in a controlled transaction by determining the division of profits that independent enterprises would have expected to realize from engaging in the transaction or transactions. The main strength of the TPS method is that it can offer a solution for highly integrated operations for which a one-sided method would not be appropriate.
5. **The transactional net margin (TNM) method** examines the net profit relative to an appropriate base (e.g. costs, sales, assets) that

a taxpayer realizes from a controlled transaction. Thus, a TNM method operates in a manner similar to the CP and RP methods. A TNM method is unlikely to be reliable if each party to a transaction makes valuable, unique contributions.

Establishing the most adequate method to apply the arm's length principle takes into account, in principle, the following elements:

- the method that is closest to circumstances in which prices are set in conditions of free competition in comparable commercial markets;
- the method by which information regarding the actual activity of affiliated organizations involved in the free transaction is available;
- the precision of the adjustments made to achieve comparability;
- the circumstances of the individual case;
- the effective activities of various affiliated entities;
- the method used must meet the circumstances of the market and the taxpayer's business;
- the documentation that the taxpayer can provide.

The circumstances of the individual case taken into account in the examination of the market price are these: the type, the condition, the quality and degree of novelty of merchandise, goods and services transferred; the market conditions when goods, merchandise or services are used, consumed, treated, processed or sold to independent entities; the activities and stages of production and distribution of entities involved; the clauses contained in contracts regarding obligations, payment terms, discounts, guarantees, risk taking; the special conditions of competition (Matei and Pirvu, 2011, p. 104).

After questioning a number of 877 companies with cross-border activities in 25 countries, Ernst and Young made a study in 2010 that clearly showed the growing importance of transfer pricing issues worldwide. Thus, over a third of chief financial officers surveyed said that tax issues regarding transfer pricing were the most important challenge for their companies. Over 70 per cent of these believed that the importance of transfer prices would increase in coming years due to the diversification of legislative regulations and the intensification of tax authorities' inspections regarding the way in which the arm's length principle was applied. Over 50 per cent of the sampled companies have been subjected to a transfer pricing investigation in the last six years, and one-third of these have proceeded to transfer pricing adjustments. Under these conditions, most respondents said that in recent years, the costs of compliance with specific requirements for transfer prices have increased significantly (Ernst and Young, 2010, pp. 5–13).

In the EU, transfer pricing is a problem for tax authorities if corporate groups aim to reduce corporate income tax by price manipulation. The corporate group tries to establish most of the taxable income in the more permissive tax jurisdictions by decreasing (increasing) prices for intra-group transactions.

To highlight the importance of transfer pricing issues in the EU, Alfons Weichenrieder developed a model of correlation between the taxation of profits and the profitability of affiliated organizations. Analysing the situation of German subsidiaries of foreign companies, the author found that an increase in corporate income tax rate in the home country by 10 percentage points caused an increase in subsidiaries' profitability (artificially generated through transfer pricing) by half a percentage point (Weichenrieder, 2007, p. 21).

Current systems of corporate income taxation in member states incite firms with cross-border activities to avoid taxation due to the existence of significant differences between corporate income tax rates and rules for determining taxable income. Economic integration has complicated the corporate income tax issues and diminished fiscal administrations' ability to monitor commercial flows and cash flows for companies with cross-border activities. Economic globalization also reduces the capacity of fiscal administrations to verify the accuracy of transfer prices used by taxpayers, due to the significant increase in foreign income and companies' diversification. To avoid the possibility of manipulating corporate income tax systems, tax authorities impose requirements concerning the preparation of some transfer pricing documentation, thereby becoming increasingly more onerous. Thus, companies are faced with situations where they must add more detail to the already complex transfer price documentation in all countries where they operate, and the risk of incurring penalties for non-compliance with the requirements of tax authorities is much higher. In addition, the application of different methods for determining the correct transfer prices is becoming increasingly complex and costly, given that new technologies and business structures (implying a greater emphasis on the firm's intangible assets) have created difficulties in the identification of comparable uncontrolled commercial transactions.

There are also substantial differences in the rules for applying the methods of transfer pricing between member states, so that EU companies are faced with uncertainty regarding the prices for intra-group transactions, because these could be considered unacceptable by tax authorities in a later audit (European Commission, 2005b). The transfer pricing adjustment made after the tax audit can lead to risk of double taxation. For example, double taxation related to transfer pricing disputes occurs when the tax authorities of a member state unilaterally adjust the price for a sale executed by a company (member of a corporate group) without offsetting this adjustment by a corresponding adjustment in the member state in which the purchase was made. Although research published by the European Commission suggests that the number of disputes between tax authorities and corporate groups regarding transfer pricing adjustments is quite limited, business representatives have complained that often litigation costs are so high that the acceptance of double taxation is a less expensive option (European Commission, 2001b, p. 223).

The specific costs that corporate groups have to incur when fulfilling their tax obligations related to transfer pricing include the following:

- the company's obligation to respect the "arm's length" principle, which means the identification of prices of comparable uncontrolled transactions, the completion of documentation and the justification of prices in case of a tax audit;
- protection against the risk of double taxation if prices are adjusted (bringing proceedings against the tax authorities, insurance costs, etc.).

According to estimates by the European Commission, compliance costs related to transfer pricing in the EU accounted for about 4–5.5 million Euros per year, i.e. 1.9 per cent of corporate income taxes payable (European Commission, 2001b, p. 267). Estimates were made on the basis of an analysis of 700 companies from 14 countries. Other authors found that these costs would amount to 2 and 4 per cent of corporate income taxes paid by companies (Lanno and Levin, 2002, p. 3).

Since many of the issues concerning tax treatment related to transfer pricing are obstacles to the proper functioning of the Single Market, limiting efficiency, effectiveness, transparency and simplicity in economic activities, the European Commission proposed in 2005 a set of rules for partial resolution of the problems encountered by European companies (European Commission, 2005b, pp. 15–17). Thus, in 2006, the European Council adopted a code of conduct on the transfer pricing documentation requested by the tax authorities.[1]

According to the code, the transfer pricing documentation must include the following:

- A set of documents with standardized information relevant to all entities of the corporate group, called "master file", which will find an overview of intra-group transactions and corporate policy on transfer pricing issues.
- A set of documents with specific information required in each member state in which the taxpayer has related party transactions, called "country-file". The country-specific documentation contains: (a) a detailed description of the local business and its business strategy; (b) a description and explanation of specific controlled transactions; (c) a comparative analysis (characteristics of property and services) and a functional analysis (assets used, risks assumed and others, contractual terms, economic circumstances and specific business strategies); (d) an explanation of the selection of the most appropriate transfer pricing method or methods; (e) relevant information on comparable domestic and/or foreign prices; (f) a description of application of the worldwide group's transfer pricing policy.

In February 2007, the European Commission published the results of the Joint Transfer Pricing Forum activities, making amendments to the code by specifying procedures regarding dispute avoidance and orientation for advance pricing agreements within the EU (European Commission, 2007b).

The measures listed above have the potential to help reduce the corporate compliance costs related to transfer pricing documentation, but they do not entirely solve the transfer pricing problem. For this reason, the European Commission has repeatedly reaffirmed the need for corporate income tax base consolidation as a solution to solving the transfer pricing problem. At the same time, the European Commission pointed to the need to ensure good governance in tax matters among member states as an essential tool for combating cross-border tax evasion and fraud, and to provide a financial base for public spending.

3.3.2 Intra-group loans

Another important instrument of the international transfer of financial funds available to corporate groups are intra-group loans. There are many types of intra-group loans, but the most used are:

- direct loans (any loan made by a parent company to its subsidiary or loan made by a subsidiary to another subsidiary, without the involvement of intermediaries);

- "back-to-back" loans (arrangements whereby a bank advances a loan on the basis of a loan advanced by another bank in another country, usually to circumvent foreign exchange restrictions – such arrangements typically involve parent and subsidiary firms where the parent company remains liable for repayment in case the subsidiary defaults);
- parallel loans (arrangement whereby two companies in different countries borrow each other's currency for a given period of time, in order to reduce the foreign exchange risk for both of them, or to obtain an attractive foreign currency interest rate).

The choice between debt and equity financing is achieved by the parent company in the interest of the corporate group. Consequently, if the parent company finances subsidiaries, there will be an arbitrage between debt and equity financing, based on several criteria. Typically, short-term liquidity needs or an investment generates an infusion of capital and short-term financing needs will be covered by a short-term loan. However, tax considerations may influence these economic considerations. In terms of tax, the financing through an intra-group loan has the advantage of interest expense tax deduction. Thus, corporate groups can realize significant tax savings, if an establishment located in a favourable tax jurisdiction borrows from other establishments in jurisdictions with higher tax according to the example below (Figure 3.6).

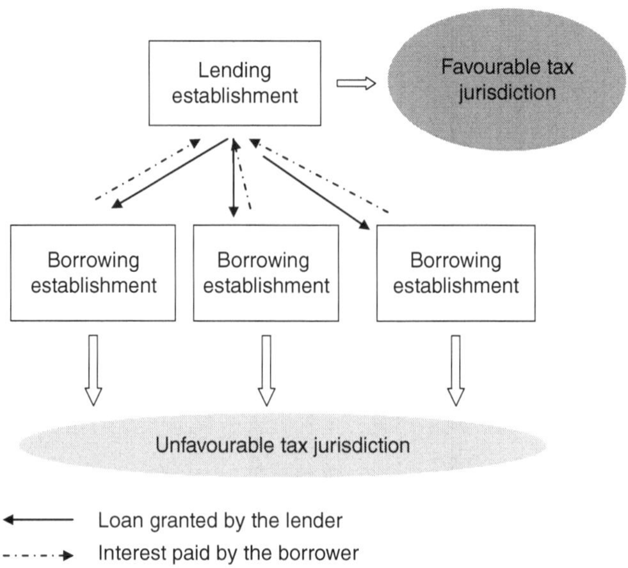

Figure 3.6 International transfer of funds through intra-group loans.

Borrowing establishments will deduct interest paid on these loans, avoiding high taxation in countries where they operate, and the lending establishment will pay a low tax on interest income, due to the permissive tax regime of the country where it operates.

To limit the ability of corporate groups to avoid taxation using intra-group loan schemes, public authorities have introduced regulations regarding the conditions under which a corporate group member may opt to change its financial structure, called "thin capitalization rules". According to these rules, when a parent company grants a loan to a subsidiary when a capital increase is necessary, the interest paid on that loan is not deductible and is treated as a a dividend, in terms of tax. This happens not only when interest rates are excessive, but also if the subsidiary had not obtained the loan from an unaffiliated entity under the same financial conditions.

The thin capitalization rules applied in most EU member states are based on the principle that the interest payments on intra-group loans are deductible for tax purposes if the debtor company can demonstrate that similar loans contracted from unaffiliated entities would be given the same conditions (the "arm's length" principle), or if the debt-equity ratio does not exceed a certain level (Table 3.1).

Table 3.1 Thin capitalization rules in EU member states

Country	**"Arm's length" principle**	**Debt-equity ratio**	**Other principles**	**Absence of thin capitalization rules**
Austria, Czech Republic, Denmark, Latvia	–	less than 4	–	–
Bulgaria, Greece, Hungary, Netherlands, Poland, Romania, Spain	–	less than 3	–	–
Belgium, Cyprus, Estonia, Finland, Ireland, Luxembourg, Malta, Slovakia	–	–	–	x
France, Germany, Italy	–	–	x	–
Lithuania, Portugal, Slovenia, Sweden, UK	x	–	–	–

Source: Author's calculations based on Deloitte (2011).

Since the regulation on intra-group loans has more nuances than those illustrated in Table 3.1, further clarifications are required as follows:

- In Bulgaria, non-deductible interest expenses relating to intra-group loans can be carried forward for a period of 50 years.
- Interest expenses relating to loans contracted by Belgian companies from the shareholders/directors – individuals are not deductible if the debt-equity ratio (for these loans) is greater than 1. Also, interest expenses relating to loans contracted by Belgian companies from entities located in more advantageous tax jurisdictions are not deductible if the debt-equity ratio (for these loans) is greater than 7.
- In France, deducting interest expenses relating to intra-group loans is deferred if the amount thereof: (a) exceeds 50 per cent of equity value, and (b) exceeds 5 per cent of the operating profit of the company. Deductible interest expenses can be carried forward for a period of 20 years.
- In Germany and Italy, the maximum deduction for interest expenses related to intra-group loans is limited to 30 per cent of operating profit.
- In Lithuania and Slovenia, debtor companies (that cannot demonstrate that the intra-group loan could be contracted under the same conditions from unaffiliated entities) have the right to deduct interest expenses related to the loan if debt-equity ratio is not more than 4 (in Lithuania) and 5 (in Slovenia).
- In Romania, the regulation on intra-group loans allows the deductibility of interest expenses, if the interest rate does not exceed 6 per cent per year.

Because in the EU there are no restrictions on the transfer of funds between residents and non-residents (however, in order to combat the phenomenon of money laundering, banks and financial institutions are obliged to monitor deposits or withdrawals that exceed a certain limit), the existence or absence of thin capitalization rules may affect international investment location decisions. Because in Belgium, Cyprus, Estonia, Finland, Ireland, Luxembourg, Malta and Slovakia, the legislation does not provide measures to protect tax bases tax avoidance actions through intra-group loans, we can assume that these locations are more attractive to corporate groups. This situation may distort the efficient allocation of resources within the

EU, representing an obstacle for the proper functioning of the Single Market.

The introduction of certain common corporate income tax rules in the EU (especially fiscal consolidation) will allow the following:

- removal of the risk of manipulation of tax systems through intra-group loans;
- promotion of the principle of neutrality, since the decisions of public authorities regarding the thin capitalization rules will not be able to represent incentives in the European locations of investments.

3.4 Conclusion

Analysis of a wide range of specific issues on corporate income taxes demonstrates that different tax regimes operate within the EU. This situation can lead to distortions in the location of foreign investment and the optimal allocation of resources. The possibility of transfer of tax bases from high tax countries to low tax countries, the costs of knowing the tax laws of each member state, the efforts to monitor transfer prices, the risk of double taxation, the general inability to offset losses in some member states against profits in another member state are further concerns relating to the failure of initiatives on corporate income tax harmonization. The initiative for the coordination of corporate income taxes is justified and it responds to the needs of companies with cross-border activities and public authorities.

4
Objectives of Corporate Income Tax Coordination in the European Union

4.1 Introduction

Corporate income tax coordination is a necessary step to achieve the objectives stipulated in the European Union (EU) Treaty. The specific objectives of corporate income tax coordination were defined by the European Commission's strategy documents and were based on studies, research and analysis. This chapter presents the specific objectives of corporate income tax coordination in the EU. It also argues for the idea that corporate income tax coordination can contribute to creating a level playing field for all Single Market participants, to limit and prevent non-taxation and abuse, and to avoid harmful tax competition.

4.2 The prevention of distortion of competition within the Single Market by fiscal policy that stimulates corporate location decisions

Foreign direct investment (FDI) flows between member states have a particular importance for the EU economy. These flows generate new jobs, representing a factor that stimulates productivity and European economic integration. Intra-EU direct investments reported by EU member states show a considerable variation in the FDI flows from year to year, depending on the economic opportunities offered by each state (Annex 3).

During 2007–2009, there was a trend of disinvestment (affecting in particular the new member states), because during recessions corporate groups focus more on activities in the markets they already serve.

Statutory rates on corporate income tax diverge significantly across EU countries (Table 4.1), and these differences are susceptible to encourage corporate decisions to locate in low tax states.

Table 4.1 Statutory corporate income tax rates in some member states

Country	Statutory corporate income tax rate (%)
Malta	35.0
France	34.4
Belgium	34.0
Italy	31.4
Spain	30.0
Romania	16.0
Latvia	15.0
Lithuania	
Ireland	12.5
Bulgaria	10.0
Cyprus	

Source: European Commission – Taxation and Customs Union (2011), p. 130.

During 2005–2010, some member states with lower corporate income tax rates were able to attract an important volume of FDI (such as Ireland or Cyprus). But some member states with higher corporate income tax rates registered similar performances (Belgium, the Netherlands and Sweden). It is obvious that the statutory tax rates cannot provide complete information on the tax burden faced by companies.

This deficiency can be removed by determining the effective tax rate. In the literature, one can find the effective marginal tax rate (EMTR) as well as the effective average tax rate (EATR). The methodology used in order to determine the two rates was created by Michael P. Devereux and Rachel Griffith (1999). The approach proposed by these two economists consists in considering a hypothetical investment in the home country of residence or in another country.

Investment decisions are affected by both rates, but in different ways. According to Michael P. Devereux, the EATR orientates the decision on the selected investment emplacement, and the volume of investment is more influenced by the EMTR (Devereux, 2006, p. 5).

The EATR allows the measurement of the effect of taxation on the impulse to invest. It represents the rate that applies to the marginal investment, showing the effect of taxes on an investment with a minimum after-tax rate of profit. Assessing the impact of corporate income tax on the capital investment level is done through the cost of capital, defined as the benefit rate (before taxes) required by companies owners.

The percentage difference between the cost of capital and the required after-tax real rate of return is the EMTR (Matei and Pirvu, 2010a, p. 112).

According to Christina Elschner and Werner Vanborren, companies will invest until the point when the marginal rate of return to capital is equal to the cost of capital. For a solicited after-tax rate of return, a restrictive fiscal system generates a high cost of capital (Elschner and Vanborren, 2009, p. 8).

Using the notes of authors Devereux and Griffith, the EMTR formula is as follows:

$$\text{EMTR} = \frac{(\tilde{p} - r)}{\tilde{p}}$$

where:

- $\tilde{p}$ is the cost of capital for a marginal investment;
- r is the discount rate;

or

$$\text{EMTR} = \frac{[c - (r + \delta)]}{c} = \left[\frac{(1 - A)}{(1 - \tau A)}\right] \times \tau$$

where:

- c is the cost of capital;
- r is the discount rate;
- τ is the tax rate on total return;
- δ is the economic depreciation;
- A is the net present value of allowances.

The EATR is the percentage difference between the net present value of a profitable investment project in the absence of tax and the net present value of the same investment in the presence of tax. The EATR is the relevant rate for analysing discrete investment choices, such as where to locate.

The formula of EATR is as follows:

$$\text{EATR} = \frac{R^* - R}{\dfrac{p}{(1 + r)}}$$

$$R^* = \frac{(p - r)}{(1 + r)}$$

$$R = \frac{(1 + \delta)(1 - \tau) - (r + \delta)(1 - A)}{1 + r}$$

where:

- R^* is the present value in the absence of the tax;
- R is the net present value in the presence of the tax;
- p is the pre-tax profit.

Analysing the evolution of the EMTR and the EATR during 1982–2005 for an estimated inflation rate of 3.5 per cent, Michael P. Devereux and Peter B. Sørensen obtained the following conclusions (Devereux and Sørensen, 2006, pp. 69–71):

- The EMTR remained fairly stable during the 1990s (26 per cent in 1982 and 25.5 per cent in 1999) and it decreased in the next period (21 per cent in 2005).
- The EATR decreased from 34.5 per cent in 1982 to 29 per cent in 2005.

Ruud de Mooij and Michael P. Devereux reached the conclusion that in all EU member states, with the exception of Belgium, the EMTR was positive, varying from 15 per cent in Malta to 0.25 per cent in Estonia. Malta, Luxembourg and Spain recorded the highest levels of EMTR, and Belgium, Estonia, Romania, Latvia and Bulgaria the lowest levels of EMTR for 2007. Therefore, the corporate tax burden generated a higher volume of investment in new EU member states (Estonia, Romania, Latvia, Bulgaria, Lithuania) and in several countries with a consolidated state in the EU (Belgium, Cyprus, Ireland, the UK). At the opposite end of the scale, in terms of EMTR, are Malta, Luxembourg, Spain, the Czech Republic, Germany and France (de Mooij and Devereux, 2009, p. 17).

Christina Elschner and Werner Vanborren determined the EATR in the 27 member states during 1998–2007, based on the following assumptions: it concerned an investment in the productive sector involving the use of assets with different depreciation rates and various sources of funding, the required real rate of return was estimated at 5 per cent and the inflation rate was estimated at 2 per cent (Elschner and Vanborren, 2009, pp. 10–19). The two economists concluded that the EATR decreased by 6.7 percentage points (from 29.1 to 22.4 per cent), while the statutory corporate income tax rate decreased by 9.6 percentage points (from 34.1 per cent in 1998 to 24.5 per cent in 2007).

Rachel Griffith and Alexander Klemm believed that EMTRs were more stable over time than EATRs due to enlargement of the tax base in parallel with reducing tax rates. The explanation of significantly reducing the EATRs must be sought in order to achieve an increase in the profitability of investments. If profitable capital is more mobile, the increasing competition for it is obvious (Griffith and Klemm, 2004, p. 28).

Using the methodology of Devereux and Griffith, several specialists determined the EATR for 2009 in the 27 EU member states, at the request of the European Commission. The study by Michael P. Devereux, Christina Elschner, Dieter Endres and Christoph Spengel shows the differences between statutory corporate income tax rates and EATRs (Figure 4.1).

Major differences between the statutory corporate income tax rate and the EATR (more than 3 percentage points) are observed for Belgium, Estonia, Germany, Greece, Lithuania, Luxembourg and Sweden. Differences between EU member states in terms of EATR are explained mainly by differences in statutory tax rates and less significantly by differences in the elements that determine the tax base (Devereux et al., 2009, p. 2).

Corporate income tax coordination could allow companies intending to operate on the territory of certain member states to know the exact tax burden they will have to bear. The absence of various tax incentives

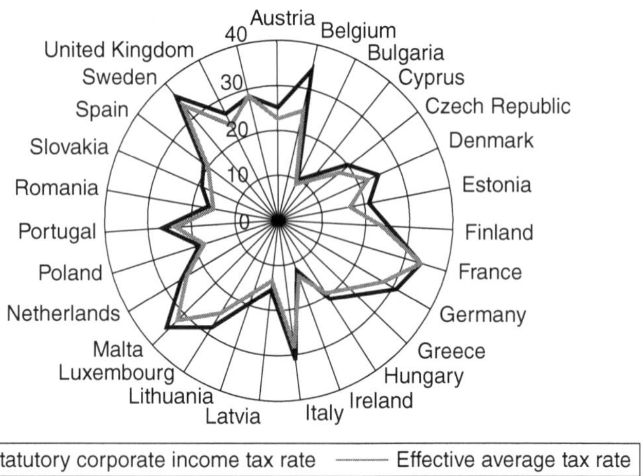

Figure 4.1 Statutory corporate income tax rates and effective average tax rates in member states (2009)

Source: Prepared by the author based on Devereux et al. (2009), p. 2.

provided through tax deductions and exceptions from the tax would create a neutral tax environment within the EU. In this way, an important objective of corporate income tax coordination would be achieved – the prevention of distortion of competition within the Single Market by fiscal policy that stimulates corporate location decisions.

4.3 Diminishing corporate tax arbitrage opportunities

Corporate groups' internal financial systems enable the exploitation of imperfections resulting from differences in national regulations of countries. In order to avoid barriers and restrictions on transactions, corporate groups frequently use tax arbitrage. Various tools through which members of a corporate group can transfer financial funds include the following: transfer pricing, advance payments and settlement delays between companies of the group, intra-group loans and dividend adjustments. In many cases, these tools are used to avoid taxation. The ability of corporate groups to avoid taxation has increased as a result of growing economic integration of markets, and tax avoidance and evasion are facilitated by the existence of tax havens.

Corporate groups' ability to make extensive use of tax havens and offshore centres as part of their tax avoidance strategies conflicts with the principle of fair competition and corporate responsibility (European Parliament, 2009).

Taking into consideration the information provided by the OECD in 2008, the Economic and Monetary Affairs Committee shows that the world's tax havens have attracted between $5 trillion and $7 trillion in assets, although the degree of secrecy surrounding these accounts makes it difficult to determine exactly just how much is located within these individual jurisdictions. Although there are no undisputed figures on the amount of tax fraud in the EU, the economic literature estimates, however, the amount to be between 2 and 2.5 per cent of GDP at EU level, i.e. between €200 and €250 billion. International tax evasion has generated the following specific situations:

- About one-third of the 700 biggest UK corporations did not pay any tax in 2005 and 2006.
- 25 per cent of those US companies with assets worth more than $250 million, or income of more than $50 million a year, also failed to pay any tax between 1998 and 2005.
- France's biggest corporations currently pay 8 per cent tax on real average benefits, whereas the official tax rate is 33 per cent.

The study "Promoting Transparency and Exchange of Information for Tax Purposes" published by the OECD on 19 January 2010 estimates that tax avoidance practices generate revenue losses amounting to $100 billion a year, and in many European countries the sums run into billions of euros (OECD, 2010b, p. 2).

The introduction of a Common Consolidated Corporate Tax Base (CCCTB) in the EU would contribute towards solving the problems of double taxation and transfer pricing. Until the achievement of this objective, the European Parliament recommended the European Commission to shift the scope of the transfer pricing inspection from transaction to company level, in order to better identify inaccurate transaction pricing.

In this respect, the comparable profits method is suggested because it focuses on comparing earnings between companies in each industrial sector. A fall in the profits of a multinational company's subsidiary, which is significantly lower than the sector-wide average, over time may be evidence of massive transfer pricing (European Parliament, 2009).

In recent years, the opening up of south-eastern Europe economies to the outside and the increasing political stability in the region has encouraged the establishment of European corporations' subsidiaries in the respective countries. Because the national legislation of certain south-eastern European countries (Croatia, Macedonia, Russia, Ukraine) was aimed partly at OECD transfer pricing guidelines, the risk of intensifying the phenomenon of tax avoidance by using international transfer pricing as an income-shifting mechanism increases significantly (PricewaterhouseCoopers, 2010, p. 71).

On the other hand, Malta does not have specific transfer pricing legislation or thin capitalization legislation. In Luxembourg, the transfer pricing documentation rules applicable to entities performing intra-group activities were introduced on 28 January 2011 for the first time.

Because corporate tax arbitrage opportunities may have important implications for EU member states' budgets, there is a growing complexity of tax issues (related to transfer pricing especially) affecting both tax administrations and corporations. The diversity of anti-avoidance rules in the EU may generate conflicts of interest between corporate groups and tax administrations, and the lack of administrative coordination between tax jurisdictions can facilitate capital flight and loss of tax revenues. Transfer pricing appears as a major tax obstacle for corporate groups. The estimates highlight that transfer pricing is an important issue for 82.8 per cent of large companies, in particular when it comes to dealing with documentation requirements, which are a difficulty for 81.9 per cent of large companies (Vanborren et al., 2004, p. 5).

The protection of tax revenues has become a major target for the financial policy of all member states, but especially for states with a high level of taxation. In this context, the introduction of a CCCTB in the EU could be a useful tool for limiting the migration of the tax base between countries, ensuring at the same time an increase in the efficiency of corporate income tax systems by a significant simplification of operations regarding the declaration of taxable income. The consolidation of the tax base will allow the determination of taxable income for corporate groups, so transaction prices will have no influence on corporate income tax paid by companies (Matei and Pirvu, 2011, p. 106).

4.4 The reduction of administrative and compliance costs associated with corporate income taxation

Administrative and tax compliance costs incurred by corporations and governments within the EU are important elements for the evaluation of the tax efficiency of the Single Market. Tax compliance costs are those costs incurred by companies to comply with tax regulations. These include the time and expenses incurred in the process of preparing, filing and paying taxes. Compliance time and costs for setting up a new subsidiary include the following: (a) record keeping for corporate tax purposes; (b) transfer pricing documentation; (c) preparation of corporate tax computations; (d) prepayments for corporate tax; (e) corporate tax returns and payments; (f) dealing with the tax authorities on corporate tax; (g) mutual agreement procedures on transfer pricing; (h) clearances and rulings for corporate tax; (i) learning and education for corporate tax. Administrative costs are those incurred by public authorities to collect taxes and to apply tax rules. These costs also include indirect costs related to disputes between taxpayers and tax authorities.

Estimating these costs is a difficult *démarche*, and the information available on this subject is scarce. A study conducted at the request of the European Commission published in October 2004, based on a sample of 700 companies in EU member states (of which 165 companies with cross-border activities) highlighted the following issues:

- Weighted total absolute compliance costs are estimated at €1,460,000 for large companies. This corresponds to 1.9 per cent of taxes paid and to 0.02 per cent of sales, respectively.

- Weighted total absolute compliance costs are estimated at €203,000 for small and medium enterprises (SMEs). This amount corresponds to 30.9 per cent of taxes paid and to 2.6 per cent of sales, respectively.

Compliance costs are higher for companies with at least one subsidiary in another EU member state compared with companies without subsidiaries in another member state. Compliance costs increase with the number of subsidiaries abroad (Vanborren et al., 2004, pp. 23–37).

Tax compliance costs are generated by both differences in tax and accounting rules across EU member states and the complex documentation related to transfer pricing that affiliated companies must prepare. These issues require specialized (on the tax systems), legal and accounting knowledge. To reduce compliance failure (which may involve fines, penalties, etc.), corporate groups are forced to hire accountants, lawyers and tax advisors for each jurisdiction in which they operate.

In this context, applying a common set of rules in order to determine the corporate income tax base will generate a substantial reduction in compliance costs incurred by corporate groups. A consolidated tax base would also allow the automatic offsetting of losses in one EU country against profits elsewhere in the EU for tax purposes. Under the new fiscal conditions, corporate groups would be less interested in using the tools and mechanisms that allow the international transfer of financial funds to avoid taxation. This creates the conditions to reduce the administrative costs of solving disputes between corporate taxpayers (which requires abuses of tax inspectors) and tax authorities (who seek to limit international tax evasion).

This approach is accepted by the Association of European Chambers of Commerce and Industry (EUROCHAMBRES), which is in favour of changing regulations on corporate income tax in EU member states so that they become sufficiently comparable, for the easy identification of differences between tax systems and procedures applicable in different countries. All these should be materialized in the creation of a CCCTB.

EUROCHAMBRES also supports measures that would help reduce those tax compliance costs considered to be much higher for companies with cross-border activities than companies with local activity and which is disproportionately high for SMEs. A CCCTB would help to reduce discretionary fiscal practices, tax compliance costs and administrative burdens, and eliminate double taxation situations. Thus, it would facilitate the offsetting of losses against profits (in this context, unrealized profits should not be taxed), and it would help to create a more transparent tax system in the EU. For these reasons, EUROCHAMBRES supports the European Commission's proposals for a common consolidated corporate income tax, if this is clear, simple and easy to use (EUROCHAMBRES, 2007, pp. 3–4).

The harmonization of the corporate income tax base is supported by most members of EUROCHAMBRES, with the exception of the British Chamber of Commerce and the Ireland Chamber of Commerce, who are not convinced of the opportunities provided by introducing this measure. The Cyprus Chamber of Commerce, although it expressed reservations about the possibility of creating a European legal framework necessary for the CCCTB, has been willing to analyse the impact of its introduction.

Similar positions were expressed by representatives of European corporations. A study by KPMG International published in 2007 shows that many companies with cross-border activities in the EU want a unique formula for calculating income taxable. This study involved financial managers, directors and tax managers of more than 400 corporate groups from all 27 EU member states and Switzerland. The study showed that many experts support the European Commission proposal for a single formula to calculate the corporate tax base at European level (European Commission, 2011c, p. 6).

4.5 Conclusion

The objectives of corporate tax income coordination within the EU are as follows: to avoid competition distortions within the Single Market by fiscal policy that stimulates FDI location, to avoid transfer of profits from high tax countries to low tax countries using transfer pricing and intra-group loans, and to reduce tax compliance and administrative costs associated with corporate income taxation. Corporate income tax coordination in the EU has the capacities required to solve problems arising from the existence of different national tax rules. For this reason, the European Commission's proposal for a partial harmonization of corporate income tax (the tax base only) is supported by business representatives in most member states, as long as the new tax mechanism is optional.

5
Coordination Systems of Corporate Income Tax in the European Union

5.1 Introduction

Certain policy documents of European Union (EU) institutions adopted after 2000 highlighted the need to increase competitiveness within the EU and identified the elimination of tax obstacles as a necessary measure to ensure a better functioning of the Single Market. In this context, favourable conditions were created, in order to debate some projects regarding corporate income tax coordination in the EU. In order to remove the tax obstacles which resulted from the existence of 27 different corporate tax systems, three coordinated systems were affirmed: European Corporate Income Tax, Home State Taxation and the Common Consolidated Corporate Tax Base (CCCTB). Because the efforts to implement the third coordinated system are the most advanced, this chapter focuses on the conceptual development of the consolidated tax base. The main provisions of the Common Consolidated Corporate Tax Base Draft Directive are also presented.

5.2 European Corporate Income Tax

European Corporate Income Tax (EUCIT) requires the creation of a common corporate base that would be mandatorily applicable in all member states. In connection with the concrete issues involved in the application of this system, the discussions held at the Conference on European business taxation in Brussels on 29–30 April 2002 – "Towards an Internal Market without tax obstacles: A strategy for providing companies with a consolidated corporate tax base for their EU-wide activities" – revealed the following:[1]

- EUCIT could be applied either to all companies in the member states, or only to companies with cross-border activities, or it could represent an additional corporate income tax.
- EUCIT could be administered directly by a European institution. In this case, the tax rate would be unique, and the tax receipts could finance the EU budget.
- In a less "federalist" vision, EUCIT would be administered by member states, which would establish their own tax rates, and tax receipts would be divided among the countries in which companies are engaged in activities, according to a predetermined formula.

EU budget financing problems could be solved by introducing a "European tax" on corporate income in addition to existing national corporate income taxes, but this measure would generate an increased corporate tax burden and reduce the incentive to invest in the EU. On the other hand, the additional application of EUCIT should be made using a European tax base as similar as possible to that used in each member state in which companies are engaged in activities. Such a tax project has little chance of implementation.

Creating a "European tax" on corporate income could lead to a significant harmonization of EU member states' tax systems. Because corporate groups could be taxed on European incomes, this system would facilitate the consolidation of business operations in the Single Market. At the same time, tax administrations would have fewer difficulties in verifying transfer pricing, international allocation of financial funds and other characteristic aspects of cross-border transactions.

On the other hand, a mandatory "European tax" on corporate income would have important political difficulties that can be intuited, taking into account the strong opposition expressed by many member states to the proposals regarding the harmonization of corporate income taxation in the early 2000s. In addition, this initiative would be rejected by business representatives. They support the idea of an optional common system to calculate the corporate tax base.

A harmonized corporate tax rate (required by one type of EUCIT) should be determined as an average between the higher tax rates, applied in the "old" member states and the lower tax rates, applied in the "new" member states. In the opinion of Margit Schratzenstaller, this situation would generate a decrease in the corporate income tax rate and the diminution of tax receipts in the "old" member states, and an increase in the corporate income tax rate would reduce foreign direct investment (FDI) flows in the "new" member states (2005, p. 36).

So taxes could not be used to offset the existing disadvantages in the new member states for foreign investors (weaker infrastructure, smaller sales market, etc.).

5.3 Home State Taxation

Home State Taxation (HST) is based on the idea of voluntary mutual recognition of tax rules by EU member states. According to this concept, the profits of a group of companies active in more than one member state would be computed according to the rules of one company tax system only, i.e. the system of the home state of the parent company or head office of the group.

Each participating member state would continue to apply its own corporate tax rate, but only for a share of the profit from economic activities conducted on its territory. This share would be established under a predetermined formula.

According to the European Commission, the application of this tax system could limit difficulties faced by small and medium enterprises (SMEs) in the EU Single Market (high compliance costs to comply with the tax systems in different member states and the difficulty of adjustment of cross-border losses). The HST was considered a tool for boosting the SME sector. The importance of this sector is illustrated by the following figures: there were about 23 million SMEs in the EU, representing 99.8 per cent of all companies, and they provided 66 per cent of existing jobs in the private economic sector, in 2001 (European Commission, 2005c, pp. 8–11).

Based on the investigations conducted by Malcolm Gammie and Sven-Olof Lodin in 2001,[2] the European Commission proposed that the HST should be applied as a voluntary time-limited pilot scheme.[3] Key points for the design of this scheme were as follows:

- The pilot scheme should be designed as a practical test. Only work with real-life data could allow experience to be gained and justify the efforts involved in the pilot scheme.
- The pilot scheme should be applied only to corporate income tax, but could be extended to local surcharges on business, depending on the individual choice of the member states.
- Taxes other than corporation taxes (notably VAT and local profit taxes) should not be included within the scope of the scheme.

However, member states could continue to apply national (profit-related) surcharges on corporate tax as established under the conditions of the pilot scheme. Other, non-profit related local or regional taxes could also continue to be levied according to the rules of the resident/host state.

- The tax rules of HST in principle should be applied to the participating company (parent company/company headquarters) and its subsidiaries and/or permanent establishments in the participating member states. A business which, while participating in the pilot project, organically grows beyond the limits set out in the SME definition should not for this reason be excluded from the project. This definition distinguishes: (a) medium-sized enterprises (headcount <250 and turnover ≤€50 million and/or balance sheet total ≤€43 million); (b) small enterprises (headcount <50 and turnover ≤€10 million and/or balance sheet total ≤€10 million); (c) micro enterprises (headcount <10 and turnover ≤€2 million and/or balance sheet total ≤€2 million). The European Commission recommended disqualification of individual companies or individuals who were running their own economic activities, because their participation in the pilot project could not provide the perspectives of some major economic benefits. As the participation in the project pilot for companies with cross-border activities through international partnerships could generate potential complications and additional technical problems in the project implementation, the European Commission recommended their qualification only in exceptional circumstances, and only if the object of such partnerships was represented by production and/or commerce in foreign markets.
- The test run period should be sufficiently long to allow it to be analysed thoroughly and to justify the changeover cost. The European Commission considered at least five years to be a suitable timeframe.
- The proposed formula for apportioning the tax base between the participating member states was simple, based on two factors with equal weight: payroll (or alternatively the number of employees) and turnover.
- Participating companies were obliged to file a tax return only in their home state. The responsible tax administrations of the other states concerned would receive copies of this tax declaration and the relevant annexes (e.g. balance sheets, profit/loss accounts, etc.). The information must be sufficient to allow the calculation of any surcharge (usually local taxes) and other national taxes. To reduce

administrative costs, the European Commission considered that for these documents there should be no imposed translation into the national language of the host states. A synthesis document provided in the national language of the host states, at the request of the tax administration, was sufficient. The corporate income tax owed in the host state, according to the distributed tax base, would be paid in that country.

- Tax audits could be carried out by the home state authorities, if need be jointly with the partner administration, but the audit should be limited to issues governing the implementation of the pilot project.
- Mergers and acquisitions that do not affect the constitutive elements of the pilot scheme (SME definition; determination of home state, etc.) should not automatically lead to the exclusion of the participating company. The responsible tax administrations had to make an assessment to determine whether the new structure generated difficulties in project implementation. Changing the country of origin during the implementation of the pilot project was not permitted.
- If the fiscal year in the home state did not coincide with the fiscal year in the host states, the parent company was obliged to organize its accounting activity in such a manner as to allow tax administrations to evaluate the request for the allocation of the tax base.
- The transfer of assets under the pilot scheme between (a) the headquarters and the permanent establishment, or (b) the parent company and subsidiary in another member state was generally possible under the domestic (group) taxation rules of the home state and would thus not give rise to a taxable event. If the transaction was covered by Directive 90/434/EEC, the rules were applied to this directive.
- Economic relations between members of a group of companies participating in the pilot project were outside the provisions of any double taxation agreements between the home state and host states.
- Third-country income (dividends, interest, royalties, income from immovable property, etc.) of the group members falling outside the scope of the pilot scheme would have to be accounted for under the normal rules. In other words, foreign source income was to be added to the income of the group member after apportionment.
- Transfer pricing adjustments fell within the competences of the tax authorities in the home state. The European Commission

recommended making these adjustments before apportioning the tax base between tax jurisdictions.

- Payments of dividends or other similar transactions made between companies that operate within the same member state, but with subsidiaries of two or more companies resident in other member states, were to be subject to taxation according to the rules of the host state.
- In order to avoid cases of tax fraud, companies that wanted to participate in the project were qualified only if: (a) they participated with all their subsidiaries (there was no possibility to declare only certain subsidiaries eligible), and (b) the parent company must have been resident in the home state for at least two years.
- In order to facilitate the implementation of the project, the European Commission recommended the member states to use a common mechanism in the multilateral agreements on avoidance of double taxation. For this purpose, the European Commission was to provide support and technical assistance to all participating member states (European Commission, 2005c, pp. 13–24).

Figure 5.1 illustrates the basic functioning of the pilot scheme.
Explanations are as follows:

- The four companies can form a "Home State Group".
- The parent company is the leader of the group. It is responsible for the functioning of the pilot project and it is a resident of member state A (the home state). If a company has residence in two countries, the home country is considered to be the country where it carries out its management functions. If this rule could not be applied, the tax administrations of the member states had to reach a common agreement on the home state.
- Member states B and C are the host states for the two subsidiaries of the parent company and the sub-subsidiary in member state C.
- The parent company establishes the taxable income of the corporate group according to the tax legislation of member state A.
- The tax base so established is apportioned among member states A, B and C following a simple key, e.g. the proportions of payroll and/or turnover in each jurisdiction.
- The parent company files a group/comprehensive tax return in member state A and pays tax.

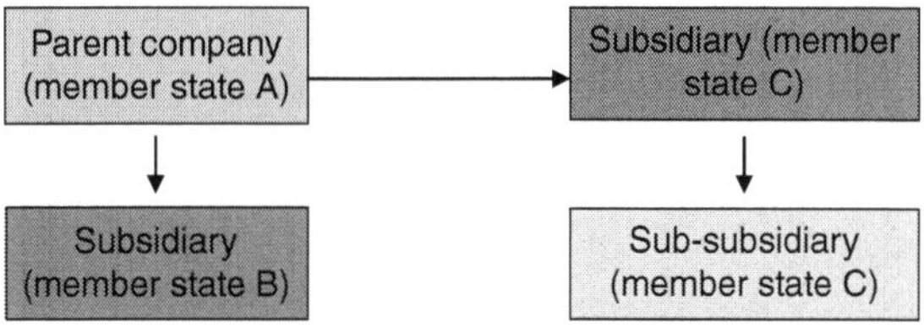

Figure 5.1 Basic functioning of the HST pilot scheme.

- The subsidiary in member state B files self-assessment documentation and pays its individual tax liability in member state B.
- The subsidiary and sub-subsidiary in member state C file self-assessment documentation and pay their individual tax liabilities in member state C.

The pilot project proposed by the European Commission had to be implemented during the period 1 January 2007 to 1 December 2011, and the following results were expected (2005c, pp. 39–63):

(1) **Economic impact assessment of the HST option**

- The existing international SMEs groups could benefit from the HST cross-border loss compensation possibilities. The estimated amount of the immediate savings in tax payments for the existent international SMEs in the EU was of €3 billion. This resulted in estimated immediate savings in tax payments equal to around €860 million;
- The quantitative compliance costs savings were estimated, under the most conservative assumptions, they equalled 0.00081 per cent in terms of EU GDP, which amounted to approximately €70 million yearly for the EU-25;
- Removing the existing tax barriers could be a strong motivation for SMEs to expand their business in other member states. Enhancing investment flows in the EU member states should lead to the improvement of technology transfer and know-how, an increase in the range of products offered to consumers, lower prices of goods under the impact of increased competition, etc. According to an optimistic scenario, applying the "Mutual recognition of tax rules in the country of origin" could generate growth of foreign investment in the EU by about 6 percentage points.

- The application of HST will also increase costs for fiscal administrations, due to an increased administrative burden and the need to coordinate with other fiscal authorities.
- The quantitative analysis of the effects of the apportionment mechanism showed that tax receipts for each member state would not have experienced substantial changes, or at least no insurmountable adverse consequences for any member state. Expanding small and medium businesses internationally would increase the tax revenues of the member states concerned.
- The increased participation of SMEs in the Single Market would generate increased tax revenues for the member states concerned.

(2) **Social impact assessment of the HST option**
The social effects of HST implementation included an increase in the number of jobs and wages (by increasing productivity), especially in host countries.

(3) **Regional impact assessment of the HST option**
Regional impact assessment suggested that most SMEs that would expand their business into another member state would have been located in border regions. Because the level of cross-border business operations are generally higher in the border regions, HST implementation had to be accompanied by additional measures to boost SME activity in more distant regions.

Applying HST would increase the complexity of operations carried out by the tax authorities in member states, because in each tax jurisdiction there would be situations where the tax rules of another country applied to certain taxpayers. This tax coordination system can work in practice as long as the tax rules and practices in member states are close enough. The main advantage of the system is determined by the implementation, which is much easier than for other tax coordination systems.

HST is a transition tool for solving the current obstacles generated by corporate income taxation in the Single Market, because its area of application is quite limited. Nearly all the SMEs in the EU-25 were micro enterprises (employing less than 10 employees), as they represented 91.3 per cent of the total number of enterprises, in 2001. They did not have the economic capacity to expand internationally in a short- to medium-term timeframe.

The starting of the HST pilot project has not received approval from member states, and it is not currently on the tax agenda of the European Commission.

5.4 The Common Consolidated Corporate Tax Base

5.4.1 Objectives of the "Common Consolidated Corporate Tax Base"

The Common Consolidated Corporate Tax Base (CCCBT) involves the rating of the taxable income of an entire corporate group according to one set of rules and the establishment of consolidated accounts for tax purposes. The consolidated tax base established is then shared between the entitled member states, based on a unique formula. Member states will charge corporate income tax according to national rates. The territorial scope of the CCCBT will be limited to the Single Market, if the European Commission's proposal is ratified by all the EU member states.

According to the European Commission, the CCCBT answers the need for economic efficiency in the Single Market (by the elimination of the problems of transfer pricing and double taxation, and by the reduction of the effective corporate income tax rate in the EU), while maintaining the independence of states to set their own tax rates (2001a, p. 11).

Concrete actions for building the CCCBT in the EU began at the ECOFIN Council in September 2004, when most member states accepted the usefulness of progress towards building a common tax base and decided to set up a working group of experts representing the member states and chaired by the European Commission to examine in detail the possible solutions.[4]

The following solutions were identified (European Commission, 2010, pp. 7–8):

- **An optional Common Corporate Tax Base (optional CCTB):** EU-resident companies (and EU-located branches of third-country companies) would have the option to compute their tax base pursuant to a set of common rules instead of any of the 27 national corporation tax systems, as the case may be. "Separate accounting" would remain in place for intra-group transactions, as the system would not involve a consolidation of tax results.
- **A compulsory Common Corporate Tax Base (compulsory CCTB):** all eligible EU-resident companies (and EU-located branches of third-country companies) would have to apply a new set of common rules for computing their tax base. The new rules would replace the current 27 national corporation tax systems. Again, in the absence of consolidation, "separate accounting" would continue to determine the allocation of profit in intra-group transactions.

- **An optional Common Consolidated Corporate Tax Base (optional CCCTB):** this alternative would replace the current 27 different corporation tax systems and the use of "separate accounting" in allocating profits within a group with a set of common rules, establishing an EU-wide consolidated tax base. Thus, the tax results of each EU-resident group member (or EU-located branch of a third-country company) would be aggregated and apportioned to each eligible jurisdiction according to a pre-established sharing mechanism (i.e. Formulary Apportionment). According to this scenario, any EU-resident company (or EU-located branch of a third-country company) would be entitled to opt for the CCCTB, provided that all eligible members of the same group do the same ("all-in all-out").
- **A compulsory Common Consolidated Corporate Tax Base (compulsory CCCTB):** all eligible EU resident companies (and EU-located branches of third-country companies) would have to apply the CCCTB rules described in (3) above.

The main objectives of the Common Consolidated Corporate Tax Base Working Group (CCCTB WG), established in 2004, were as follows:

- to discuss the principles that will govern the CCCBT;
- to examine the technical definition of a common consolidated tax base for companies in more than one member state;
- to establish fundamental structural elements of a consolidated tax base;
- to formulate a mechanism for the allocation of the consolidated tax base between different member states.

The documents resulting from the discussions of the CCCTB WG are prepared by the Directorate-General for Taxation and Customs Union and published on the website of the European Commission after each meeting. So far, 13 meetings of the CCCTB WG have been held. In late 2008, the European Commission hoped to translate the results of the CCCTB WG into a legislative proposal, applicable from 2010. However, it was only in March 2011 that the European Commission succeeded in publishing a proposal for a CCCTB.

This proposal aims to enable companies to opt for a simplified tax system (without changing the current national tax rates), in order to reduce tax compliance costs and remove the existing tax obstacles that companies face when they operate in several member states. According to the proposal for the EU directive on the CCCTB, this is an important initiative to eliminate the obstacles that stand in the way of the fair and efficient functioning of the Single market, representing a stimulation tool for the increase of the EU corporate sector. In this way, the number of jobs affected now by the international economic crisis will also increase.

The main objective of the CCCTB, identified during discussions of the CCCTB WG, is to eliminate the obstacles that resulted from the existence of 27 corporate tax systems in the EU (Directorate-General Taxation and Customs Union, 2006, p. 3). The proposal for an EU directive on the CCCTB includes the following strategic objectives: the re-launching of the Single Market in the context of Europe 2020 initiatives,[5] the simplification of tax rules, the reduction of compliance costs and the removal of tax obstacles for companies with cross-border activities.

The expected results of the application of the CCCTB are as follows: (a) to allow cross-border loss-offset; (b) to reduce occurrences of double or over-taxation; (c) to reduce undue or unintended tax planning opportunities for companies by the parallel application of 27 corporate tax systems in the EU; (d) to introduce a one-stop shop approach for tax declarations and assessment; (e) to provide companies with the option to apply a common system for taxation in the EU; (f) to reduce transfer pricing compliance obligations (European Commission, 2011a, pp. 15–16).

From the legal point of view, the CCCTB will be implemented into a directive, which means that the unanimous agreement of all member states will be required. Since the unanimous support of member states is unlikely, it was established that the proposal for the EU directive on the CCCTB could be implemented under enhanced cooperation between some member states.

The idea of the CCCTB for companies with activities in several countries is not new. A system for fiscal consolidation (profits are taxed in each state after the allocation of the tax base according to certain criteria) operates successfully in the USA.

5.4.2 Eligible organizations for the "Common Consolidated Corporate Tax Base"

The EU directive on the CCCTB shall apply to entities subject to corporate tax in the EU member states or subject to a similar tax system (specified in an annex of the regulation), organized in groups, regardless of their size.

The European Commission estimates that, by reducing tax obstacles and administrative burdens, the CCCTB will encourage, in particular, the expansion of cross-border activities of SMEs, which are most affected by the high compliance costs of the current situation. Therefore, the CCCTB has particular importance as part of the effort to support and encourage SMEs to take advantage of the Single Market's potential (European Commission, 2011a, p. 21).

Eligible organizations for the CCCTB include the following:

- companies established under the laws of a member state and which take one of the forms listed in the annex to the proposal for the introduction of the CCCTB;
- third-country companies with a permanent establishment located in member states, which would qualify for consolidation if they have been resident in the member states, and having similar forms as resident companies in these countries.

A resident taxpayer shall form a group with: (a) all its permanent establishments located in other member states; (b) all permanent establishments located in a member state of its qualifying subsidiaries resident in a third country; (c) all its qualifying subsidiaries resident in one or more member states; (d) other resident taxpayers that are qualifying subsidiaries of the same company which is resident in a third country and fulfils the eligibility criteria. A non-resident taxpayer shall form a group with all its permanent establishments located in member states and all its qualifying subsidiaries resident in one or more member states, including the permanent establishments of the latter located in member states.

If a company is resident in more than one member state, it shall be considered to be resident in the member state in which it has its place of effective management. If the place of effective management of a shipping group member or of a group member engaged in inland waterways transport is aboard a ship or boat, it shall be deemed to be situated in the member state of the home harbour of the ship or boat, or, if there is no such home harbour, in the member state of residence of the operator of the ship or boat (European Commission, 2011a, p. 19).

Requirements to form a group for consolidation (group membership) refer to the ownership (more than 75 per cent of equity) or rights to profits (more than 75 per cent of rights giving entitlement to profit) and control (more than 50 per cent of voting rights). Qualifying subsidiaries shall be all immediate and lower-tier subsidiaries in which the parent company holds the following rights: (a) a right to exercise more than 50 per cent of the voting rights; (b) an ownership right amounting to more than 75 per cent of the company's capital or more than 75 per cent of the rights giving entitlement to profit. The two thresholds should be met throughout the tax year; otherwise, the company should leave the group immediately. There should also be a nine-month minimum requirement for group membership. A taxpayer in respect of which a declaration of insolvency is made or which is liquidated shall leave the group immediately (European Commission, 2011a, p. 39).

The existence of complex relationships between companies residing in EU member states and companies residing in non-EU countries requires some clarification regarding eligible structures for the CCCTB. The following examples (see Figures 5.2–5.7) present some structures eligible for tax consolidation within the EU (see the document "Eligibility Tests for Companies and Definition of a CCCTB Group", published on the occasion of the CCCTB workshop held in Brussels on 20 October 2010[6]):

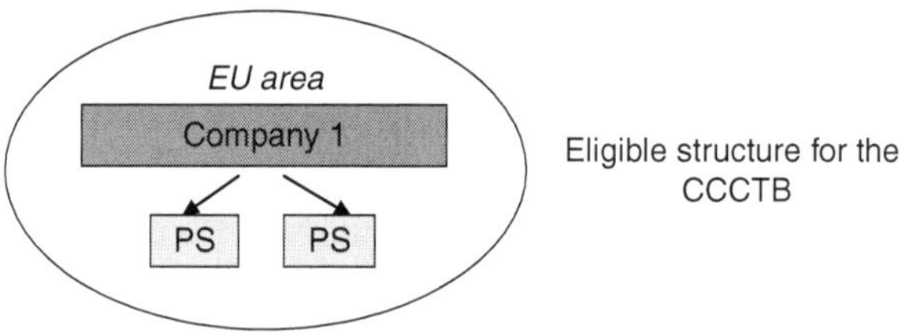

Figure 5.2 Example A of eligible structure for tax consolidation in the EU.

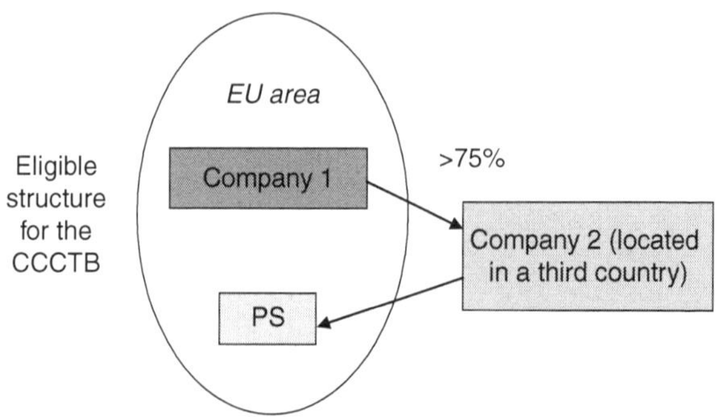

Figure 5.3 Example B of eligible structure for tax consolidation in the EU.

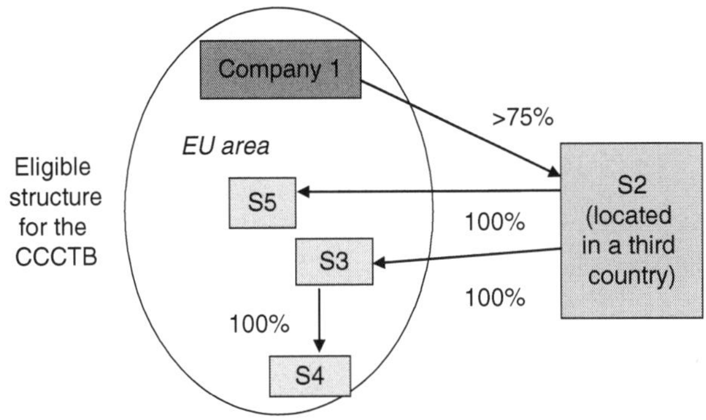

Figure 5.4 Example C of eligible structure for tax consolidation in the EU.

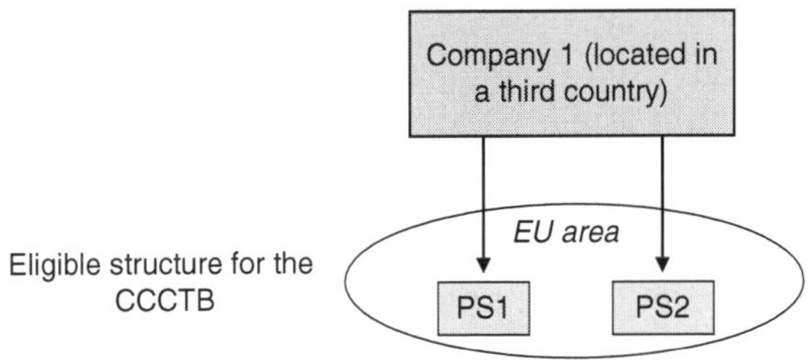

Figure 5.5 Example D of eligible structure for tax consolidation in the EU.

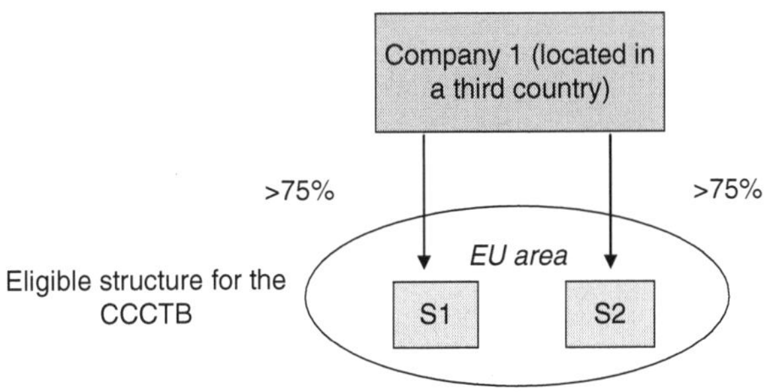

Figure 5.6 Example E of eligible structure for tax consolidation in the EU.

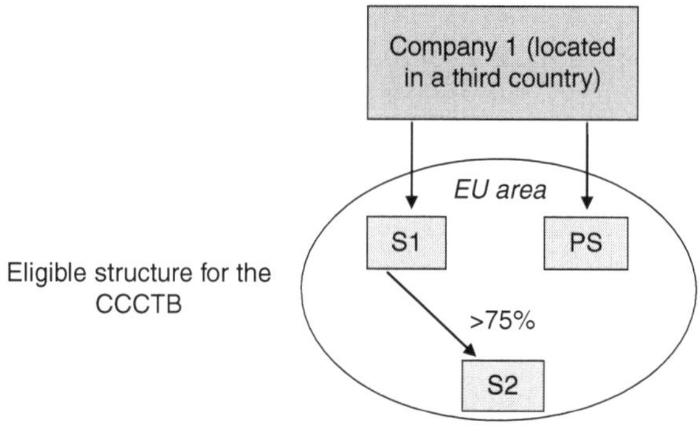

Figure 5.7 Example F of eligible structure for tax consolidation in the EU.

- An EU resident taxpayer (Company 1) and its two permanent establishments (PS1 and PS2) located in (an) other member state(s) form a CCCTB group.
- An EU resident taxpayer (Company 1) with a >75 per cent subsidiary located in a third country (Company 2) is eligible to form a CCCTB group with the permanent establishment (PS) (located in a member state) of Company 2.
- An EU resident taxpayer (Company 1) holds a >75 per cent subsidiary (S2) located in a third country that in turn has three 100 per cent-owned subsidiaries (S3, S4 and S5) located in the EU. Company 1 and subsidiaries 3, 4 and 5 are eligible to form a CCCTB group, since Company 1 owns subsidiaries 3, 4 and 5 >75 per cent.
- A non-resident taxpayer (Company 1) has two permanent establishments (PS1 and PS2) in the EU. Both PS1 and PS2 are eligible to form a CCCTB group.
- A non-resident taxpayer (Company 1) holds a direct share of >75 per cent in two EU-resident subsidiaries (S2 and S3). Subsidiaries 2 and 3 are eligible to form a CCCTB group.
- A non-resident (Company 1) with a permanent establishment (PS) and a 100 per cent-owned subsidiary (S1), both located in the EU. The subsidiary holds a share of >75 per cent in another subsidiary (S2). Subsidiaries 1 and 2 and the permanent establishment are eligible to form a CCCTB group.

A reorganization of companies within the group or the cross-border transfer of the registered office of a company which remains part of the group should not give rise to any profit or loss in order to determine the consolidated tax base.

5.4.3 General principles of the "Common Consolidated Corporate Tax Base"

The CCCTB must meet the legal standards applied when designing a tax system: neutrality, equity and certainty. The system should ensure fiscal neutrality in the Single Market, since jurisdictional differences between the national tax bases will not affect the location of capital. A brief analysis of the system, in terms of tax equity, reveals that a CCCTB would contribute to the reduction of corporate tax arbitrage opportunities, which generate advantages for companies with cross-border activities compared to companies with only local activities. The existence of some common tax and accounting rules for calculating taxable corporate income will increase the transparency and stability of the fiscal framework in the EU member states.

In 2004, the CCCTB WG set out the specific principles of the CCCTB, as follows (Directorate-General Taxation and Customs Union, 2004, pp. 3–5):

- **Vertical equity**

The burden of taxation should be shared in accordance with taxpayers' respective ability to pay, sometimes referred to as "the ability to pay" principle. It is difficult to see how this principle (normally applied to personal taxation) could or should be applied to company taxation. However, the "ability to pay" could be relevant when considering whether or not unrealized profits should be taxable. The concept that higher profits should be taxed at higher rates is not often applied to companies other than in the case of certain reliefs for small companies in some countries.

- **Horizontal equity**

Taxpayers in the same economic circumstances should receive equivalent treatment. In the context of international company taxation, equity relates mainly to the fair allocation of the tax base between states where international companies operate. Traditionally, inter-country equity can be satisfied by (1) source country entitlement (the source country has the prior right to tax profits earned within its jurisdiction), and (2) non-discrimination (countries agree not to discriminate against foreign companies). In this way, different companies operating in a particular country are treated in a similar manner.

- **Efficiency (neutrality)**

Generally, taxes should be neutral to ensure that investment decisions take into account the "best" location from an economic perspective. This avoids "locational inefficiency", whereby investments are not placed where the productivity of capital is highest. However, taxation policy may be used to correct "market failures", whereby distortions or inefficiencies in a particular market economy can be "corrected" by the use of specific tax incentives. Determining whether a tax policy is correcting a market failure or is inefficient can be difficult.

The CCCTB will ensure the efficiency of the Single Market, since all investors will be able to easily determine the tax burden (by opting for the CCCTB application) and they will be able to compare the effective levels of company taxation in EU member states.

- **Effectiveness**

Effectiveness is essentially the capacity of the tax base to achieve its basic objectives. Together with the tax rate, these would be to generate revenues and set the desired economic incentives. Within a single country, or within the EU with a CCCTB, such incentives may increase competitiveness but in the international context this depends on interaction with other systems, for example, incentives which reduce the effective rate in a source country may have no effect if a parent company is taxed on a residence basis and the tax rate in the country of residence is above that of the source country. Such incentives simply shift tax revenue between the source country and the resident country.

- **Simplicity, transparency and certainty**

The simpler a tax base is, the lower the administrative or compliance costs should be, for both administrations and business. These costs are difficult to measure, so international comparisons – measuring the incentive provided by a tax base with "low" costs against a "high" cost tax base – are difficult. The rules must also be certain and clear, which links in to the requirement for transparency. Certainty is desirable to assist business planning, but also to provide a degree of revenue certainty for administrations, for example, if the rules governing loss-offset are unclear, then neither business nor government can predict tax payments and revenues. The rules must also provide an appropriate level of protection against tax evasion and the unacceptable use of purely artificial tax avoidance schemes.

- **Flexibility**

Markets and business practices change over time, so the tax base should be responsive and capable of change as well. This is particularly relevant for a CCCTB which it might be more difficult to "change" than the existing national tax bases. However, too much flexibility can endanger certainty from a business perspective.

5.4.4 Defining and assessing the tax base

The CCCTB involves the use of common rules for determining taxable corporate income.

The working documents of the CCCTB WG on the issue of accounting rules made reference to the International Financial Reporting Standards (IFRS). These have the advantage (in addition to their wide international recognition) of being easily adaptable to the needs of the new tax system, because – with effect from 1 January 2005 – European Community-wide rules apply, requiring companies listed on regulated capital markets to prepare their consolidated balance sheets according to the IFRS. In 2003 and 2004, the European Commission published two regulations,[7] by means of which the majority of the available International Accounting Standards (later called the International Financial Reporting Standards) were "approved", thus transforming these financial reporting requirements into mandatory European legislation.

In addition, the national legislatures were empowered to extend the application of the IFRS in the case of unlisted companies. In this context, the IFRS are applied to a wide extent in EU companies.

By comparing the tax and accounting rules in EU member states with the IFRS, some experts (Gammie et al., 2005, pp. 23–65; Oestreicher and Spengel, 2007, pp. 27–34) showed that these standards could provide the basic elements for creating a common EU tax base. Thus, areas such as the recognition of assets and liabilities, the determination of costs, depreciation and the treatment of onerous contracts are now governed by the IFRS in all EU member states.

Since the rules for determining taxable income vary widely across member states, many complex and controversial issues exist concerning the calculation of the CCCTB. These include: defining business income and expenses for tax purposes, treatment of dividends and capital gains, etc.

The calculation of the CCCTB can start with a comparison of opening and closing balance sheets or profit and loss statements. In the first case, it is necessary to prepare a model of "fiscal balance" in accordance with some commonly defined rules, which include the profit and loss statement. In the second case, it is necessary to provide only the profit and loss statement as defined by mutual agreement of the CCCTB. The European Commission does not support the idea of "fiscal balance", because it represents an additional administrative burden (European Commission, 2007a, p. 10).

According to the proposal for the EU directive on the CCCTB, the tax base shall be calculated for each fiscal year (12 months) using the following formula:

$$TB = TR - (ER + DE + ODI)$$

where: TB – tax base; TR – total revenues; ER – exempt revenues; DE – deductible expenses; ODI – other deductible items.

For the purposes of calculating the tax base, transactions shall be measured at:

- the monetary consideration for the transaction, such as the price of goods or services;
- the market value where the consideration for the transaction is wholly or partly non-monetary;
- the market value in the case of a non-monetary gift received by a taxpayer;
- the market value in the case of non-monetary gifts made by a taxpayer other than gifts to charitable bodies;
- the fair value of financial assets and liabilities held for trading;
- the value for tax purposes in the case of non-monetary gifts to charitable bodies.

The tax base, income and expenses shall be measured in euros during the tax year, or translated into euros on the last day of the tax year at the annual average exchange rate for the calendar year issued by the European Central Bank or, if the tax year does not coincide with the calendar year, at the average rate from daily observations issued by the European Central Bank through the tax year. This shall not apply to a single taxpayer located in a member state that has not adopted the euros. Nor shall it apply to a group if all group members are located in the same member state and that state has not adopted the euros.

Generally, any revenues from corporate economic activities will be subject to tax consolidation: income from selling goods and services, receipts from disposal of assets and rights of use of assets, interest, dividends and other profit distributions, royalties, subsidies and grants (subsidies directly linked to the acquisition, construction or improvement of fixed assets may be exempt from taxation), gifts, etc.

As some corporate revenues have some particularities, which require a separate tax approach, the CCCTB WG focused on foreign income, capital gains and income from intra-group transactions. The main proposals in this area are listed below.

Foreign income can either be excluded completely from the CCCTB or it can be incorporated into the CCCTB and a method devised for including it in the consolidation and sharing mechanism. The issue arises because the different methods of avoiding double taxation currently followed by member states under their existing legislation and bilateral treaties with third countries must be taken into account. In 2007, the European Commission considered it preferable to design a method which incorporated foreign income in the CCCTB, supplemented where appropriate by a form of relief to avoid double taxation (European Commission, 2007a, p. 11). According to the proposal for the EU directive on the CCCTB, dividends, receipts from the sale of shares of a company that is not part of the group and profits of foreign permanent establishments should be exempt. Interest incomes and royalties should be taxable, being granted a withholding tax exemption for such income (European Commission, 2011a, p. 22).

Capital gains are considered as ordinary business income in most member states, so they are subject to corporate income tax. In certain circumstances, however, the exemption from capital gains tax is practised in Cyprus, Luxembourg, Sweden and the UK. The CCCTB WG believes that both capital gains and losses must be considered when determining the taxable income of companies.

Revenues from intra-group transactions are determined by the transfer price. In order to avoid transfer pricing issues, there are a number of ways of eliminating intra-group transactions when consolidating the tax base. They could be ignored, recognized at cost or recognized at the current arm's length price. Each has advantages and disadvantages, and the European Commission must decide which method is preferable, or whether it would be possible to permit each group a choice of methods (European Commission, 2007a, p. 11).

The following shall be exempt from corporate tax:

- subsidies directly linked to the acquisition, construction or improvement of fixed assets, subject to depreciation;
- proceeds from the disposal of pooled assets, including the market value of non-monetary gifts;
- received profit distributions;

- proceeds from a disposal of shares;
- income of a permanent establishment in a third country.

Provisions relating to income exempted from taxation do not apply where the entity which made the profit distributions (Controlled Foreign Company) is tax resident in a low-tax third country, meaning a country which operates:

- under its general tax regime, a statutory corporate tax rate lower than 40 per cent of the average statutory corporate tax rate applicable in the Member States[8];
- a special regime that allows for a substantially lower level of taxation than the general regime.

Deductible expenses shall include all costs of sales and expenses net of deductible VAT incurred by the taxpayer with a view to obtaining or securing income, including costs of research and development and costs incurred in raising equity or debt for the purposes of the business.[9] Deductible expenses shall also include gifts to charitable bodies,[10] which are established in a member state or in a third country which applies an agreement on the exchange of information on request comparable to the provisions of Directive 2011/16/EU.[11] The maximum deductible expense for monetary gifts or donations to charitable bodies shall be 0.5 per cent of revenues in the tax year.

The costs relating to the acquisition, construction or improvement of fixed assets[12] not subject to depreciation shall be deductible in the tax year in which the fixed assets are disposed of, provided that the disposal proceeds are included in the tax base. The total amount of deductible expenses for a tax year shall be increased by the value of stocks and work-in-progress at the beginning of the tax year, and reduced by the value of stocks and work-in-progress at the end of the same tax year. No adjustment shall be made in respect of stocks and work-in-progress relating to long-term contracts.

The following expenses shall be treated as non-deductible:

- profit distributions and repayments of equity or debt;
- 50 per cent of entertainment costs;
- the transfer of retained earnings to a reserve which forms part of the equity of the company;
- corporate tax;
- bribes;

- fines and penalties payable to a public authority for breach of any legislation;
- costs incurred by a company for the purpose of deriving income (such costs shall be fixed at a flat rate of 5 per cent of that income unless the taxpayer is able to demonstrate that it has incurred a lower cost);
- monetary gifts and donations other than those made to charitable bodies;
- costs relating to the acquisition, construction or improvement of fixed assets except those relating to research and development (the depreciation shall be deducted in the year of acquisition or entry into use, whichever comes later);
- taxes listed in Annex III of the draft directive, with the exception of excise duties imposed on energy products, alcohol and alcoholic beverages, and manufactured tobacco.

For certain categories of expenditure, additional clarifications were made.

Depreciation of fixed assets

Fixed assets should be depreciable for tax purposes, subject to certain exceptions. Long-life tangible and intangible assets should be depreciated individually, while others should be placed in a pool. The depreciation base shall comprise any cost directly connected with the acquisition, construction or improvement of a fixed asset. Costs shall not include deductible VAT. In the case of fixed assets produced by the taxpayer, the indirect costs incurred in production of the asset shall also be added to the depreciation base in so far as they are not otherwise deductible.

The depreciation shall be deducted by the economic owner. A fixed asset may be depreciated by no more than one taxpayer at the same time. If the economic owner of an asset cannot be identified, the legal owner shall be entitled to deduct depreciation. In that case, the interest element of the lease payments shall not be included in the tax base of the legal owner. In the case of leasing contracts in which economic and legal ownership does not coincide, the economic owner shall be entitled to deduct the interest element of the lease payments from its tax base. The interest element of the lease payments shall be included in the tax base of the legal owner.

The useful life of a fixed asset shall be determined as follows:

- buildings: 40 years;
- long-life tangible assets other than buildings: 15 years;

- intangible assets: the period for which the asset enjoys legal protection or for which the right is granted or, if that period cannot be determined, 15 years.

Fixed assets that are not the subject of physical and moral depreciation, such as land, antiques, jewellery, etc. will not be amortized, unless the taxpayer shows that these assets registered a continuous decrease in value. According to the proposal for the EU directive on the CCCTB, fixed assets that are not depreciated individually shall be depreciated together in one asset pool at an annual rate of 25 per cent of the depreciation base.

Provisions

Provisions represent an important part of the tax base in that they accelerate tax relief. The tax treatment of actual expenditure under most of the categories of provisions currently recognized across the EU is tax deductible. According to the proposal for the EU directive on the CCCTB, where at the end of a tax year it is established that the taxpayer has a legal obligation, or a probable future legal obligation, arising from activities or transactions carried out in that, or previous tax years, any amount arising from that obligation which can be reliably estimated[13] shall be deductible, provided that the eventual settlement of the amount is expected to result in a deductible expense. Where the obligation relates to an activity or transaction that will continue over future tax years, the deduction shall be spread proportionately over the estimated duration of the activity or transaction, having regard to the revenue derived thereof. These amounts shall be reviewed and adjusted at the end of every tax year. In calculating the tax base in future years, account shall be taken of amounts already deducted. In the case of pension provisions, actuarial techniques shall be used in order to make a reliable estimate of the amount of benefits that employees have earned in return for their service in the current and prior period. The pension provision shall be discounted by reference to Euribor for obligations with a maturity of 12 months, as published by the European Central Bank. The calculations shall be based on the yearly average of that rate in the calendar year in the course of which the tax year ends.

Bad debt deductions

According to the proposal for the EU directive on the CCCTB, a deduction shall be allowed for a bad debt receivable where the following conditions are met:

- at the end of the tax year, the taxpayer has taken all reasonable steps to pursue payment and reasonably believes that the debt will not be satisfied wholly or partially; or the taxpayer has a large number of homogeneous receivables and is able to reliably estimate the amount of the bad debt receivable on a percentage basis, through making reference to all relevant factors, including past experience where applicable;
- the debtor is not a member of the same group as the taxpayer;
- where the bad debt relates to a trade receivable, an amount corresponding to the debt shall have been included as revenue in the tax base.

Stocks and work-in-progress

The cost of stock items and work-in-progress that are not ordinarily interchangeable and goods or services produced and segregated for specific projects shall be measured individually. The costs of other stock items and work-in-progress shall be measured by using the first-in first-out (FIFO) or weighted-average cost method. A taxpayer shall consistently use the same method for the valuation of all stocks and work-in-progress having a similar nature and use. The cost of stocks and work-in progress shall comprise all costs of purchase, direct costs of conversion and other direct costs incurred in bringing them to their present location and condition. Costs shall be net of deductible VAT. A taxpayer who has included indirect costs in valuing stocks and work-in-progress before opting for the system provided for by this directive may continue to apply the indirect cost approach. Stocks and work-in-progress shall be valued on the last day of the tax year at the lower of cost and net realizable value. The net realizable value is the estimated selling price in the ordinary course of business less the estimated costs of completion and the estimated costs necessary to make the sale.

Local taxes

Local business taxes applied in some member states may be deductible from the consolidated tax base and thus included in the mechanism for sharing the CCCTB or retained at national level and deducted only from that part of the tax base distributed among member states. Most experts seemed to prefer that local business taxes should be deducted not from the consolidated tax base, but should be deducted from each individual member state's share of the consolidated tax base (Directorate-General Taxation and Customs Union, 2008, p. 4).

Losses incurred by companies that opted for the system provided for by the EU directive on the CCCTB will be deducted in subsequent tax years. Unrelieved losses incurred by a taxpayer or a permanent establishment under the rules of the EU directive on the CCCTB or under national corporate tax law before entering a group may not be set off against the consolidated tax base. Such losses shall be carried forward and may be set off against the apportioned share or processed according to the national corporate tax law that would be applicable to the taxpayer in the absence of the system provided for by the directive. A reduction of the tax base on account of losses from previous tax years shall not result in a negative amount. The oldest losses shall be used first. Where, as a result of a business reorganization, one or more groups, or two or more members of a group, become part of another group, any unrelieved losses of the previously existing group or groups shall be allocated to each of the members, on the basis of the factors applicable to the tax year in which the business reorganization takes place, and shall be carried forward for future years (European Commission, 2011a, p. 35).

In terms of defining and evaluating aspects of the CCCTB, the proposal for an EU directive is based on the conclusions of the working group, internal researches and consultations with representatives from the business and academic community. For some elements of the CCCTB, member states may make further adjustments to the national tax bases after apportionment. If the European Commission does not manage well enough any "intervention" of member states affecting the national tax bases after apportionment, conditions to stimulate the movement of profits within the corporate group may arise. Also, this situation could lead to increased complexity of the CCCTB system.

5.4.5 Opportunities for consolidation and formula for allocating the consolidated tax base

The CCCTB WG identified two options for consolidating the corporate tax base, as follows:

- completely ignoring intra-group income and expenditure other than that related to depreciable assets;
- including intra-group income and expenditure other than that related to depreciable assets by each group company and netted off when the consolidation is carried out.

The following examples[14] illustrate possible scenarios for consolidating the corporate tax base.

Example 1: Sale of goods without stocks

Company A and company B belong to the same CCCTB group. Company A produces intermediate products that are sold to B for 4000 m.u. To produce these goods A needs third party inputs as electricity (60 m.u.), raw materials (1000 m.u.) and wages (2000 m.u.). Company B purchases intermediate products from A (4000 m.u.) and from third parties (500 m.u.). In addition, B uses third party electricity (30 m.u.) and wages (1000 m.u.) to produce goods that are sold to third parties for 6000 m.u.

Company A		**Company B**	
Cost of electricity	−60 m.u.	Cost of electricity	−30 m.u.
Cost of raw materials	−1000 m.u.	Cost of purchase	−(4000 + 500) m.u.
Cost of wages	−2000 m.u.	Cost of wages	−1000 m.u.
Sales to B	+4000 m.u.	Sales to third	+6000 m.u.

Option (i): determination of the consolidated tax base by subtracting total expenses from the total revenues of the group

Company A		**Company B**	
Cost of electricity	−60 m.u.	Cost of electricity	−30 m.u.
Cost of raw materials	−1000 m.u.	Cost of purchase	−(**4000** + 500) m.u.
Cost of wages	−2000 m.u.	Cost of wages	−1000 m.u.
Sales to B	+**4000** m.u.	Sales to third	+6000 m.u.

In order to determine the consolidated tax base, representing 1410 m.u., the total costs of the group are subtracted from sales of B (i.e. 6000 – 60 – 30 – 1000 – 500 – 2000 – 1000). The value of the tax base remains unchanged regardless of the price at which Company A sells intermediate products of Company B. Thus, transfer pricing influence is eliminated, Company A has the potential to sell at a price equal to the incurred costs (3060 m.u.).

Option (ii): determination of the consolidated tax base by adding individual tax bases of companies

Company A		Company B	
Cost of electricity	−60 m.u.	Cost of electricity	−60 m.u.
Cost of raw materials	−1000 m.u.	Cost of raw materials	−1000 m.u.
Cost of wages	−2000 m.u.	Cost of wages	−2000 m.u.
Sales to B	+4000 m.u.	Sales to B	+4000 m.u.
Tax base	940 m.u.	Tax base	470 m.u.

Summing the values of the two tax bases, one arrives at the same amount of consolidated tax base: 1410 m.u., but the transfer pricing problem is not eliminated. So, if in the country where Company A operates the corporate tax rate is higher than in the country where Company B operates, the use of some lower transfer prices will generate a lower tax base in the country with a high level of profit rate and a higher tax base in the country with a low level of profit rate.

Example 2: Sale of goods with stocks

Using the same data as in example 1, now consider the existence of stocks at Company B.

Company A		Company B	
Cost of electricity	−60 m.u.	Cost of electricity	−30 m.u.
Cost of raw materials	−1000 m.u.	Cost of raw materials	−(4000 + 500) m.u.
Cost of wages	−2000 m.u.	Cost of wages	−1000 m.u.
Valuation of stocks	0	Valuation of stocks	+5300 m.u.
Sales to B	+4000 m.u.	Sales to third	0

Option (i): determination of the consolidated tax base by subtracting total expenses from the total revenues of the group

Stocks are valued at the group level, representing: 60 + 30 + 1000 + 500 + 2000 + 1000 = 4590 m.u. If Company B does not sell any finished products (they are stored), the consolidated tax base is 0.

Company A		Company B	
Cost of electricity	–60 m.u.	Cost of electricity	–30 m.u.
Cost of raw materials	–1000 m.u.	Cost of raw materials	–(4000 + 500) m.u.
Cost of wages	–2000 m.u.	Cost of wages	–1000 m.u.
Valuation of stocks	0	Valuation of stocks	+4590 m.u.
Sales to B	+4000 m.u.	Sales to third	0

If the intra-group transaction is done at the cost amount, the consolidated tax base will be 0.

Company A		Company B	
Cost of electricity	–60 m.u.	Cost of electricity	–30 m.u.
Cost of raw materials	–1000 m.u.	Cost of raw materials	–(**3060** + 500) m.u.
Cost of wages	–2000 m.u.	Cost of wages	–1000 m.u.
Valuation of stocks	0	Valuation of stocks	+4590 m.u.
Sales to B	+**3060** m.u.	Sales to third	0

Option (ii): determination of the consolidated tax base by adding individual tax bases of companies

Company A		Company B	
Cost of electricity	–60 m.u.	Cost of electricity	–30 m.u.
Cost of raw materials	–1000 m.u.	Cost of raw materials	–(4000 + 500) m.u.
Cost of wages	–2000 m.u.	Cost of wages	–1000 m.u.
Valuation of stocks	0	Valuation of stocks	+5300 m.u.
Sales to B	+4000 m.u.	Sales to B	0
Tax base	+940 m.u.	Tax base	0

In this situation, the consolidated tax base will have a value of 940 m.u. If the intra-group transaction is made at the cost amount we have:

Company A		Company B	
Cost of electricity	−60 m.u.	Cost of electricity	−30 m.u.
Cost of raw materials	−1000 m.u.	Cost of raw materials	−(3060 + 500) m.u.
Cost of wages	−2000 m.u.	Cost of wages	−1000 m.u.
Valuation of stocks	0	Valuation of stocks	+4590 m.u.
Sales to B	+3060 m.u.	Sales to B	0
Tax base	0	Tax base	0

This time the consolidated tax base will be 0, and companies will be interested in making intra-group transactions at prices equal to costs in order to reduce income tax costs.

Example 3: Sale of assets

Company A sells an asset (market value of 5000 m.u.) to company B for a sales price of 5000 m.u. Assumption: pools are calculated entity by entity (necessary for the calculation of the asset factor for the sharing mechanism) and depreciation is at the rate of 20 per cent on a reducing balance basis.

Option (i): ignoring completely

Using this alternative, intra-group purchase and sales proceeds are ignored, but as noted above the assets cannot be completely ignored.

Company A		Company B		Group
Asset leaving	−4000 m.u.			−4000 m.u.
Sale of asset to B	+4000 m.u.	Acquisition of asset	**4000** m.u.	+4000 m.u.
		Depreciation	−800 m.u.	−800 m.u.
Tax base	−800 m.u.			

Option (ii): included in each group company and netted off when consolidated

Company A		**Company B**		**Group**
Asset leaving	−4000 m.u.			−4000 m.u.
Sale of asset to B	+5000 m.u.	Acquisition of asset	5000 m.u.	+5000 m.u.
		Depreciation	-1000 m.u.	−1000 m.u.
Elimination of the intra-group profit				−1000 m.u.
Adjustment to the depreciation: 800 – 1000 =				−200 m.u.
Tax base	−800 m.u.			

The size of the tax base remains unchanged, regardless of the value of assets involved in sales.

According to the proposal for the EU directive on the CCCTB, the European Commission opted for the method of ignoring profits and losses from intra-group transactions (arising from transactions directly carried out between members of a group). For the purpose of determining whether there is an intra-group transaction, both parties to the transaction must be group members at the time that the transaction is effected, and the associated revenues and expenses are recognized.

Artificial transactions carried out for the sole purpose of avoiding taxation shall be ignored for the purposes of calculating the tax base. Interest paid to an associated enterprise resident in a third country shall not be deductible where there is no agreement on the exchange of information comparable to the exchange of information on request provided for in Directive 2011/16/EU and where one of the following conditions is met: (a) a tax on profits is provided for, under the general regime in the third country, at a statutory corporate tax rate lower than 40 per cent of the average statutory corporate tax rate applicable in the member states; (b) the associated enterprise is subject to a special regime in that third country which allows for a substantially lower level of taxation than that of the general regime. Interest paid to an entity resident in a third country with which there is no agreement on the exchange of information comparable to the exchange of information on request provided for in Directive 2011/16/EU shall be deductible, in an amount not exceeding that which would be stipulated between independent enterprises, where one of the following conditions is met: (a) the amount of that interest is included in the tax base as income of the associated enterprise; (b) the interest is paid to a company whose principal class of shares is regularly traded on one or more recognized stock exchanges; (c) the interest is paid to an entity engaged, in its country of residence, in the active conduct of a trade or business. This shall be understood as an independent economic enterprise carried on for profit and in the context of which officers and employees carry out substantial managerial and operational activities.

The tax base shall include the non-distributed income of an entity resident in a third country where the following conditions[15] are met: (a) the taxpayer by itself, or together with its associated enterprises, holds a direct or indirect share of more than 50 per cent of the voting rights, or owns more than 50 per cent of the capital, or is entitled to receive more than 50 per cent of the profits of that entity; (b) under the general regime in the third country, profits are taxable at a statutory corporate tax rate lower than 40 per cent of the average statutory corporate tax rate applicable in the member states, or the entity is subject to a special regime that allows for a substantially lower level of taxation than that of the general regime; (c) more than 30 per cent of the income accruing to the entity falls within one or more of the categories;[16] (d) the company is not a company whose principal class of shares is regularly traded on one or more recognized stock exchanges.

Where an entity is treated as transparent in the member state of its location, a taxpayer holding an interest in the entity shall include its share in the income of the entity in its tax base. Transactions between a taxpayer and the entity shall be disregarded in proportion to the taxpayer's share of the entity. Accordingly, the income of the taxpayer derived from such transactions shall be considered to be a proportion of the amount which would be agreed between independent enterprises calculated on an arm's length basis which corresponds to the third party ownership of the entity.

The formula used to allocate the consolidated tax base between member states that are entitled to levy corporate income taxes generated the most discussion in the CCCTB WG, but also among specialists. Ana Agúndez-García believes that it is necessary for this formula to be transparent and simple, and not impose excessive compliance and administration costs, in order to reduce the possibility of creating tax-induced distortions to the allocation of investment by EU companies across the Single Market (Agúndez-García, 2006, pp. 32–38). Considering these principles, the CCCTB WG discussed several ways of allocating the consolidated tax base between those member states that are entitled to levy corporate income taxes, including a microeconomic approach (factors based on characteristics of companies and value added by companies) and a macroeconomic approach (GDP, VAT receipts and other macroeconomic variables).

Starting from the practical experience of countries that use such a formula (the USA and Canada), some authors (Hellerstein and McLure, 2004, p. 211) proposed the following formula based on the characteristics of the companies (the size of capital, labour, the volume of sales by destination):

$$TB_i = CTB[\alpha(\text{no. of employees}_i \times \text{payroll}_i/\text{no. of employees}_{group} \times \text{payroll}_{group}) + \beta(\text{assets}_i/\text{assets}_{group}) + \gamma(\text{sales}_i/\text{sales}_{group})]$$

where:

- TB_i is the apportioned share of a group member: company "i";
- CTB is the consolidated tax base of a group;
- α, β, γ is the weight given to each factor, so that $\alpha + \beta + \gamma = 1$.

An apportionment based on a formula containing company-specific factors allows the correlation between the real economic activity of a company and the apportioned share of the consolidated tax base to each individual entity. Correct determination of the consolidated tax base depends, however, on the manner of collecting information with respect to factors included in the distribution formula. Whatever the nature of the allocation factors used, the risk of the different ways that individual public authorities implement the CCCTB system cannot be entirely eliminated. Member states may try to attract unprofitable activities onto their territory, using the reduction of non-harmonized taxes to increase their share of the consolidated tax base. For example, reducing social security contributions may stimulate employment and increase the share of the labour factor in a particular tax jurisdiction.

According to Dragos Negrescu and Anton Comanescu, these deficiencies are added to the specific problems of each individual factor, described below (Negrescu and Comanescu, 2007, pp. 61–63).

"**Assets**" is a factor whose inclusion has a serious justification, because profits are, ultimately, the return on investment. Measuring this indicator can cause difficulties. Firstly, there are problems of evaluation, especially for intangible assets (such as intellectual property rights), for which there are no relevant market prices. Another problem is the high mobility of this factor that may make possible its movement to jurisdictions with lower tax rates. This problem is amplified in the case of leased intra-group assets, because access to better tax treatment without affecting the optimal location is possible by registering these assets in jurisdictions with lower tax rates and renting them to members of the group from other jurisdictions.

Implications of the "**labour**" factor (number of employees and/or payroll) are various. The number of employees may have a low relevance, because there is no systematic correlation between this and the value added. Also, the measurement of this factor would be problematic in the case of temporary employees. The payroll is a better correlation of the value added to the company, but it must be taken into account that in the new member states the wages are lower compared to those of Western EU countries.

Using sales measured "at origin" (taking into account the place from which the goods are shipped) or "at destination" (taking into account the place where the goods are ultimately delivered) generates a series of difficulties for the evaluation of the factor "**sales**". Choosing sales "at origin" will be an incentive to locate subsidiaries in jurisdictions with lower tax rates. Choosing sales "at destination" will stimulate consumption and imports, at the expense of exports. In terms of political feasibility, the choice of sales "at destination" would balance the sharing tax revenue between the net producing countries and the net consuming countries. In addition, sales "at destination" are less mobile and controllable by the taxpayers. Other problems could be generated by identifying the exact place of sale for certain services, intangible property and electronic commerce.

It is acknowledged that "**demand**" in the member state of consumption is already taxed in the EU via VAT. However, other factors (such as assets and payroll) are also subject to other taxes than corporate income tax in the member state of production. Moreover, the inclusion of a factor in the formula does not imply a new taxation of this factor, but the allocation of taxing rights among taxing jurisdictions on the basis of this factor. There was also a concern that compensating consuming states via corporate taxation would duplicate the effect of VAT in the EU. However, only a part of the tax base – which would depend on the weight of the sales factor in the formula – would be attributed to consuming states; manufacturing states would be remunerated via the labour and the asset factor as supply based factors (Directorate-General Taxation and Customs Union, 2007, p. 13).

Another way to build formula apportionment in the EU considers the value added to a company by its activities in a member state, according to the following formula:

$$TB_i = CTB\ (VA_i/VA_{group})$$

where VA is the value added.

Hellerstein and McLure (2004) identified two methods in order to determine the value added to a company:

Method of calculating the value added based on production allows the possibility of measuring the total economic value to a company, over a period of time, as follows:

$$\text{Value added} = \text{The total value of outputs (production)} \\ - \text{The total value of inputs (consumption)}$$

The total value of outputs (production) includes the sales and stocks of finished goods.

The total value of inputs (consumption) includes balance purchases and stocks of raw materials used in the production process.

Method of calculating the value added based on distribution measures the total remuneration of factors of production, as follows:

$$\text{Value added} = \text{Labour remuneration} + \text{Interest payments} \\ + \text{Profit before tax}$$

Apportionment based on a formula containing the value added to a company generates a more equitable situation for member states, compared with apportionment based on a formula containing company-specific factors. Thus, a company that has suffered tax losses may receive a share of the consolidated tax base, but because the situation of tax loss may not be accompanied by a large positive value added, the member state whose resident the company is will collect a lower corporate income tax. The value added approach has downsides, which imply that it most likely must be rejected as a viable alternative. Since value added is dependent on prices, an element of transfer pricing will resurface. Even though it is much more difficult to manipulate the value added measure than the profit figure, member states may not agree on the allocated value added and a new kind of transfer pricing issue may arise.

Formula apportionment in the EU may include macroeconomic factors, such as GDP, value added tax, etc. The allocation of the consolidated base among member states in relation to their GDP, national VAT base or some other macroeconomic variable would be very simple and prevent any manipulation by companies. The CCCTB WG does not regard this as either a realistic, or an appropriate allocation method. It means that taxes would have to be paid to member states participating in the CCCTB, even in cases where the group has no or very limited economic activity in the country (Directorate-General Taxation and Customs Union, 2007, p. 13).

Ana Agúndez-García (2006) evaluated the three approaches of EU formula apportionment according to the following tax policy objectives: equal earned income,[17] equal capacity to earn income,[18] the benefit principle,[19] neutrality,[20] enforceability/tax planning,[21] simplicity/cost effectiveness.[22] The approach based on macroeconomic factors registered maximum scores for neutrality, enforceability/tax planning and simplicity/cost effectiveness and minimum scores for equal earned income, equal capacity to earn income and the benefit principle. The value added approach registered average scores for five of the tax policy objectives. The approach based on company-specific factors registered maximum scores for the equal capacity to earn income and the benefit principle, and minimum scores for equal earned income and neutrality.

Because none of the three approaches of EU formula apportionment can fully achieve all the objectives of fiscal policy, it is important to clarify the priorities of member states with respect to a common tax system: which aspects are essential and which ones can be sacrificed.

In late 2007, the CCCTB WG published a paper presenting the European Commission's proposal on the mechanism for allocating the consolidated tax base to the various member states. The document mentions that the European Commission tried to create a sharing mechanism that was easy to apply and to check for taxpayers and tax administrations, and fair and equitable for all member states in order not to generate undesirable effects in terms of tax competition. To avoid the handling of the system by taxpayers, the CCCTB WG focused on the factors that cannot be transferred between different tax jurisdictions artificially (Directorate-General Taxation and Customs Union, 2007, p. 6).

The formula for the allocation of the consolidated tax base, as presented in the working document in 2007 is presented below:

$$\text{Taxbase} = \left(\frac{1}{m} \frac{\text{Sales}^{\text{A}}}{\text{Sales}^{\text{Group}}} + \frac{1}{n} \left(\frac{1}{2} \frac{\text{Payroll}^{\text{A}}}{\text{Payroll}^{\text{Group}}} + \frac{1}{2} \frac{\text{Number\_of\_employees}^{\text{A}}}{\text{Number\_of\_employees}^{\text{Group}}} \right) + \frac{1}{o} \frac{\text{Assets}^{\text{A}}}{\text{Assets}^{\text{Group}}} \right) * \text{CCCTB}$$

with $\frac{1}{m}+\frac{1}{n}+\frac{1}{o}=1$

where m, n and o are weights of the apportionment factors.

The European Commission services consider that an equal weighting of the three factors labour, assets and sales could be assumed.

The CCCTB WG chose both production factors (labour and assets) and factors of company performance (sales) for creating the EU apportionment formula.

Regarding the labour factor, the European Commission made the following specifications:

- The labour factor shall consist, as to one half, of the total amount of the payroll of a group member as its numerator and the total amount of the payroll of the group as its denominator, and as to the other half, of the number of employees of a group member as its numerator and the number of employees of the group as its denominator. Where an individual employee is included in the labour factor of a group member, the amount of payroll relating to that employee shall also be allocated to the labour factor of that group member. The number of employees shall be measured at the end of the tax year. The definition of an employee shall be determined by the national law of the member state where the employment is exercised.
- If a person is employed by a company that is resident in a member state, but effectively performs her/his services for another company possibly in another member state, it would be counted for the "payroll" allocation factor of the latter company.[23] Where employees provide their services for different entities during a tax year, their cost should be shared based on number of months.

Regarding the asset factor, the European Commission made the following specifications:

- For reasons of practicality and simplicity it is suggested that only fixed tangible assets (land and buildings, plant and machinery, other fixtures and fittings, tools and equipment) should be taken into account. This means that intangibles, financial and current assets (including inventory) would be excluded from the denominator and numerator of the formula. Although inventory (stocks) could represent a very important component of assets for certain sectors (e.g. trading companies), the European Commission services proposed the exclusion of inventory from the asset factor because inventory could be rather mobile and therefore their inclusion could be prone to manipulation (e.g. establishment of a warehouse in a low tax country in order to shift part of the tax base in this country via an increased asset factor).

- An asset shall be included in the asset factor of its economic owner. If the economic owner cannot be identified, the asset shall be included in the asset factor of the legal owner. If an asset is not effectively used by its economic owner, the asset shall be included in the factor of the group member that effectively uses the asset. However, this rule shall only apply to assets that represent more than 5 per cent of the value for tax purposes of all fixed tangible assets of the group member that effectively uses the asset. Except in the case of leases between group members, leased assets shall be included in the asset factor of the group member that is the lessor or the lessee of the asset. The same shall apply to rented assets.
- Land and other non-depreciable fixed tangible assets shall be valued at their original cost. An individually depreciable fixed tangible asset shall be valued at the average of its value for tax purposes at the beginning and at the end of a tax year. Where, as a result of one or more intra-group transactions, an individually depreciable fixed tangible asset is included in the asset factor of a group member for less than a tax year, the value to be taken into account shall be calculated with regard to the whole number of months. The pool of fixed assets shall be valued at the average of its value for tax purposes at the beginning and at the end of a tax year. Where the renter or lessee of an asset is not its economic owner, it shall value rented or leased assets at eight times the net annual rental or lease payment due, less any amounts receivable from sub-rentals or sub-leases. Where a group member rents out or leases an asset but is not its economic owner, it shall value the rented or leased assets at eight times the net annual rental or lease payment due. Where, following an intra-group transfer in the same or the previous tax year, a group member sells an asset outside the group, the asset shall be included in the asset factor of the transferring group member for the period between the intra-group transfer and the sale outside the group. This rule shall not apply where the group members concerned demonstrate that the intra-group transfer was made for genuine commercial reasons.

Regarding the sales factor, the European Commission made the following specifications:

- The sales factor shall consist of the total sales of a group member (including permanent establishments). Sales shall mean the proceeds of all sales of goods and supplies of services after discounts and returns, excluding value added tax, other taxes and duties. Exempt revenues, interest, dividends, royalties and proceeds from the disposal of fixed assets shall not be included in the sales factor, unless they are revenues earned in the ordinary course of trade or business. Intra-group sales of goods and supplies of services shall not be included.
- Sales of goods shall be included in the sales factor of the group member located in the member state where dispatch or transport of the goods to the person acquiring them ends. If this place is not identifiable, the sales of goods shall be attributed to the group member located in the member state of the last identifiable location of the goods. Supplies of services shall be included in the sales factor of the group member located in the member state where the services are physically carried out. Where exempt revenues, interest, dividends and royalties and the proceeds from the disposal of assets are included in the sales factor, they shall be attributed to the beneficiary. If there is no group member in the member state where goods are delivered or services are carried out, or if goods are delivered or services are carried out in a third country, the sales shall be included in the sales factor of all group members in proportion to their labour and asset factors. If there is more than one group member in the member state where goods are delivered or services are carried out, the sales shall be included in the sales factor of all group members located in that member state in proportion to their labour and asset factors.

Calculations for the allocation of the consolidated tax base will be made annually. A positive consolidated tax base (net profit) will be allocated immediately, and a negative consolidated tax base (net loss) will be offset by future profit of the group. Where a company leaves a group of companies that opted for the CCCTB, the tax base consolidation and distribution will be made for the fraction of the tax period in which the firm was a member of the group.

According to the proposal for the EU directive on the CCCTB, the European Commission opted for an equal weight to each factor of apportionment formula (1/3). It also states that the consolidated tax base is allocated only if it is positive. If a company enters a group or leaves it during a fiscal year, its share is calculated taking into account the proportion of the number of calendar months the company was part of the group during the fiscal year.

The asset factor of a financial institution[24] shall include 10 per cent of the value of financial assets, except for participating interests and its own shares. Financial assets shall be included in the asset factor of the group member in the books of which they were recorded when it became a member of the group. The sales factor of a financial institution shall include 10 per cent of its revenues in the form of interest, fees, commissions and revenues from securities, excluding value added tax, other taxes and duties. Financial services shall be deemed to be carried out, in the case of a secured loan, in the member state in which the security is situated or, if this member state cannot be identified, the member state in which the security is registered. Other financial services shall be deemed to be carried out in the member state of the borrower or of the person who pays fees, commissions or other revenues. If the borrower or the person who pays fees, commissions or other revenues cannot be identified, or if the member state in which the security is situated or registered cannot be identified, the sales shall be attributed to all group members in proportion to their labour and asset factors.

Sales of a group member conducting its principal business in the field of the exploration or production of oil or gas shall be attributed to the group member in the member state where the oil or gas is to be extracted or produced. If there is no group member in the member state of exploration or production of oil and gas, or the exploration or production takes place in a third country where the group member which carries on the exploration or production of oil and gas does not maintain a permanent establishment, the sales shall be attributed to that group member.

The revenues, expenses and other deductible items of a group member whose principal business is the operation of ships or aircraft in international traffic or the operation of boats engaged in inland waterways transport shall not be apportioned according to the apportionment formula but shall be attributed to that group member. Such a group member shall be excluded from the calculation of the apportionment formula.

5.4.6 Administrative framework

The administrative framework of the CCCTB should be designed to be as efficient as possible, both for taxpayers and tax authorities. For this purpose, the CCCTB WG proposed in 2006 the substantiating administrative framework of the CCCTB to adopt the approach of a "one stop shop" for tax declarations and assessment. So that, under the CCCTB, groups of companies would have to apply a single set of tax rules across the EU and deal with only one tax administration. Groups of companies should be able to deal with a single tax administration ("principal tax authority"), which should be that of the member state in which the parent company of the group (principal taxpayer) is resident for tax purposes. Groups of companies will apply a single set of tax rules across the EU and will deal with only one tax administration (one stop shop).

A company that opts for the CCCTB ceases to be subject to national corporate tax arrangements in respect of all matters regulated by the common rules. A single taxpayer shall opt for the CCCTB by giving notice to the competent authority of the member state in which it is resident or, in respect of a permanent establishment of a non-resident taxpayer, in which that establishment is situated. In the case of a group, the principal taxpayer shall give notice, on behalf of the group, to the principal tax authority. Such notice shall be given at least three months before the beginning of the tax year in which the taxpayer or the group wishes to begin applying the system. The notice to opt for the CCCTB shall cover all group members. However, shipping companies subject to a special taxation regime may be excluded from the group. The following information shall be included in the notice to opt for the CCCTB: (a) the identification of the taxpayer or of the members of the group; (b) the proof of compliance with conditions related to property and rights to profit; (c) identification of any associated enterprises; (d) the legal form, statutory seat and place of effective management of the taxpayers; (e) the tax year to be applied.

The principal tax authority shall transmit the notice to opt for the CCCTB immediately to the competent authorities of all member states in which group members are resident or established. Those authorities may submit to the principal tax authority, within one month of the transmission, their views and any relevant information on the validity and scope of the notice to opt for the CCCTB. When the notice to opt has been accepted, a single taxpayer or a group, as the case may be, shall apply the CCCTB system for five tax years. Following the expiry of that initial term, the single taxpayer or the group shall continue to apply the system for successive terms of three tax years unless it gives notice of termination. A notice of termination may be given by a taxpayer to its competent authority or, in the case of a group, by the principal taxpayer to the principal tax authority in the three months preceding the end of the initial term or of a subsequent term.

Where a taxpayer or a non-taxpayer joins a group, the term of the group shall not be affected. Where a group joins another group or two or more groups merge, the enlarged group shall continue to apply the system until the later of the expiry dates of the terms of the groups, unless exceptional circumstances make it more appropriate to apply a shorter period. Where a taxpayer leaves a group or a group terminates, the taxpayer or taxpayers shall continue to apply the system for the remainder of the current term of the group (European Commission, 2011a, pp. 38–40).

The quantification of the consolidated tax base will be done by the tax authorities on the basis of the tax return filed. In the case of a group, the principal taxpayer shall file the consolidated tax return of the group with the principal tax authority. The return shall be treated as an assessment of the tax liability of each group member. Where the law of a member state provides that a tax return has the legal status of a tax assessment and is to be treated as an instrument permitting the enforcement of tax debts, the consolidated tax return shall have the same effect in relation to a group member liable for tax in that member state. Where the consolidated tax return does not have the legal status of a tax assessment for the purposes of enforcing a tax debt, the competent authority of a member state may, in respect of a group member which is resident or situated there, issue an instrument of national law authorizing enforcement in the member state. That instrument shall incorporate the data in the consolidated tax return concerning the group member. Appeals shall be permitted against the instrument exclusively on grounds of form and not to the underlying assessment. The procedure shall be governed by the national law of the relevant member state. The tax return of a single taxpayer shall be filed within the period provided for in the law of the member state in which it is resident or in which it has a permanent establishment. The consolidated tax return shall be filed in the nine months that follow the end of the tax year. The tax return of a single taxpayer shall include the following information: (a) the identification of the taxpayer; (b) the tax year to which the tax return relates; (c) the calculation of the tax base; (d) identification of any associated enterprises. The consolidated tax return shall include the following information: (a) the identification of the principal taxpayer; (b) the identification of all group members; (c) identification of any associated enterprises; (d) the tax year to which the tax return relates; (e) the calculation of the tax base of each group member; (f) the calculation of the consolidated tax base; (g) the calculation of the apportioned share of each group member; (h) the calculation of the tax liability of each group member. The consolidated tax return and supporting documents filed by the principal taxpayer shall be stored on a central data base to which all the competent authorities shall have access. The central data base shall be regularly updated with all further information and documents and all decisions and notices issued by the principal tax authority.

Where the principal taxpayer fails to file a consolidated tax return, the principal tax authority shall issue an assessment within three months based on an estimate, taking into account such information as is available. The principal taxpayer may appeal against such an assessment.

After verification, the principal tax authority may issue an amended assessment not later than three years after the final date for filing the consolidated tax return or, where no return was filed, before that date. This will happen not later than three years following issuance of an assessment. An amended assessment may not be issued more than once in any period of 12 months. An amended assessment may be issued within six years of the final date for filing the consolidated tax return where it is justified by a deliberate or grossly negligent misstatement on the part of a taxpayer, or within 12 years of that date where the misstatement is the subject of criminal proceedings. Such an amended assessment shall be issued within 12 months of the discovery of the misstatement, unless a longer period is objectively justified by the need for further inquiries or investigations. Any such amended assessment shall relate solely to the subject matter of the misstatement. No amended assessment shall be issued in order to adjust the consolidated tax base where the difference between the declared base and the corrected base does not exceed the lower of €5000 or 1 per cent of the consolidated tax base. No amended assessment shall be issued in order to adjust the calculation of the apportioned shares where the total of the apportioned shares of the group members resident or established in a member state would be adjusted by less than 0.5 per cent.

On the request of the competent authority of the member state in which it is resident or in which its permanent establishment is situated, a taxpayer shall provide all information relevant to the determination of its tax liability. On the request of the principal tax authority, the principal taxpayer shall provide all information relevant to the determination of the consolidated tax base or of the tax liability of any group member. The principal tax authority may initiate and coordinate audits of group members. An audit may also be initiated on the request of a competent authority. The principal tax authority and the other competent authorities concerned shall jointly determine the scope and content of an audit and the group members to be audited. Where the competent authority of the member state in which a group member is resident or established disagrees with a decision of the principal tax authority, it may challenge that decision before the courts of the member state of the principal tax authority within a period of three months.

Appeals against amended assessments or assessments shall be heard by an administrative body that is competent to hear appeals at first instance according to the law of the member state of the principal tax authority. If, in that member state, there is no such competent administrative body, the principal taxpayer may directly lodge a judicial appeal (European Commission, 2011a, pp. 46–47). The administrative and judicial appeal is detailed in the draft directive on the CCCTB.

In order to solve any disputes between taxpayers and tax administrations, the CCCTB WG envisaged the creation of an arbitration panel, and in order to clarify technical issues related to the application of the CCCTB, the CCCTB WG envisaged the creation of an interpretation body, however, the proposal for a directive on the CCCTB does not make references to either of these bodies.

In order to properly conduct the administrative relations within the CCCTB system, EU member states should intensify the exchange of information in tax matters. Therefore, intense efforts by the European Commission in recent years to encourage the cooperation and collaborative actions between member states in tax matters can be interpreted as a preamble to the proposed directive for corporate income taxation.

5.5 Conclusion

The need for corporate income tax coordination within the EU is pressing, however, the implementation of one of the three systems proposed by the European Commission will not be easy. The EUCIT is a project without a realistic chance of implementation because many EU member states have expressed strong opposition to the compulsory introduction of harmonization rules in the field of direct taxation. The HST and CCCTB allow corporate groups to opt for a common system of taxation in the EU member states, but they would generate increased tax administrative costs. Of the three systems of corporate income tax coordination in the EU, the CCCTB has the most likely chance of application in the future. The proposal for a European Council directive on the CCCTB outlines the general legal and institutional framework for an optional common system for calculating the tax base within the EU. The system's internal mechanisms are not sufficiently detailed, such that the CCCTB seems like a complicated system and difficult to implement, after a first reading of the draft directive. The apportionment formula has certain limitations, recognized even by the draft directive (the European Commission has proposed special regimes for companies operating in the oil and gas industry, financial services, insurance undertakings and shipping). But the proposal for a European Council directive on the CCCTB represents a first attempt to make progress in an area as controversial as the convergence and harmonization of the corporate tax base in the EU.

6
Effects of Corporate Income Tax Harmonization/Coordination in the European Union

6.1 Introduction

In order to assess the effects of introducing corporate income tax harmonization/coordination within the European Union (EU), numerous studies and tests have been conducted by independent experts and specialized services of the European Commission or at its request. The attention of experts has mainly turned to estimates of the economic impact of corporate income tax harmonization/coordination (change in GDP, welfare and tax revenues), but other aspects have not been neglected, including tax compliance costs and location decisions for foreign direct investment (FDI). Since it seems unlikely that the member states will unanimously agree to corporate income tax harmonization/coordination within the EU, this chapter is intended to give readers a basic understanding of the adopting of harmonized corporate income tax regulations via enhanced cooperation.

6.2 Results of studies requested by the Directorate-General for Taxation and Customs Union

Corporate income tax harmonization is likely to have positive effects on some member states, but also negative effects on others. Variations in harmonization efficiency can be higher if the differences between the initial tax rates (or tax rules for determining the tax base) are higher. If these differences are significant, the process of tax harmonization will generate winners and losers.

In the early 2000s, the specialty literature asserted several models of corporate income tax harmonization, whose economic effects were only intuited (not scientifically validated or documented). At the request of the Directorate-General for Taxation and Customs Union, the study entitled "Economic effects of tax cooperation in an enlarged European Union. Simulations of corporate tax harmonisation and savings tax coordination"[1] was published in 2004. The overall objective of the study was to evaluate the economic effects of tax coordination within the EU, and the specific objective was to estimate the effects of corporate income tax harmonization. The authors analysed two tax harmonization scenarios in terms of their effects on the size of GDP, tax revenues and welfare for EU member states, as follows:

1. Full tax harmonization of corporate tax bases and tax rates, based on:
   - a weighted average corporate tax rates applied in the member states;
   - an unweighted average corporate tax rate.
2. Harmonization of corporate tax bases, based on:
   - current nominal corporate tax rates;
   - budget neutral tax revenues;
   - a minimum corporate tax rate.

The two scenarios have been tested in CETAX, a simulation model based on the OECDTAX model developed by Peter Birch Sørensen. The CETAX model is a computable general equilibrium model describing the international spillover effects of national tax policies via the world capital market. It features private portfolio composition, endogenous corporate financial policies, incorporation of a housing market, a distinction between foreign direct investment and foreign portfolio investment, explicit modelling of the financial sector and a detailed description of tax systems. The model can be used both to analyse the effects of unilateral changes in tax policies and of various forms of international tax cooperation (Jesper and Svensson, 2004, p. 62).

The full tax harmonization scenario was based on a corporate income tax rate of 27.2 per cent (unweighted average of current rates) and 32.6 per cent, respectively, representing the GDP-weighted average of current rates.[2]

The partial tax harmonization (only tax bases) scenario with a minimum tax rate focused on three sub-scenarios based on the following tax rates: 20, 25 and 30 per cent.

Testing the full tax harmonization scenario generated the following results:

- the gain in GDP was around 0.8 and 4 per cent, respectively;
- welfare for the EU-25 as a whole grew by 0.4 and 0.1 per cent, respectively;
- aggregate tax revenues for the EU-25 as a whole decreased by 0.6 per cent and remained at the same level, respectively.

In almost all the EU-25 countries, the increase in tax revenues generated a reduction of GDP, while the increase in GDP determined the reduction of tax revenues. Exceptions to this rule were found only in Latvia, Lithuania and Hungary, but in these countries the variations for full harmonization were almost negligible: the increase in GDP was 0.1–0.4 per cent, leaving tax revenues constant or an increase in tax revenues of 0.3–0.4 per cent.

Testing the partial tax harmonization scenario (the harmonization at unweighted averages and weighted averages) showed that GDP gains were more modest (between 0.2 and 0.35 per cent), welfare increased by about 1 and 1.5 per cent, respectively, and tax revenue decreased by about 0.2 and 0.3 per cent, respectively. These reductions are the result of the effect of narrowing the tax base in large countries; they cannot be compensated for by extending the tax base in small countries.

Using a minimum tax rate of 20, 25 and 30 per cent generated a decreasing gain in GDP and welfare and increasing tax revenues.

The largest gains in GDP were obtained for Luxembourg, Belgium, the Netherlands, the UK and the Czech Republic (more than 1.8 per cent), and the largest losses in GDP were obtained for Germany and Malta. Economically developed countries in Northern and Western Europe (except Germany and Austria) would have been more advantaged (in terms of GDP and welfare gains) by the harmonizing corporate income tax base. Also, most new member states would be faced with a reduction in tax revenues.

In summary, the conclusions resulting from the application of the two tax harmonization scenarios are as follows (Table 6.1):

Table 6.1 The effects of corporate income tax harmonization in the EU

	Full tax harmonization		**Harmonization of corporate tax bases**	
	Unweighted averages	**Weighted averages**	**Unweighted averages**	**Weighted averages**
Change in GDP (%)	0.79	0.38	0.17	0.34
Change in welfare (%)	0.21	0.07	0.04	0.06
Change in total tax revenues (%)	−0.56	0.01	−0.17	−0.29

Source: Results of the study "Economic effects of tax cooperation in an enlarged European Union. Simulations of corporate tax harmonisation and savings tax coordination" (Jesper and Svensson, 2004, pp. 18–25).

It can be acknowledged that full harmonization based on weighted averages would generate the greatest benefits for the EU as a whole. In political terms, such a solution was not feasible, because countries that had to reduce their tax rates to the level of the lower harmonized tax rate (weighted average of tax rates applied in the member states) could be forced to compensate tax revenue losses by raising taxes on labour. The impact of this measure could be an increase in unemployment. Conversely, the tax rates should be adjusted upwards in low tax member states. This measure was likely to generate capital outflows and significant changes in long-term economic growth.

Testing the partial tax harmonization scenario based on a neutral tax revenue budget included considering some adjustments in tax revenues in order to maintain an unchanged level of public expenditure. The authors also considered changing the tax rates for wages, indicating that further adjustments could be made by changing the tax rates for other types of income (interest, dividends, etc.) or for consumption. In this case, the effects on GDP and welfare were similar to those described in the situation in which the existing tax rates were maintained.

The most important conclusion of the study concerned the fact that, regardless of the scenario applied, some member states would suffer tax revenues losses, so that implementation of a compensation mechanism proved indispensable. The authors stated that, in order to develop measures of common fiscal policy in the field of corporate income taxation, future studies should consider the dynamic effects of several concrete proposals for tax harmonization.

A significant limit of the study was the fact that the impact of the "crowding" of investments in the developed countries of the EU was not analysed. The effects of crowding limited the international mobility of capital, which meant that the effectiveness of tax competition was, in turn, limited. Since the new member states did not recover the economic development gap, they cannot offer investors the same location advantages as the more developed countries of the EU, so that maintaining a lower level of taxation is justified. Thus, full harmonization increases the risk of capital outflows in new member states in response to the increase in taxes.

In fact, even the authors highlight a number of limitations of the study, as follows:

- Some country-specific policies may not be fully captured.
- The study cannot be regarded as an assessment of the gains of moving to an EU tax system for multi-jurisdictional corporate taxation based on consolidation of firms' EU-wide income.
- The study does not estimate the gains related to lower compliance and administrative costs that would result from the harmonization of corporate tax bases.
- The model does not capture the dynamics of fiscal interactions between member states, i.e. the reactions of member states to each other's fiscal policies.
- The model does not take into account some dynamic effects, e.g. a possible increase in the number of new start-up firms as a consequence of tax reforms.
- The use of a limited number of sub-scenarios. (Jesper and Svensson, 2004, p. 39)

These limitations of the study do not diminish the undeniable merit of trying to achieve, for the first time, a comprehensive analysis of the effects of harmonizing corporate income taxes in all EU member states.

The conclusions of the study convinced the European Commission that the general usefulness of full corporate income tax harmonization is reduced (in terms of GDP and welfare), such that the attention of this institution turned to the harmonization of the tax base as a solution for the problems generated by the existence of different taxation systems within the EU.

6.3 Evaluation of corporate income tax harmonization effects by independent researchers

In 2006, a new evaluation of the effects of corporate income tax harmonization was made in terms of using the same simulation model (CETAX). The CETAX model described a stationary equilibrium under the following conditions (Brøchner et al., 2006, p. 6):

- It includes 35 countries representing the EU and the Rest of the World.
- One country in the Rest of the World is a tax haven that facilitates tax evasion.
- Each country produces the same homogeneous good, which is traded in an integrated international goods market.
- Labour is immobile across countries, whereas capital is imperfectly mobile.
- The supply of capital to an individual country is thus an increasing function of the rate of return offered in that country.
- The model is specifically designed to allow for higher capital mobility within the EU than between the EU and the Rest of the World.

In terms of inputs that targeted the year 2004, Jens Brøchner, Jesper Jensen, Patrick Svensson and Peter Birch Sorensen tested three scenarios, as follows:

1. full tax harmonization of corporate tax bases and tax rates;
2. harmonization of corporate tax bases;
3. enhanced cooperation between a subset of the member states.

Full harmonization of corporate tax bases and tax rates, using a tax rate of 27.2 per cent (unweighted average corporate tax rate) led to gains in both GDP and welfare (around 0.8 and 0.2 per cent, respectively) and to a significant drop in tax revenues (around 0.2 per cent). The tax rate of 32.6 per cent (weighted average corporate tax rates applied in the member states) reduced to more than half the gains in both GDP and welfare (below 0.4 and 0.1 per cent, respectively). The aggregate tax revenue for the EU-25 countries was virtually constant. Luxembourg, Belgium, the Netherlands, the Czech Republic and France registered the largest gains in GDP (over 2.3 per cent), and Estonia, Germany and Slovenia the most significant losses in GDP (more than 1.5 percentage points). Potential welfare losses were recorded only in Ireland, Cyprus, Estonia, Hungary, Poland, Slovakia and Slovenia. Fourteen EU member states would have recorded tax revenue losses (between 0.2 and 1.3 percentage points).

Testing harmonization of corporate tax bases generated better results in terms of gains in GDP and welfare in the case of weighted average tax rates (around 0.35 and 0.05 per cent). In this case, tax revenue losses were 0.1 per cent. Similar results were obtained for the testing of enhanced cooperation (loss of tax revenue was, however, smaller).

Testing of the three scenarios allowed the authors to determine two major causal factors for most of the economic effects of corporate income tax harmonization. Firstly, full tax harmonization of corporate tax bases and tax rates generate a reduction of the disparities between the effective tax rates applied in the member states. The situation created by full tax harmonization will allow a more efficient allocation of capital within the EU, which can be regarded as value added in economic terms. This gain will always appear after full tax harmonization; it will certainly not materialize after partial harmonization, because the latter scenario will not generate a reduction of the disparities between effective tax rates applied in the member states. Secondly, in all cases where the public budget is balanced by adjusting public transfers, corporate income tax harmonization will generate an increase of the tax burden in some countries and its reduction in others. A higher tax burden leads to higher tax revenue collection, but it generates a loss in GDP due to distortions occurring in the business environment. In the reverse situation, a lower tax burden generates a decrease in the amount of tax revenues and a rise in GDP resulting from the stimulation of economic efficiency.

Analysis of gains and losses from corporate income tax harmonization in the EU shows that the aggregate effect of changes in taxation dominates the effect of efficient allocation of capital. Larger changes in the tax revenues frequently determine higher changes in GDP.

Because corporate income tax harmonization in the EU will generate antagonistic effects for different member states (the scale of changes in GDP, welfare and tax revenues is quite large), the authors opined that an EU-wide consensus for a major reform of the corporate income tax system (meaning the introduction of harmonized tax rules) would not arise. In contrast, enhanced coordination between a number of relatively homogeneous member states (in terms of per capita gross national product (GNP), tax rates and tax bases) was considered viable. Such an approach could lead to less radical policy changes, but small gains from corporate income tax harmonization (Brøchner et al., 2006, p. 26).

The conclusions of the study made by Jens Brøchner, Jesper Jensen, Patrick Svensson and Peter Birch Sørensen proved to be correct. During 2006–2008, many member states stated they were firmly against full and partial harmonization of corporate income taxes. Some of these states claimed the need to maintain national sovereignty in tax matters, and others claimed the losses in tax revenues was a reason.

In 2007, the effects of corporate income tax coordination in the EU were simulated by Albert van der Horst, Leon Bettendorf and Hugo Rojas-Romagosa using the CORTAX model[3] (it describes 17 European member states and the USA).

Testing several scenarios regarding corporate income tax coordination in the EU (Home State Taxation, European Union Company Income Tax, Compulsory consolidation) and using an apportionment formula based on three factors (capital, production and employment), the three authors reach the following conclusions:

- Benefits from the introduction of common rules for all EU member states in the field of corporate income tax will be higher if these rules are binding and the tax rates are harmonized.
- Welfare losses will have the highest values when the labour factor has the largest share in the distribution formula.
- Harmonizing the tax base and maintaining the sovereignty of member states in determining corporate income tax rates will lead to important effects of reallocation of capital within the EU.
- The welfare effects of consolidation will be unevenly distributed between member states, given the diversity in the current corporate income tax systems. (van der Horst et al., 2007, p. 31)

The calculations are based on a series of unrealistic assumptions, as follows: tax compliance costs are equal to 10 per cent of corporate income tax, transfer prices are completely eliminated and tax allowance rate is restricted between 5 and 15 per cent. Even if it has certain limitations, the study by Albert van der Horst, Leon Bettendorf and Hugo Rojas-Romagosa is an important step in the examination of the dynamic effects of corporate income tax coordination in the EU.

6.4 Economic effects of enhanced cooperation between a group of member states

Under conditions where some member states experience a disadvantaged position in terms of tax revenues or changes in GDP, it is unlikely that corporate income tax coordination in the EU will come about through unanimous agreement of all member states. A potential solution to achieving this important step in the process of tax harmonization in the EU is the enhanced cooperation procedure by which a subset of member states would be able to coordinate their corporate income tax systems.

Enhanced cooperation is a tool that allows for nine or more countries to make progress in relation to a political measure that is important for the whole EU, but is blocked by a small minority of member states. The possibility of concluding an enhanced cooperation agreement among a subset of member states was established in the Treaty of Amsterdam (1997) and the Treaty of Nice (ratified in 2003). The conditions under which member states may conclude an enhanced cooperation agreement were amended in the Lisbon Treaty (entered into force on 1 December 2009). Thus far, the following rules apply:

- Enhanced cooperation can be used only when other attempts to unify the positions of all member states have failed, therefore, it is a mechanism of last resort.
- At least nine member states (one-third of EU member states) must participate in the agreement.
- The agreement must be approved by the European Council by qualified majority on a proposal of the European Commission and after the European Parliament's approval.
- Any member state wishing to join enhanced cooperation already in progress may submit a request to the European Commission and the European Council. The European Commission shall decide in the first instance whether or not to authorize the member state joining the enhanced cooperation agreement. Where appropriate, the European Commission finds that the conditions of participation are fulfilled and adopts any transitional measures necessary for the application of the acts already adopted within the enhanced cooperation agreement. If it considers that the conditions of participation are not fulfilled, the European Commission indicates the arrangements for their achievement and sets a deadline to review the request. In the case of the European Commission issuing a refusal, the member state may appeal to the European Council to deliver a decision on its request.
- All members of the European Council may participate in its deliberations, but only members of the European Council representing the member states that participate in enhanced cooperation shall take part in the vote.

- Enhanced cooperation must contribute to furthering the process of integration within the EU and must not undermine the Single Market or the EU's economic and social cohesion. Furthermore, it must not create a barrier to or discrimination in trade between the member states and it must not distort competition between them. An enhanced cooperation agreement shall respect the competences, rights and obligations of those member states which do not participate in it.

In order to arrive at enhanced cooperation, the participating member states should reach an agreement on the following issues:

- the common policy which should be implemented (including benefits from enhanced cooperation);
- rules for sharing/division of the benefits from enhanced cooperation.

Making an enhanced cooperation agreement between a group of member states in order to introduce measures of corporate income tax coordination should be preceded by the steps listed above.

Results of the simulation achieved by Jens Brøchner, Jesper Jensen, Patrick Svensson and Peter Birch Sørensen in 2006 highlighted that benefits from tax harmonization would be lower in the case of enhanced cooperation between a group of the member states (Austria, Belgium, Finland, France, Germany, Greece, Ireland, Italy, Luxembourg, the Netherlands, Portugal and Spain), compared with a situation in which all EU member states would introduce a set of common corporate tax rules. Full harmonization of corporate tax bases and tax rates would not change the size of GDP, tax revenues or welfare for the member states that did not participate in enhanced cooperation. Instead, member states participating in the enhanced cooperation agreement would be put in the position of loser or winner, depending on the particularities of national systems of corporate income tax.

At a corporate income tax rate of 31.5 per cent, Austria, Germany, Ireland and Spain will record losses in GDP (between 0.1 and 2.6 percentage points), Germany and Ireland will record welfare losses of 0.1 and 0.3 per cent, Finland, France, Italy, Luxembourg, the Netherlands and Portugal will record losses in tax revenues (between 0.1 and 0.8 percentage points). The simulation was based on the reduction of the corporate income tax rate in Austria, Belgium, France, Germany, Greece, Italy, the Netherlands and Spain, and its increase in Finland, Ireland, Luxembourg and Portugal (Brøchner et al., 2006, pp. 18–33).

Depending on the degree of economic homogeneity of the member states participating in the enhanced cooperation agreement, the introduction of the CCCTB will generate different effects on welfare. These effects were analysed by Hendrik Vrijburg and Ruud A. de Mooij in 2010. The main conclusions reached by the two authors, based on simulations with three different-sized countries (considering that capital is a perfectly mobile factor at the international level), are as follows:

- Participating countries in an enhanced cooperation agreement may prefer enhanced cooperation over global harmonization when they are small relative to the other countries.
- Non-participating countries in an enhanced cooperation agreement may prefer the formation of enhanced cooperation by other countries over both full harmonization and decentralization.
- Small countries may gain from forming an enhanced cooperation agreement with other small countries, although this is not guaranteed.
- The formation of an enhanced cooperation agreement always leads to a higher tax in countries participating in enhanced cooperation.
- Tax rates in different countries can be strategic complements or strategic substitutes, depending on country size and substitution possibilities between public and private consumption (Vrijburg and de Mooij, 2010, pp. 31–32).

Customizing aspects of enhanced cooperation for the introduction of the CCCTB, Leon Bettendorf, Albert van der Horst, Ruud de Mooij and Hendrik Vrijburg tested (using the CORTAX model) the effects of enhanced cooperation agreement between some of the member states under two different conditions:

1. The enhanced cooperation agreement was concluded between states where the corporate sector was of minor importance (new member states).
2. The enhanced cooperation agreement was concluded between states where the corporate sector had great importance (member states in northwest Europe).

In the case of enhanced cooperation between new member states with low corporate sector significance, these member states will record significant increases in the level of welfare due to an improved business environment, however, most states with large corporate sectors will be affected by the reduction in the level of welfare under the impact of capital outflows. According to data for 2005, Bulgaria, Hungary and Portugal would register the largest gains in welfare.

In the case of enhanced cooperation between member states with large corporate sectors, the only countries affected by the reduction of welfare will be France and the Netherlands. The new member states will not record any losses or gains because the distribution of corporate income tax base is accomplished exclusively between countries participating in enhanced cooperation (Bettendorf et al., 2010, pp. 23–26).

The results of the study by Leon Bettendorf, Albert van der Horst, Ruud de Mooij and Hendrik Vrijburg suggest that the introduction of the CCCTB through an enhanced cooperation agreement between states with large corporate sectors is preferred in the context of the current political and economic conditions. The positive economic impact caused by an enhanced cooperation agreement could in reality be of a much greater magnitude, because the CORTAX model cannot quantify the effects of the reduction of tax compliance costs. In any event, however, some of the member states participating in an enhanced cooperation agreement will record losses for which compensation measures must be established.

6.5 Conclusion

All the research on the effects of corporate income tax harmonization/coordination within the EU shows that the benefits of harmonization will vary from state to state. If a limited number of member states introduce the CCCTB, some of the corporate groups within the EU will find themselves in the following situation: for some of their companies they will be able to apply a common set of rules for the calculation of the corporate tax base, and for others they will have to maintain the existing systems of documentation for financial and accounting reporting in member states not participating in the enhanced cooperation agreement. In this context, companies with cross-border activities would not receive all the benefits of introducing a common consolidated tax base. On the other hand, the effects of the adoption of strategic behaviour in the field of corporate income tax by member states not participating in enhanced cooperation agreements are uncertain. If these member states adopt measures to stimulate FDI, in order to counter the emergent pole of attraction for corporate groups, the benefits from introducing a common set of rules for the calculation of the corporate tax base will be much reduced, so this approach would be doomed to failure.

7
Impact Assessment of the Common Consolidated Corporate Tax Base

7.1 Introduction

This chapter presents several impact assessments of the Common Consolidated Corporate Tax Base (CCCTB). Several variants on the proposal were analysed: a mandatory CCCTB across all 27 European Union (EU) member states, an optional CCCTB for companies, and a mandatory CCCTB adopted by a subset of EU member states under the enhanced cooperation framework. Assessing the various options with respect to the practical impacts of introducing a CCCTB was aimed at the impact on the size of the tax bases, and on the distribution of corporate tax bases among the EU member states, the impact on tax compliance costs and the impact on some macroeconomic indicators.

7.2 Effects of corporate tax base consolidation and distribution

Assessing the economic effects of tax base consolidation and applying the EU apportionment formula is a difficult approach, because the centralized data about corporate groups in the EU are insufficient and the numbers of factors that can influence business activities are very large. An early study made to assess the impact of introducing rules for the consolidation and distribution of the corporate tax base in the EU was conducted by Clemens Fuest, Thomas Hemmelgarn and Fred Ramb (2006).

In the absence of a complete data base on companies in all the EU member states, the authors focused on parent companies in Germany (1844 companies) and their foreign subsidiaries (5827 companies) during 1996–2001. The analysis was based on the following assumptions:

a compulsory CCCTB, the absence of tax consolidation, the absence of common accounting rules, eliminating the payroll factor and using sales "at origin".

Particular conditions of analysis made by the three authors generate the following results:

- The consolidation and distribution of the corporate income tax base will generate tax revenue losses for small states that use tax incentives, since the tax bases attracted to these countries are large comparative with the real economic activity taking place within their territory (measured by assets, turnover and payroll).
- Offsetting losses against profits in cross-border business will generate a significant decrease in the total tax base. Reduction of the total tax base was estimated at 20 per cent. (Fuest et al., 2006, pp. 19–20)

Starting from the premise that companies with cross-border activities will not change their location options after the introduction of the CCCTB in the EU, Michael P. Devereux and Simon Loretz (2006) estimated the effects of the EU apportionment formula on corporate tax revenues in 22 member states. The authors did not make a full analysis (for all member states), as the available data base did not contain information on the number of employees and payroll for companies in certain states (essential elements in order to determine the tax base allocated to member states). The study was based on the financial statements of approximately 400,000 companies owning assets with a value of at least €2 million during 2000–2004.[1]

Michael P. Devereux and Simon Loretz considered the possibility that some of the companies included in the data base may refuse to participate in the CCCTB, given its optional nature. The results arrived at by the authors of the study are as follows:

- All the old EU countries (except Great Britain, Sweden and Ireland) would have recorded losses of corporate tax revenues. All the new EU countries (except Latvia) would have recorded gains in corporate tax revenues.
- The largest gain in corporate tax revenues would have been obtained by Estonia, and the largest loss of corporate tax revenues would have been obtained by Finland.
- The EU as a whole would have recorded a loss of corporate tax revenues of 2.4 per cent.

In 2008, Michael P. Devereux and Simon Loretz extended the analysis on the impact of the CCCTB in the EU, moving their attention to the effects on economic efficiency. In their research, the two authors started from the following assumptions:

- In the absence of capital export neutrality (effective tax rate on capital should be the same in the Single Market), taxation can generate losses in efficiency through misallocation of resources.
- Taxation in the EU should not favour one company over another (with which it is in competition).
- In order to ensure optimal conditions for increasing the efficiency of the Single Market, the offsetting of losses against profits in cross-border businesses can be binding or optional. (Devereux and Loretz, 2008, p. 1)

Observations made for 4567 corporate groups (323,442 companies) that carried out activities in the 27 member states during 2001–2005 allowed the measurement of changes in corporate tax revenues. The main results reached by the two authors are as follows:

- The effective average tax rate (EATR) registered significant differences among EU member states (from 40.1 per cent in Malta to 20.9 per cent in Belgium) during 2001–2005.
- The introduction of voluntary international loss consolidation under the existing tax system will considerably reduce the differences in EATR between member states (from 29.9 per cent in Malta to 18.3 per cent in Italy).
- More favourable results in terms of the reduction of the EATR were obtained in the case of an obligatory system of international consolidation and apportionment formula (from 28.6 per cent to 19.7 per cent in the EU as a whole). Also, the spread between countries in terms of EATR was reduced significantly (from 21.6 per cent in Cyprus to 18 per cent in Italy), thus creating the prerequisites to ensure the conditions for tax neutrality in the EU. (2008, pp. 14–29)

These results are clear evidence of the positive impact (in terms of economic efficiency) of the introduction of the CCCTB.

In 2010, Leon Bettendorf, Albert van der Horst, Ruud de Mooij and Hendrik Vrijburg conducted a further simulation based on the CORTAX model (regarding the effects of the introduction of the CCCTB on welfare in member states). This led to new results, caused by changes in national tax systems.

In a first step, the authors analysed the implications of the introduction of the CCCTB on welfare in member states, taking into account all the companies (domestic or foreign) operating in the EU. Results of this simulation show a modest gain in EU-wide welfare: 0.006 per cent of GDP. However, the absence of differences in the rules for the determination of the tax base generates an improvement in the allocative efficiency of capital in the EU. Under these conditions, the most important benefits of the introduction of the CCCTB could be obtained by Poland and Spain, and the most disadvantaged countries would be Belgium and Estonia. Most member states will have winning positions (14 of the 27 member states).

In a second step, the authors analysed the implications of corporate tax base consolidation and distribution in the EU. The consolidation of the common tax base using the apportionment formula will generate a reduction in corporate tax revenues of 0.1 per cent of GDP in the EU as a whole, due to offsetting losses against profits in cross-border activities. This reduction will have a greater significance for countries with high corporate income tax rates (for example, Malta) or for countries where the corporate sector has high importance (for example, Belgium). All member states will suffer losses in corporate tax revenues. In order to offset the losses in corporate tax revenues, public authorities will probably react by decreasing financial transfers to beneficiaries (individuals) of the public budget or by increasing personal income tax rates. Choosing one or the other of the two options will generate different effects in terms of welfare. In the first situation, there will be an increase in the average level of welfare in the EU by 0.1 per cent of GDP. All member states (except for France and the Netherlands) will record an increase in welfare (due to incentives to invest). The most advantaged countries will be Bulgaria and Portugal, with an increase in welfare of more than 0.3 per cent of GDP. In the second case, the average level of welfare will be lower: 0.01 and 0.03 per cent of GDP in the EU as a whole. A larger number of member states will be faced with a reduction in welfare (Bettendorf et al., 2010, pp. 17–25).

Like any general equilibrium model, CORTAX includes simplifying assumptions and specifications that are not undisputed, and it cannot take away the uncertainty about the strength of certain behavioural effects of tax policies. In addition, CORTAX does not capture the long-term dynamic gains from further integration in the Single Market, e.g.

in terms of an increase in the number of internationally active firms (European Commission, 2011b, p. 6).

Also, the results of simulations using the CORTAX model cannot be appreciated as precise estimates regarding the effects of the introduction of the CCCTB, since the reactions of representatives of companies and public authorities to the new fiscal environment can only be intuited. Maintaining national corporate income tax rates will stimulate the transfer of the corporate income tax base from high tax member states to more favourable tax jurisdictions. The EU apportionment formula cannot avoid this risk. Obviously, the reallocation of the tax base between the member states will be more difficult than at present (using transfer pricing and intra-company loans), but the CCCTB will certainly influence the size of tax revenues in the member states. Counter measures to reduce tax revenue losses, adopted by national authorities, are also unknown elements that prevent a clear knowledge of the economic situation of each member state after the introduction of the CCCTB.

Estimates of the effects of corporate tax base consolidation and distribution in the EU have some drawbacks, because they fail to take into account all the elements on which the CCCTB was founded. For this reason, the results obtained by different experts do not reflect an accurate picture of the impact of the introduction of the CCCTB.

7.3 Impact assessments published by the European Commission

One of the studies published at the request of the European Commission is entitled "Study on the impact of reforms of corporate income taxation systems at the EU level on the size of the tax bases of the EU companies, using the model 'European Tax Analyzer' ". The report assesses the impact of a Common Corporate Tax Base (CCTB) on the size of the corporate tax bases of EU companies, using the "European Tax Analyzer" model. The European Tax Analyzer is a computer-based model firm approach for the computation and comparison of international company tax burdens. The estimates on both the size of the corporate tax bases and the effective average tax burdens are derived by simulating the development of a corporation over a ten-year period. In a first stage, this report applies the proposed options for a CCTB for both an average EU-27 large corporation and an average EU-27 small and medium-sized corporation. In a second stage, the report examines how the results will be affected by alternative assumptions on the economic data of the model companies. Finally, in a third stage, the effects of major tax reforms in five member states (Germany, France, Italy, the Netherlands and Spain) during 2006 and 2008 were examined. Financial data were extracted from the AMADEUS data base. The size of the sample used was about 1,147,483 companies in 24 member states, 19,211 of which are large companies and 1,128,272 of which are small and medium enterprises (SMEs). The following elements of the tax base will be taken into account (Spengel et al., 2008, pp. 36–37):

- A depreciation rate for pooled assets of 20 per cent. Special rules applied to buildings (individual straight-line depreciation with a rate of 2.5 per cent) and intangible assets (individual straight-line depreciation with a general rate of 6.67 per cent if useful lifetime doesn't require a different rate).
- The weighted-average cost method (WAC) was chosen for valuation of inventories.
- All direct costs were treated as production costs.
- International Financial Reporting Standards' (IFRS) rules for the calculation of pension provisions were applied. Pension provisions were treated as deductible contributions when certain requirements are met.
- Losses were carried forward indefinitely without the possibility for losses carried back within a single company.

Exercising the option concerning the application of the CCCTB for only large companies will generate an increase of the future value of the tax base by 6.2 per cent in EU-27 countries. Bulgaria will record the largest increase in the tax base (13.1 per cent) and Cyprus will record the largest decrease in the tax base (6.7 per cent). The biggest change in the value of the tax base will be registered in the case of large transport companies (over 50 per cent). Increasing the value of the tax base will be lower if the option concerning the application of the CCCTB is exercised by SMEs (only 5.57 per cent). In this case, Hungary will record the highest increase in the tax base (15.4 per cent) and Cyprus will record the largest decrease in the tax base (6.9 per cent). The biggest change in the value of the tax base will be registered in the case of energy companies (over 30 per cent). In both cases, only two member states will face a decrease in the tax base (Bulgaria and Cyprus). These countries practise the lowest corporate income tax rates (10 and 12.5 per cent).

Countries affected most by the introduction of a CCTB were Bulgaria, Hungary, Latvia, Lithuania and Portugal. Sensitivity analyses reveal Greece, France and Slovakia as countries with a strong impact as well.

At the request of the European Commission – TAXUD, PricewaterhouseCoopers has made a study on the impact of income tax reforms at the EU level on European business taxpayers (published on 9 July 2008). The study had two objectives:

1. to assess the impact of alternative tax scenarios on the size of multinationals' taxable profits and on their effective tax rates;
2. to assess the impact of alternative tax scenarios on the size of multinationals' tax-related compliance costs.

Data have been collected from 21 multinational groups operating in the 27 EU countries during 2005–2006. The study covered two scenarios: (1) a Common Corporate Tax Base (CCTB), and (2) a Common Consolidated Corporate Tax Base (CCCTB).

The CCTB scenario (harmonized corporate tax base but with no cross-border tax consolidation) revealed an enhancement of the current average tax base of companies by 11 per cent and the aggregate tax base by 3 per cent. According to the first scenario, Luxembourg and Belgium will register the largest change in the average tax base (5 and 3 per cent), and Spain will record the biggest drop in the average tax base (3 per cent). Germany and Belgium will register the largest change in the aggregate tax base (4 and 3 per cent), and Sweden will record the biggest drop in the aggregate tax base (9 per cent). The CCCTB scenario revealed an enhancement of the current average tax base of companies by 5 per cent and the aggregate tax base by 2 per cent. According to the second scenario, Great Britain and Luxembourg will register the largest change in the average tax base (8 and 4 per cent), and France will record the biggest drop in the average tax base (5 per cent). Great Britain will register the largest change in the aggregate tax base (11 per cent), and France will record the biggest drop in the aggregate tax base (4 per cent). The average tax charge of the companies studied over the same period increased by 14 per cent. The aggregate tax charge increased by 4 per cent (PricewaterhouseCoopers, 2008, pp. 7–27).

The results for the CCCTB scenario showed an important difference between the predicted impact of time spent in the country where the principal taxpayer and the principal tax authority are located and in other countries. It is anticipated that the time in the principal taxpayer country will increase by 15 per cent and time spent in other countries will reduce by 23 per cent. Overall, a reduction by 8 per cent of time spent on tax compliance activities was anticipated (European Commission, 2011b, pp. 5–7).

The CORTAX model was used in a study conducted at the request of the European Commission by Leon Bettendorf, Albert van der Horst, Ruud de Mooij, Michael Devereux and Simon Loretz in 2009. In the first stage, three variants of the CCCTB were tested, as follows:

1. The first variant adopted all the proposals of the CCCTB WG.
2. The second variant changed the depreciation rates for buildings and equipment (from 25 per cent – as per the CCCTB WG proposal – to 20 per cent).
3. The third variant set the depreciation rates for fixed assets as the average of current rates existing in EU countries.

The authors used the Orbis data base edited by Bureau van Dijk Electronic Publishing.

The results show that the first variant will lead to a widening of the corporate tax base in the EU, the second variant implies a slight narrowing of the corporate tax base in the EU and the third variant will have a negligible effect on the size of the corporate tax base in the EU.

In the second stage, the authors simulated the effects of introducing the CCCTB by all companies (with local and cross-border activities), and only by companies with cross-border activities. Applying the CCCTB rules (as proposed by the CCCTB WG) will reduce the level of welfare in the EU by 0.2 per cent of GDP in the first case, and by 0.1 per cent of GDP in the second case. Therefore, with regard to the effects on welfare, introducing the CCCTB only in companies with cross-border activities should be the better solution. In this case, tax compliance costs should be reduced by 30 per cent (Bettendorf et al., 2009, pp. 32–59).

The study is limited in terms of the information volume, compared with other similar studies (based on the CORTAX model) because it does not provide information regarding the volume and distribution of the corporate tax base between EU member states, after the application of the CCCTB. The European Commission justified this situation when it stated that the objectives of its legislative initiative were not defined in terms of the distribution of income or revenue neutrality for member states (European Commission, 2011b, p. 4).

In 2010, another study was conducted by Ernst and Young, at the request of the European Commission. It concerned a comprehensive analysis of the effects of the introduction of the CCCTB. Thus, three scenarios were tested: (1) mandatory participation for eligible corporations in the 27 member states; (2) voluntary participation for eligible corporations in the 27 member states; (3) mandatory participation for eligible corporations in the nine member states planning to sign an enhanced cooperation agreement (Austria, Belgium, France, Germany, Hungary, Italy, Luxembourg, the Netherlands and Spain). For each scenario, a static analysis and a dynamic analysis were made regarding changes in the value of the corporate tax base, consolidation and distribution of the tax base. The reference year was 2005 and the number of member states analysed was 24 (Cline et al., 2010, p. 4).

Calculations regarding changes in the value of the corporate tax base revealed the following situation:

- Three EU member states (Belgium, France and Sweden) will register a significant increase in the corporate tax base (more than 5 per cent).
- Six EU member states (Austria, Latvia, Lithuania, Luxembourg, Romania and Slovakia) will record a modest increase in the corporate tax base (less than 5 per cent).
- Tax and accounting rules set by the CCCTB WG will not generate changes in the corporate tax base of greater than or less than 1 per cent for nine EU member states (Denmark, Estonia, Germany, Greece, Hungary, Italy, the Netherlands, Spain and the UK).
- Six EU member states (Bulgaria, the Czech Republic, Finland, Ireland, Poland and Portugal) will register a small decrease in the corporate tax base (less than 5 per cent).

The AMADEUS data base (over 6 million companies) was the main source of information for the static analysis. This analysis aimed to determine changes in the value of corporate tax revenues (collected from eligible corporate groups in the 27 member states – about 200,000 groups).

Mandatory participation of eligible corporate groups in the CCCTB system would have generated an average increase in corporate tax revenues of 0.2 per cent for the EU as a whole. Denmark and the Netherlands would have recorded the most significant reductions in corporate tax revenues (8.3 and 7.6 per cent), and France and Greece would have recorded the largest increase in corporate tax revenues (6 and 4 per cent).

Voluntary participation of eligible corporate groups in the CCCTB system would have caused an average reduction in corporate tax revenues of 0.6 per cent for the EU as a whole. In this case, the number of member states that will register losses in corporate tax revenues is lower (compulsory CCCTB would cause losses in corporate tax revenues for 12 member states and the optional CCCTB would cause losses in corporate tax revenues for 14 member states). The largest losses in corporate tax revenues would have been recorded in Germany (7.7 per cent), and the highest gains in corporate tax revenues would have been recorded in the UK (2.2 per cent).

Mandatory participation in the case of an enhanced cooperation agreement would have caused an average increase in corporate tax revenues of 0.1 per cent in the participating countries. The largest losses in corporate tax revenues would have been registered in the Netherlands (8.5 per cent), and the largest gains in corporate tax revenues would have been registered in France (5.7 per cent).

The dynamic analysis of the effects of the introduction of the CCCTB started from the assumption that changes between effective tax rates in the member states and the cost of capital for new investment were governed by a certain correlation. Thus, if the effective tax rate increases after the application of the CCCTB, the cost of capital should follow the same trend, leading to the decline of the investment and therefore a reduction in employment and GDP. If the effective tax rate decreases after the application of the CCCTB, this situation would generate increased investment and would have a positive economic impact.

In this context, determinations made by the representatives of Ernst and Young reveal a number of changes in GDP, in employment and in the volume of FDI.[2]

The introduction of a mandatory CCCTB in all member states would lead to a decline in GDP by 0.2 per cent, employment by 0.3 per cent and in the volume of FDI by 1.1 per cent, in the EU as a whole. Bulgaria, Romania, Latvia and Luxembourg would record the most significant losses in GDP (over 2 percentage points) and employment (about 1 percentage point). The decrease in the effective tax rate will generate a growth in the volume of FDI (over 11 per cent) for Bulgaria and Romania, so that the negative effects could be mitigated in the medium term. Belgium and France would have a net gain status after the introduction of the CCCTB.

If the reductions in corporate tax revenues from the introduction of the CCCTB require adjustment measures in personal income tax rates, economic indicators will register new changes. The inclusion of the effect of these adjustment measures in the analysis model would result in changes to the values of analysed indicators by 0.1–0.3 percentage points.

The introduction of voluntary CCCTB in all member states would lead to a decline in GDP by 0.1 per cent, employment by 0.1 per cent and volume of FDI by 0.5 per cent, in the EU as a whole. France and Spain would be the only states in a position of economic advantage. In terms of losses in GDP, the most disadvantaged countries would be Luxembourg and Latvia, and in terms of losses in FDI, the most disadvantaged countries would be Romania and Austria.

The introduction of mandatory CCCTB in a group of member states (the enhanced cooperation agreement) would generate more pronounced negative economic effects compared with those suggested by the previous scenarios. The whole group of the member states would record losses in GDP (0.3 per cent), employment (0.2 per cent) and volume of FDI (2.2 per cent). The only advantaged states would be France and Spain (Cline et al., 2010, pp. 65–77).

Therefore, a voluntary CCCTB in all member states would be the most advantageous scenario.

The study on the economic and budgetary impact of the introduction of a CCCTB in the EU has many limitations, some of them even recognized by the authors:

- The analysis was focused on a very short period of time (2005), so the results of the study are strongly influenced by particular economic and political conditions.
- The analysis did not include all EU member states (lack of information about Cyprus, Malta and Slovenia).
- The information regarding payroll was estimated by the authors, because the companies' financial statements do not always include this information. Thus, the tax base distributed to member states based on a three-factor apportionment formula may have other values than those revealed in the study.
- The authors formulated, in the case of the dynamic analysis, the hypothesis that the decrease in the corporate tax revenues would generate adjustments in personal income tax rates. Public authorities may choose other solutions, however: adjusting public expenditure, introducing new taxes to compensate losses in tax revenue, etc.

Differences between the estimates regarding the effects of the introduction of the CCCTB can be observed. Therefore, the real impact of the European Commission's proposal for a CCCTB is very difficult to quantify. The number of participating member states and corporate groups that opt for the CCCTB has a very important influence on the determinations made by various experts. In any event, the application of the CCCTB will generate winners and losers among the member states. According to the European Commission, no conclusions should be drawn about the final impact on overall tax revenues, as these will depend on member states' own policy choices with regard to possible adaptations of the mix of different tax instruments or applied tax rates. The introduction of the common tax base provisions unrelated to consolidation (CCTB) could lead to broader tax bases than the current ones for most EU-based companies. However, the magnitude of this increase seems to depend essentially on the depreciation rules applied. The common tax base would also reduce the substantial variation in tax bases across European countries that currently exist, partly due to differences in fiscal depreciation schemes and inventory valuations (European Commission, 2011b, pp. 5–7).

In this context, the proposal for a directive on the introduction of the CCCTB provides, as an exception to the apportionment rules, that in the case of obtaining an unfair result in terms of corporate tax receipts, a safeguard clause that allows the use of other apportionment methods will apply. In addition, the directive will contain a clause to assess the impact after five years of its entry into force (European Commission, 2011a, p. 64).

7.4 The impact of distribution factors on revenue from corporate income tax in economically less developed member states

The determination of the sales factor depending on the dispatch/destination of goods, i.e. the place where services are effectively provided, is a mechanism by which less developed member states will be disadvantaged in the process of allocating the consolidated tax base. According to information provided by Eurostat in 2009, the purchasing power in the new member states is lower than the European average (Figure 7.1).

Therefore, if the sales "according to the destination" factor is used, we can see that a part of the tax base created within a narrow outlet state will migrate to a state with a large outlet.

In principle, countries where the purchasing power is low (Bulgaria, Romania, Latvia, Lithuania, Poland, Estonia) will record reductions in corporate income tax revenues, because the domestic markets of these countries will not absorb the entire quantity of goods and services produced by controlled foreign subsidiaries, so that some of the profits of these subsidiaries will be taxed in other countries. On the other hand, statistics on intra-EU trade show that most new EU

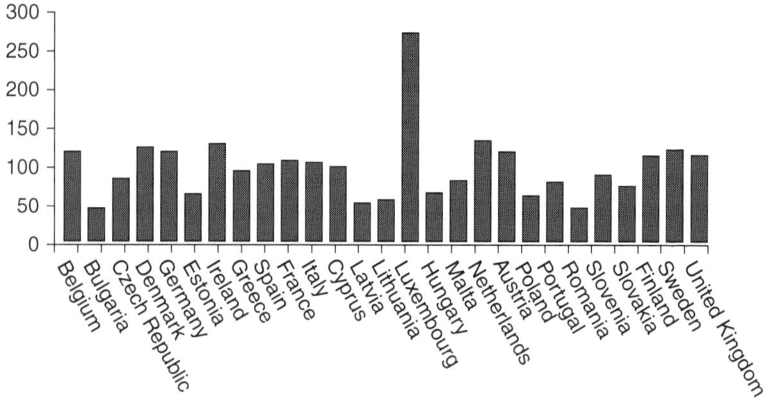

Figure 7.1 GDP per capita in purchasing power standards in 2009 (EU-27 = 100)
Source: Eurostat, GDP per inhabitant in purchasing power standards, date accessed 30 September 2011.

member states appear as net importers in relation to other member states. For example, in Romania, Bulgaria and Latvia, arrivals were 30 per cent higher than dispatches in 2009. Machinery and transport equipment and other manufactured goods were between 50 and 70 per cent of arrivals in the new EU member states. Because most of the industrial goods that are subject to foreign trade are manufactured by companies organized in groups, the above statistics show us that despite the low purchasing power, less developed EU countries (with an intra-trade balance deficit) would benefit from the transfer of a part of the tax base created by groups of companies in other member states. The volume index of GDP per capita in Purchasing Power Standards (PPS) is expressed in relation to the European Union (EU-27) average set to equal 100. If the index of a country is higher than 100, this country's level of GDP per head is higher than the EU average and vice versa. Basic figures are expressed in PPS, i.e. a common currency that eliminates the differences in price levels between countries allowing meaningful volume comparisons of GDP between countries.

Due to differences in annual earnings between EU member states (Figure 7.2), the payroll factor may disadvantage less developed EU states.

Annual earnings of employees in Romania and Bulgaria were eight times lower than the European average in 2006. In other new EU member states (Latvia, Lithuania, Estonia, Slovakia) annual earnings

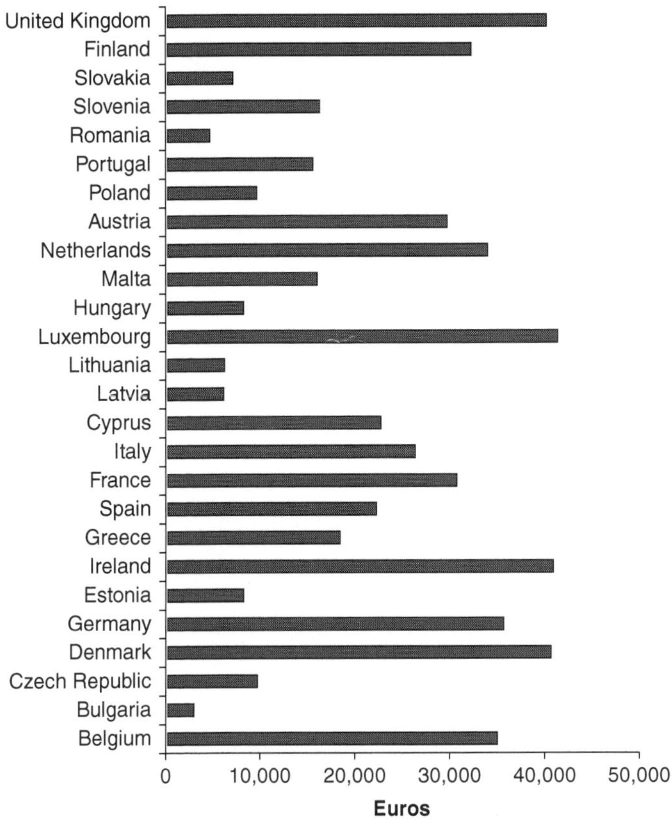

Figure 7.2 Annual earnings in 2006 (EU-27 = €27,768)
Source: Eurostat Pocketbooks (2009–2010), Labour market statistics, date accessed 30 September 2011.

were about four times lower than the European average. Therefore, the payroll factor is a potential risk factor in moving the tax base from less developed EU countries to more developed EU countries.

To prove this assumption, a research case study applied to some controlled subsidiaries in Romania was conducted (Pirvu, Banica, Hagiu, 2011). Because wage levels in Romania are about six times lower than those registered in the EU, Romania and other less developed countries of the EU will be disadvantaged in the process of allocating the consolidated tax base. Results of the simulation show that the EU apportionment formula would generate a decrease in the Romanian corporate tax revenues. The elimination of the payroll from this formula generates a mean change in corporate income tax revenues (thereby increasing them).

7.5 Conclusion

Impact assessments identify the CCCTB's winners and losers. The consolidation and distribution of the tax base will determine losses in tax revenue in the EU due to offsetting losses against profits in cross-border activities. The magnitude of these losses could be lower than those estimated in studies (or gains in tax revenue could be recorded) if the current tax deductions and exemptions for companies in the member states are removed. The CCCTB apportionment formula could affect small open economies. To ensure broad support for the project, the European Commission should provide some compensation for losses in GDP, FDI or tax revenues suffered by some member states. Such a compensation mechanism would be very complex and would limit the efficiency of the CCCTB system, so it seems unlikely that this proposal will be taken into account.

8

Supporters and Opponents of Corporate Income Tax Coordination in the European Union

8.1 Introduction

Corporate income tax coordination has not only many supporters, but also opponents among experts, politicians and business representatives. Controversies surrounding corporate income tax coordination are generated by uncertainty about its effects. The publication of the proposal for a CCCTB on 16 March 2011 intensified the debate on the need and appropriateness of introducing common rules on taxation in the European Union (EU). It was also an opportunity to clarify the positions of individual member states regarding the trend towards harmonization of corporate income taxes within the EU. The presentation of some reasoned opinions by some member states' national parliaments on the proposal for a European Council directive on a CCCTB highlights the fears, misunderstandings and hopes of representatives from nine member states.

8.2 Political reactions regarding the trend towards corporate income tax harmonization

Many obstacles exist in the way of the process of tax harmonization in the EU. The problems that occurred during the efforts to ratify the Lisbon Treaty show that many European citizens do not like the idea of transforming the EU into a superstate and granting greater powers to the European institutions. Because tax diversity is considered to be a form of independence and sovereignty of the state, the reluctance of some politicians with respect to the proposal to introduce common tax rules within the EU is normal.

Approaching the issue of tax harmonization in terms of political considerations, we wondered why some European politicians support this process and ignore voters' preferences, agreeing to give up control of one of the most important levers of economic policy: taxation. We found an answer in the study by Masimiliano Trovato, who argues that if capital and labour move easily between countries, and developments in technology allow people to communicate easily among themselves and to establish fruitful business relationships, regardless of where they are located, tax bases tend to become increasingly mobile. Public authorities can do little or nothing to prevent this trend. The role of politics in the fiscal area will diminish, perhaps with increased globalization. Thus, at the cost of a short-term loss of their fiscal powers, politicians try to counteract the effects of globalization by reapplying their tax powers on a much larger scale (Trovato, 2007, p. 2).

The issue of corporate tax harmonization raised many political controversies in EU member states, generated by the doctrinal orientation of the empowered political parties. Thus, in England and Ireland economic policy is focused on the role of the free market in the allocation of resources, promoting a principle according to which state intervention through taxes should be minimal. The Continental European countries promote the importance of maintaining the state as a "dynamic player agent", regulating some economic and social mechanisms if taxation generates minimum distortions in the working of the market economy. The Scandinavian countries promote the idea of universal social assistance and the important role of state involvement through tax levels to ensure proper social development. The simple presentation of the main characteristics of the economic and social models in the EU countries is sufficient to guess the position of their political leaders in relation to the idea of corporate tax harmonization. Thus, countries with a predominantly neo-liberal political ideology (the UK and Ireland) will not approve the idea of eliminating tax competition between governments, because it is the engine of efficiency and economic progress, whereas countries with a predominantly socialist political ideology should be interested in an increase of corporate tax discipline and in the removal of uncertainty related to the decrease of government tax revenues as a result of foreign investment migration to advantageous locations in terms of tax. Conversely, the positions of politicians regarding tax harmonization depend on the real interests of their constituents, which are in direct relationship with changes in the economic and social environment (and not with political ideology), and the constraints they are subject to. Thus, political leaders in the new member states (that impose smaller income tax rates for companies), regardless of their doctrinal orientation, should have a hostile position towards corporate tax harmonization, because their economies will lose a substantial advantage in the attraction of foreign direct investment (FDI) (Matei and Pirvu, 2010b, p. 29).

After the publication of the first report of the Primarolo Group, in which a number of "harmful tax measures" in the member states have been identified, many political leaders expressed their concern that tax competition in the EU will reduce the amount of public goods and services.

This idea is founded on socialist doctrine principles, represented by the governments of many European countries in the late 1990s and early 2000s. The German and French ministers, Oskar Lafontaine and Dominique Strauss-Kahn, indicated in 1998 that their main concerns were Luxembourg's lack of withholding tax on savings, which attracted hundreds of billions of Deutschmarks' worth of German savings, and the low tax rates on foreign companies offered by such countries as Ireland (*New York Times,* 10 December 1998). Oskar Lafontaine caused many debates in the European media when he spoke out in favour of tax harmonization across Europe. In 1999, Oskar Lafontaine identified tax harmonization as one of the key issues of Germany's presidency of the EU (*The Guardian,* 3 February 1999). In 2002, the French Prime Minister Lionel Jospin proposed, in terms of corporate tax, a harmonized tax base and a fixed minimum rate (*Je m'engage,* Jospin's election manifesto, 22 March 2002). In 2004, the German Chancellor Gerhard Schröder and French President Jacques Chirac announced their plans to promote corporate income tax harmonization by setting a minimum tax rate applicable across the EU. This measure should have prevented the so-called "fiscal dumping" carried out by the new member states. The leaders of the two countries considered that it was unacceptable for the new member states to use EU funds to finance their low taxes (*European Voice,* 27 June 2004). The Franco-German proposal was supported by the Finance Minister, Gerrit Zalm. He stated that the new member states benefited from an unfair competitive advantage over the old member states, through lower corporate income taxes (*Law and Tax News,* 7 June 2004). Therefore, the accession of new countries to the EU intensified political disputes on corporate income tax harmonization.

A study on the attitude of Members of the European Parliament (MEPs) about the introduction of a minimum corporate income tax rate across the member states, after questioning 156 MEPs from March to July 2007, revealed the situation shown in Table 8.1 (European

Table 8.1 Results of the MEPs' questionnaire regarding the introduction of the minimum rate of corporate income taxation in the EU, according to the doctrine of the political group to which respondents were affiliated

Classification according to political group	Political doctrine	Share of respondents in the parliamentary group (%)	Average score
Alliance of Liberals and Democrats for Europe (ALDE)	Liberal	17.31	−0.11
European People's Party (EPP-ED)	Conservative, Christian democrat	19.78	−0.72
European United Left/Nordic Green Left (GUE-NGL)	Socialist, communist	1.2	1.4
Independence and Democracy Group (IND/DEM)	Eurosceptic	29.17	−3.71
Identity Tradition and Sovereignty Group (IST), dissolved in November 2007	Nationalist	17.39	1
Non-attached members (NI)	–	23.08	−4
Party of European Socialists (PES)	Social democrat	23.15	2.02
Greens – European Free Alliance (Greens-EFA)	Green, regionalist	14.29	3.17
Union for Europe of the Nations (UEN)	National conservative	22.73	−1.8

Source: Osterloh and Heinemann (2009), p. 16.

Parliament Members' responses were recorded on a scale from −4, representing total disagreement with the introduction of the minimum rate, to +4, representing total agreement with the introduction of the minimum rate).

It can be observed that parliamentary representatives of a socialist orientation take a more favourable stance regarding corporate tax harmonization (including via tax rates) compared with parliamentary representatives of a liberal orientation. In terms of the respondents' origins, the survey results in the European Parliament showed that representatives from Poland, the Czech Republic and Great Britain mainly opposed the corporate tax harmonization idea, and representatives from Portugal, Austria and Belgium were the most vehement supporters of the idea. The grouping of the respondents according to time of accession to the EU of the represented countries generated the following result: almost all the parliamentarians from the new member states opposed the idea of minimum corporate income tax rate introduction, a position also inferred above (Osterloh and Heinemann, 2009, pp. 31–32).

During 2004–2010, the political leaders of some member states (Ireland, the UK, Poland, Latvia and Slovakia) came out against the CCCTB project. None of the member states declined to participate in debates of the CCCTB Working Group (WG).

8.3 Opinions from the European business environment regarding the trend towards corporate income tax harmonization

In their turn, business representatives were actively involved in the discussion of technical issues related to the CCCTB. Many professional organizations and organizations representing business were represented at the meetings of the CCCTB WG. Among them were the following: European Association of Tax Law Professors (EATLP), Union des Industries de la Communauté Européenne (UNICE), Fédération des Experts Comptables Européens (FEE), Confédération Fiscale Européenne (CFE), Association of European Chambers of Commerce (EUROCHAMBRES), European Banking Federation (EBF), The European Round Table of Industrialists (ERT), Centre for European Policy Studies (CEPS), American Chamber of Commerce (AMCHAM), European Association of Craft and Small and Medium-sized Enterprises (UEAPME), Comité Européen des Assurances (CEA), European Business Initiative on Taxation (EBIT), European Association of Co-operative Banks (EACB), European Fund and Asset Management Association (EFAMA), European Federation for Retirement Provisions (EFRP) and European Savings Banks Group (ESBG).

According to EUROCHAMBRES, different tax systems – and thus tax divergences – represent real obstacles for companies which operate across Europe, hampering the functioning of the Single Market and undermining the competitiveness of European businesses. The need to comply with a multiplicity of different rules results in unacceptable costs and represents an obstacle to cross-border economic activity.

It also impacts heavily on investors' choices and business locations. In this respect, EUROCHAMBRES supports the European Commission's suggestions for the creation of a CCCTB, which could be instrumental in achieving a better functioning Single Market, addressing the tax obstacles that exist for corporate taxpayers operating in more than one member state. EUROCHAMBRES believes that the CCCTB should be consolidated and be as large as possible, eliminating the co-existence of 27 different tax bases as well as the costs and uncertainties of complying with transfer pricing rules. Because the CCCTB would allow for automatic cross-border consolidation of profits and losses, unrealized profits should not be taxed. EUROCHAMBRES (2007) considered that introducing the CCCTB should be expedited, since tax stability and the reduction of compliance costs were important incentives for investors.

The Union des Industries de la Communauté Européenne (currently, BUSINESS EUROPE[1]) welcomes the efforts of the European Commission to address cross-border obstacles in the corporate tax field with its proposal for a CCCTB. To attract the interest and support of the business community, the CCCTB needs to meet at least the following key conditions: (a) to be optional for companies, i.e. not replace national corporate tax systems; (b) to allow for the consolidation of profits and losses from the start; (c) to reduce compliance costs with a "one stop shop"; (d) to leave any decision on tax rates to national governments (BUSINESS EUROPE, 2011).

According to the UEAPME,[2] a common tax base on company profits would provide SMEs with the right incentives to go international and make the most of the Single Market. A common tax base could dramatically reduce compliance costs for small companies operating cross-border in the EU. The UEAPME considers that the proposal for a CCCTB is too complex and not in line with the needs of SMEs. For this reason, the UEAPME requested the European Commission to provide a small business-friendly version of the CCCTB. The organization also raised doubts on the CCCTB being optional. This would add a 28th tax system to the 27 existing ones, complicate the status quo, oblige member states to run two systems at the same time and create an extra opportunity for "tax engineering" (UEAPME, 2008 and 2011).

The Association of Chartered Certified Accountants (ACCA)[3] (2010) shares the European Commission's view that simplifying procedures, improving efficiency and reducing compliance costs in taxation matters are integral to strengthening the Single Market. A clear, simple and user-friendly CCCTB would help enhance the competitiveness of European businesses and attract investment, as underscored in the new Europe 2020 Strategy. While focusing on large companies, it would also potentially help SMEs operating across borders (ACCA, 2010).

8.4 Political views on the CCCTB draft directive

On 16 March 2011 (with the publication of the proposed directive on the CCCTB), a procedural process started, a process that included a technical and political debate between member states and the European Commission. Under the Treaty of Lisbon, the member states' national parliaments had the opportunity to express reasoned opinions regarding compliance of the future legislation with the principle of subsidiarity,[4] within a period of eight weeks.

Some member states have submitted reasoned opinions to EU officials expressing concerns over the subsidiarity aspect of the proposal. In addition, some of the representatives from these countries had considerations regarding the principle of proportionality. The following guidelines should be used to examine whether the above-mentioned condition is fulfilled:

- The issue under consideration has transnational aspects which cannot be satisfactorily regulated by actions of member states.
- Actions by member states alone or lack of European Community action would conflict with the requirements of the Lisbon Treaty (such as the need to correct distortion of competition, or avoid disguised restrictions on trade, or strengthen economic and social cohesion) or would otherwise significantly damage member states' interests.
- Action at European Community level would produce clear benefits by reason of its scale or effects compared with action at the level of the member states.

Further to this, some excerpts from negative reasoned opinions submitted by some member states' national parliaments are presented below.

8.4.1 Reasoned opinion by the House of Representatives of the Kingdom of the Netherlands on the proposal for a European Council directive on a CCCTB

The introduction of the proposed CCCTB directive would not be advantageous to all parties concerned, so that it is necessary to make an assessment, comparing the advantages for some with the disadvantages for others. In making that assessment, the House of Representatives observes that the positive gain in prosperity for the EU as a whole is very limited. The House of Representatives notes that the introduction of the proposed CCCTB directive would even have a negative effect on the GDP of the EU as a whole. For a number of member states, including the Netherlands, the introduction of the proposed CCCTB directive would reduce the general level of prosperity.

The House of Representatives considers that the EU action goes beyond what is necessary in order to achieve the objectives of the Treaty and therefore takes the view that the proposal is not proportionate. The main reason for this is that the proposal would result in two different systems of corporate taxation. For the member states this would mean an increase in implementation costs, because both systems would have to be operated. The financial and administrative burdens involved would only be proportionate if they were offset by substantial advantages. The proposed formula for apportioning the total (cross-border) consolidated profits would place at a disadvantage member states with large services sectors, because such factors as non-material and financial assets are not included in the apportionment model. The Netherlands is among the countries which would be disproportionately disadvantaged by this.

The above observations concern the view adopted by the parliamentary parties which jointly hold an ample majority in the House of Representatives. Certain other parties consider that the introduction of the proposed CCCTB directive might possibly have positive effects.

The House of Representatives considers this proposal undesirable in that it would bring about a shift in the field of direct taxation from national to European level (European Parliament, 2011a).

8.4.2 Reasoned opinion by the House of Commons of the United Kingdom of Great Britain and Northern Ireland on the proposal for a European Council directive on a CCCTB

The future European Commission directive would have to be transposed into national law. Member states would be required to manage two distinct tax systems, their existing national system, which is covered by existing legislation, and a CCCTB. According to the UK Government, this would not require an adjustment to existing legislation in the UK, but would increase costs: new costs associated with the need for coordination with other administrations; and one-off costs such as the need for employee training and upgrading of IT systems.

The UK Government believes there are significant shortcomings in the European Commission's estimates of the impact of the proposal on the UK and in the impact assessment as a whole. It does not accept the assumption that a CCCTB is necessary to address the broader objectives of the proposal or that 27 different national corporate tax systems inherently impede the proper functioning of the internal market. It is not convinced that a CCCTB is necessary to improve the simplicity and efficiency of corporate tax systems in the EU. It considers that the fiscal impediments to cross-border activity that the proposal claims to tackle – compliance costs, double taxation and over-taxation – can be addressed through other routes, such as informal coordination or bilateral solutions. It remains to be convinced, therefore, that the European Commission has provided a sufficiently strong justification that action at EU level is required and that the proposal is compliant with the requirements of subsidiarity and proportionality; when negotiations begin the Government will be pressing the European Commission for any further analysis it is able to provide on compliance with subsidiarity and proportionality. There is insufficient evidence in the form of qualitative and quantitative indicators in the impact assessment that action at EU level would produce clear benefits by reason of its scale or effects compared with action at the level of the member states.

The House of Commons considers that the draft directive on a CCCTB does not comply with the principle of subsidiarity (European Parliament, 2011b).

8.4.3 Reasoned opinion by Dáil Éireann of the Republic of Ireland on the proposal for a European Council directive on a CCCTB

It is clear from the impact assessment that the proposal may have significant and possibly unequal cost implications between individual member states. There is a lack of concrete and quantified evaluations to justify such a policy outcome, particularly against the clear risk of decreasing budget revenues from corporate taxes, along with the estimated reductions in GDP, employment and foreign direct investment that a number of member states will experience. Also, by linking the financial impact from the directive to national policy decisions on direct tax, there is a potential blurring of the competency responsibilities involved. Under the Treaties the European Commission does not have competence in the area of direct corporate tax. No EU legislation should be proposed that indirectly impacts on national sovereignty as a means of remedying any negative financial impact that flows there from. The European Commission has not adequately met the procedural requirements to provide a detailed statement with sufficient quantitative and qualitative indicators, to allow national parliaments to fully assess all the subsidiarity implications in a cross-border proposal of this nature; it is therefore hard to conclude with insufficient evidence that EU legislative action is both necessary and of greater benefit than individual action. In its current form, the CCCTB proposal does not comply with the principle of subsidiarity (European Parliament, 2011c).

8.4.4 Reasoned opinion by the House of Representatives of the Republic of Malta on the proposal for a European Council directive on a CCCTB

The reasons why the Maltese Parliament believes that this proposal by the European Commission violates the principle of subsidiarity are as follows:

- On a general note, the new rules under the proposal for a CCCTB are in themselves a source of uncertainty since they do not benefit from a history of interpretation, either from tax administrations or even from tribunals. Furthermore, since the CCCTB is optional, companies have to contend with not only 27 different valid rule books, but also the CCCTB. While one could argue that there could be some advantages for large enterprises under this system, small companies might find it difficult to find the best system for them. This applies both to companies that are members of a group as well as those that are not. The latter are given an option under the proposed directive to apply the CCCTB as well. Moreover, while the proposal does not affect the tax rates applied by the member states, because the proposal is not neutral with regard to income, it is quite possible that member states could be forced to change rates in each case. While the goal of the CCCTB is to create a coordinated action, given the fact that the CCCTB is optional and also applies to companies that do not belong to a group, this means that it will not have this effect. Therefore, the aims of this directive will not be achieved more efficiently at EU level.
- While the CCCTB can offer some form of reduction in compliance costs, the choice between a separate calculation of profit and the CCCTB cannot be the appropriate proposal. Furthermore, the idea of a one stop shop gives the impression that all taxpayers are dealing with a single tax administration. However, while under the normal system companies and individuals deal with the respective tax authorities, under the CCCTB, individual companies would have to

interact more with the leading taxpayer, both upon consolidation as well as during audits by the leading competent authority. This is because the individual companies have an obligation under the CCCTB to keep all records and supporting documents. Moreover, it is not clear whether the CCCTB is required to bring about a reduction in compliance costs in terms of tax return estimates. This goal can be achieved through other subsidiary and proportional means. For example, with the introduction of electronic means at member state level, those costs could be reduced by a significant margin. Furthermore, companies that adopt the CCCTB (whether or not as part of a group) would have to incur additional costs because of change. This is of particular relevance for small and medium-sized enterprises. Therefore, no action is really necessary at EU level to achieve this goal. The Maltese Parliament considers that action in the member states should be sufficient to reduce administrative burdens.

- One of the objectives of the CCCTB is the removal of the complicated transfer pricing system that currently applies to group transactions. The Maltese Parliament is also of the opinion that the CCCTB does not eliminate transfer pricing as it still applies to companies that do not adopt the CCCTB or between group companies in different CCCTBs. The proposal itself acknowledges that the CCCTB will not eliminate disputes between member states. Furthermore, there is already a mechanism to deal with disputes between member states on this issue, i.e. agreements on the avoidance of double taxation and the Arbitration Agreement. In the same way, the EU Joint Transfer Pricing Forum combines the administration of tax by member states and those of commercial representatives to resolve transfer pricing issues. In this regard, the Forum has achieved a number of results, including the proposed code of conduct giving guidelines on value, which were approved by the Council of the EU. Therefore, no action is needed at EU level to achieve this goal, as the required mechanisms already exist. It does not appear that this goal would be better achieved through the CCCTB proposal, as the CCCTB itself recognizes that there could be some disputes.
- The CCCTB aims to take full account of cross-border commercial activities and thus avoid extra tax so as to consolidate profit and loss at EU level. While consolidation achieves this result, the member states could take action at national level to reduce group losses and in the Court of Justice. Action at EU level is not necessary to achieve such an objective, as actions on such issues can adequately be taken at national level.

- Another aim of the CCCTB is to reduce additional opportunities or those not indicated in corporate tax planning through the application of 27 parallel corporate tax systems in the EU by including a general rule against abuse, supplemented by measures designed to curb specific types of practices. The Maltese Parliament is of the opinion that existing mechanisms regulate harmful tax practices within the EU, i.e. the Code of Conduct Group (Business Taxation). Recommendations are made by this Group and subsequently approved by the Economic and Social Committee. Henceforth, the Maltese Parliament is of the opinion that it is not necessary for action to be taken at EU level to achieve this objective, as the mechanisms already exist and it does not appear that this goal would be better achieved by the CCCTB.
- The apportionment formula corresponds to the element of consolidation in the proposal. The Maltese Parliament is of the opinion that this formula causes distortions with regard to comparative and competitive advantages of the member states, it benefits economies that are still dependent on economic sectors that involve intensive work and it penalizes those economies where the level of productivity is relatively high and/or would be moving towards economic activities of added value and/or where the size of the market is restricted.

Accordingly, the Maltese Parliament believes that the formula does not satisfy the premise of the objective that it can be better achieved at EU level. Rather, the proposed action at European level could have negative effects (European Parliament, 2011d).

8.4.5 Reasoned opinion by the Riksdag of the Kingdom of Sweden on the proposal for a European Council directive on a CCCTB

The explanatory memorandum of the Swedish Government reiterates that the proposal for a European Council directive on a CCCTB falls within the national competence of each member state to safeguard welfare by raising and using tax revenues in an appropriate way. Corporate taxation is closely integrated with both other parts of the tax system and with the member states' economic and political affairs. Viewed from this perspective, the member states are better placed than the EU to assess how corporate taxation should be designed in order to achieve political and economic objectives both nationally and within the EU. National corporate tax systems are generally designed in a way that suits the structure of the economy in each individual member state (banking and finance, industry, agriculture, etc.). It could therefore be argued that there is a risk that the CCCTB could reduce competition and thus have a negative impact on productivity within the EU. In addition, the legal basis for the proposal is Article 115 – Treaty on the Functioning of the EU, whereby the European Council shall issue directives for the approximation of laws that directly affect the establishment or functioning of the internal market. In the Government's opinion, parts of this proposal go further. This applies, for example, to the change in the apportionment of tax revenues to which the apportionment key gives rise. What commitments or concessions a member state should make in relation to other member states with regard to the apportionment of tax revenues is first and foremost a question that the member states are best placed to assess. Nor is there any need for a change in the apportionment of taxes between the member states to enable the internal market to function better. The Government does, however, agree with the European Commission that several of the advantages of the CCCTB that are highlighted for businesses would best be achieved through legislation at EU level. This applies, for example, to some of the administrative simplifications that can be expected and reduced documentation requirements within the EU, the risk of double taxation and the possibility of cross-border offsetting of losses. Although objections can be raised against parts of the proposal from the point of view of subsidiarity, the Government considers that, overall, there is no reason to question the European Commission's assessment that the proposal complies with the principle of subsidiarity (European Parliament, 2011e).

8.4.6 Reasoned opinion by the Sejm of the Republic of Poland on the proposal for a European Council directive on a CCCTB

The EU shall act only within the limits of the competences conferred upon it by the member states in the Treaties to attain the objectives set out therein. Competences not conferred upon the EU in the Treaties remain with the member states. The Sejm takes the view that the EU lacks the competence to adopt provisions which concern the rules for establishing a corporate tax base. The Sejm holds the view that the European Commission, in adopting a draft directive on a CCCTB, has therefore exceeded the competences conferred upon the EU and undertaken actions in an area that belongs to the exclusive competence of the member states. The scope of the EU's competences as regards taxation is determined by Article 113 of the Treaty on the Functioning of the EU, which allows for the establishment of laws only in regard to indirect taxation. However, the draft directive concerns a CCCTB in respect of income tax. The Sejm of the Republic of Poland, having considered the proposal for a European Council directive on a CCCTB, finds said proposal to be non-compliant with the principle of subsidiarity as laid down in Article 5(3) of the Treaty on the EU (European Parliament, 2011f).

8.4.7 Reasoned opinion by the National Council of the Slovak Republic on the proposal for a European Council directive on a CCCTB

It should first of all be stated that a position of opposition to the harmonization of direct taxes is in the long-term strategic interests of the Slovak Republic at different EU levels. It was actually at the Slovak Prime Minister's suggestion that the conclusions of the summit of heads of state or government of the Eurozone countries held on 11 March 2011 explicitly emphasized in a separate sentence that direct taxation should remain under the competence of member states. Furthermore, in its "Government Programme Statement for the Period 2010–2014", the Government of the Slovak Republic pledged that it would not consent to European tax harmonization in the field of income tax. Fiscal sovereignty in the field of direct taxation is considered, along with independent budgetary policy, to be a key component of national sovereignty.

We should also like to draw attention to the costs associated with the introduction of a new system with a Common Corporate Tax Base and a possible increase in the administrative burden. We affirm that a system based on a voluntary principle is highly disadvantageous.

Another adverse aspect is a potential decrease in the flexibility of EU member states to react to changing economic situations and business environments through tax policy, as has hitherto been the case. It is proposed that the CCCTB system should be introduced in the form of a directive, making the implementation of amendments more time-consuming than it is at present in national legislations.

We should also like to state that the adoption of this directive would have a negative impact on GDP growth and employment and we also expect a negative effect on the revenue side of member states' budgets. The EC has submitted a legislative proposal, the impacts of which cannot be satisfactorily quantified. We consider a fundamental shortcoming of the proposal for a directive to be the fact that the European Commission does not include in its impact assessment an analysis of the actual impact of the introduction of the CCCTB on member states' budget receipts, while referring to the complexity of such a calculation, since the resultant tax receipts will depend on "national policy choices with regard to possible adaptations of the mix of different tax instruments or applied tax rates". The European Commission is thus proposing a new corporate tax regime without knowing what impact it will have on member states' budgets.

Another aspect requiring attention is the cost associated with the introduction of an optional CCCTB system for member states' tax administrations. The fact that the CCCTB regime has to be optional in nature on the one hand offers advantages to companies operating across borders, which would be able to profit from such a regime, but on the other hand creates 28 tax systems operating in parallel (introducing the CCCTB system alongside the 27 existing national tax systems). We can therefore assume that this measure will not lead to any desirable reduction in administrative costs for companies, nor will it lead to more efficient collection of corporate income taxes, since it will require additional costs for the administration of a dual system and the collection of corporate income tax (European Parliament, 2011g).

8.4.8 Reasoned opinion by the Chamber of Deputies of Romania on the proposal for a European Council directive on a CCCTB

The formula adopted for apportioning the tax base uses three criteria – labour, assets and sales – which could be considered to be unbalanced, non-equivalent or inequitable. The proposed formula would have adverse effects on the revenues of some member states, including Romania.

The tax revenues of states depend both on the nominal value of the rate of taxation and on the tax base. Tax sovereignty in the field of corporate tax requires retaining control both over the tax base and over the rate of taxation. Limiting the possibilities for exercising that control means there will be a loss of tax sovereignty. Application of the CCCTB will have direct effects on the tax base of each member state, as well as indirect effects on the rate of taxation, since the member states will have to adjust this to offset the effects, on tax revenues, of a change in the tax base. It follows that implementing the directive would result in a significant limitation of member states' tax sovereignty. There is a contradiction between the need to remove tax obstacles in the Single Market and member state tax sovereignty. The question is to what extent one can justify limiting the competences of the member states in the field of corporate taxation for the sake of the functioning of the Single Market (Article 115 – Treaty on the Functioning of the EU). Until now, EU legislative action in the field of direct taxation has been limited to specific areas. This proposal seeks to significantly expand EU action in the field of corporate taxation. The need for legislative action at EU level therefore has to be justified using objective criteria. The European Commission has not, moreover, provided any convincing justification for the way in which the choice made by each member state concerning its own tax rules has to be limited along the lines proposed. The concept of subsidiarity would therefore permit EU action to be expanded, within the limits of its competences. Article 5 of the Treaty on the EU states that, under the principle of conferral, the EU shall act only within the limits of the competences conferred upon it by the member states in the Treaties. In terms of this proposal for a directive, the legal basis for which is Article 115 – Treaty on the Functioning of the EU, the Commission is obliged to provide qualitative and quantitative justification, in respect of subsidiarity, for an expansion of EU action. For these reasons, the Permanent Bureau of the Chamber of Deputies has decided to issue a reasoned opinion to the effect that the proposal for a directive does not comply with the principle of subsidiarity (European Parliament, 2011h).

8.4.9 Reasoned opinion by the National Assembly of the Republic of Bulgaria on the proposal for a European Council directive on a CCCTB

According to the position submitted by the Council of Ministers, the Republic of Bulgaria is opposed to the introduction of a CCCTB at EU level. The Republic of Bulgaria is of the opinion that the introduction of a CCCTB for all member states would deprive the EU of the competitive advantages created by the diversity of tax regulations and tax rates and that this would in turn result in foreign investment being diverted from the EU to countries with more favourable tax regimes. Most controversial of which is the proposed mechanism for apportioning the common consolidated base. Bulgaria is of the opinion that the three factors incorporated in the apportionment formula are not objective criteria on the basis of which the share of each company of the common base group could be calculated. The proposed apportionment mechanism does not adequately reflect the specific characteristics of the economy of each member state or the differences in their economic development and standard of living. Even if the draft directive does not envisage harmonizing tax rates, member states can only counteract the negative effects of the introduction of a consolidated tax base by changing the tax rates. That would in turn deprive member states of an essential mechanism for regulating macroeconomic stability and the possibility of ensuring a balanced budget. Another important issue is the proposal for a common administrative framework. The Republic of Bulgaria is of the opinion that the section on administrative procedures has not been adequately developed. The vast differences between the administrative procedures for corporate taxation in the member states have not been taken into account, nor have the differences in the structure, staffing and organization of tax administrations. On the one hand, the introduction of two parallel procedures for administering corporate taxation would lead to a considerable increase in the administration and businesses costs while, on the other hand, it could lead to discrimination against different taxpayer groups when dealing with the same obligations of these groups. Corporate income tax in Bulgaria is administered in accordance with the Corporate Income Tax Act and the Tax Insurance Procedure Code. The adoption of the directive would lead to a complete change in the rules for taxing a company's profit and income, regardless of whether it is part of a European group, and to the introduction of a new administrative framework in the Tax Insurance Procedure Code. The proposal for a directive envisages a complete separation of fiscal regulations from accounting regulations by introducing a tax balance with taxable incomes and costs as the basis for determining the common tax base. The administration of two parallel regimes for corporate taxation would lead to a significant increase in both administrative and business costs as regards compliance with tax obligations and application of the new accounting procedures.

The Budget and Finance Committee (BFC) of the National Assembly of the Republic of Bulgaria believes that the proposal for a European Council directive on a CCCTB does not comply with the tax policy and national interests of the Republic of Bulgaria. The BFC also points out that the proposal does not comply with the principles of subsidiarity and proportionality. The EC has not presented sufficient quantitative and qualitative indicators to prove that the objectives of the proposed actions could not be adequately achieved independently by each member state in compliance with the requirements of Article 5(3) of the Treaty on the EU on the application of the principles of subsidiarity and proportionality of the Lisbon Treaty. With regard to the principle of proportionality, as enshrined in Article 5(4) of the Treaty on the EU, the BFC considers that the proposal for a directive goes beyond what is necessary to achieve the objectives of the Treaties, as it imposes an additional administrative and financial burden on the member states (European Parliament, 2011i).

On 9 June 2011, outside the deadline for submission of a reasoned opinion on the proposal for a European Council directive on a CCCTB, the Senate of the Parliament of the Czech Republic delivered a resolution. According to this resolution, the Senate of the Parliament of the Czech Republic finds that the European Commission's impact assessment lacks concrete and quantified evaluations of budgetary consequences of introducing a CCCTB for individual member states; the policy of fiscal consolidation, as set out in the Convergence Programme, cannot be pursued in a credible manner without this evaluation. It is convinced that making the CCCTB regime optional may, on the one hand, enable the targeting of businesses with cross-border activities, for which the regime can be beneficial, but, on the other hand, the optionality creates yet another, parallel 28th tax regime alongside the existing 27 national tax regimes; it can thus be argued that additional expenditures will be required to ensure the administration of a dual system of corporate taxation. Also, the Committee for European Affairs of the Chamber of Deputies recommended the government not to support steps towards harmonization of the corporate tax base calculation because the proposal does not comply with the subsidiarity principle.

On 16 May 2011, the Majority in the two Committees of the Danish Parliament stated that they were not at this stage capable of giving a final assessment as to whether the proposal complies with the subsidiarity principle. It therefore recommended the need for further clarification of the many unanswered questions raised by the proposal.

The Republic of Slovenia is reserved in its response to the proposal for a European Council directive on a CCCTB. On 24 June 2011, the Committee on EU Affairs of the National Assembly of the Republic of Slovenia expressed the opinion that the Republic of Slovenia believes that the proposal is very difficult to implement, in particular for small economies. At a systemic level, the proposal has both positive and negative effects, taking into account the nature of eventual final solutions. The Republic of Slovenia believes that the proposal for a European Council directive on a CCCTB lacks sufficient clearly reasoned arguments to be unconditionally supported. Nevertheless, the Republic of Slovenia is willing to discuss the effects of the proposal for a European Council directive on a CCCTB, the effects of the CCCTB, and in particular the method of setting up the CCCTB.

The European Union Policies Committee of the Italian Chamber of Deputies considers the proposal for a European Council directive on a CCCTB to be compliant with the principle of subsidiarity pursuant to Article 5 of the Treaty on the EU. According to the Committee, the justification for the proposal in terms of compliance with the principle of subsidiarity, based on the report illustrating it and the impact assessment, is very carefully argued and correct. A gradual harmonization of corporate taxation is necessary and urgently needed for the sound operation of the internal market, in order to revive the competitiveness of the European economy and to guarantee a fair distribution of the tax burden, also to address damaging tax competition between the member states.

Similar views were expressed by the Finance and Budget Committee of the Belgian House of Representatives and the Joint Committee of the Spanish Parliament. The Portuguese Parliament does not raise any subsidiarity issues (IPEX,[5] 2011).

The CCCTB project was backed by France and Germany. At the Franco-German summit, held in Paris on 16 August 2011, the French president Nicolas Sarkozy and the German chancellor Angela Merkel urged member states to conclude discussions on the introduction of the proposed directive by late 2012, thus paving the way for an agreement on the proposal.

Following concerns expressed by some member states' national parliaments on compliance with the principle of subsidiarity, the Committee of the Regions proposed a number of amendments to the proposal for a European Council directive on a CCCTB, as follows:

- The introduction of a new condition regarding eligible companies is proposed: the company is subject to the rules for partnerships.
- The following sentence is proposed: "Recurring costs relating to environmental protection and reducing greenhouse gases shall also be regarded as deductable expenses."
- It is proposed that the report on the operation of the CCCTB directive contains an analysis of the effects of the directive on local and regional communities.

8.5 Conclusion

The harmonization of the corporate tax base in the EU is supported by most European professional organizations and organizations representing business interested in tax simplification, in the reduction of effective tax rates in the EU and a decrease in compliance costs. Representatives of public authorities from member states are interested in the effects of introducing the CCCTB in terms of revenue and public expenditure. Adopting the CCCTB involves practical difficulties that are hard to ignore, evidenced in the reasoned opinions submitted by some member states' national parliaments. The most mentioned difficulties are as follows:

- Member states' tax administrations will have to manage two corporate tax systems simultaneously, which will increase their administrative costs.
- The apportionment formula disadvantages some member states, who will record losses in their GDP and tax revenue.

The CCCTB project in its present form has no chance of adoption. Given the state of the debate regarding the CCCTB, there is likely to be some form of coordination in the field of corporate income taxes (if not at the level of the entire EU, at least among a group of member states) in the near future.

Conclusions

The enlargement of the European Union (EU) and the expansion of economic globalization have intensified the debates regarding the imperfections of the Single Market and of the tax competition between member states. In recent years, these debates have resulted in the affirmation of some proposals for the harmonization of national tax systems for companies with cross-border activities.

Revealing the many difficulties faced by companies with cross-border activities due to the different existing tax systems in the 27 member states (mainly the costs of compliance with national tax laws and the inability to offset losses against profits) convinced many experts and politicians that the introduction of measures to harmonize legislation regarding corporate income tax in the EU is necessary. The issue of corporate income tax harmonization should be studied in the broader context of EU tax harmonization. The process of tax harmonization within the EU was generated by the need to reduce disparities between member states' tax systems in the context of free movement of goods and services, thereby contributing to the better functioning of the Single Market.

The main conclusions resulting from the analysis of progress in EU tax harmonization relate to the following issues:

- Currently, the EU has a harmonized and coordinated fiscal policy in indirect taxes, based on the principle of free movement of goods, services, capital and labour.
- Although the member states have, in principle, the freedom to set their own rules regarding the action of national tax systems, this freedom is conditioned by compliance with the priority objectives of the EU's founding treaties. Member states should avoid discriminatory

tax measures (which may lead to disadvantageous treatment for individuals, goods and services or capital from other member states).

- Sometimes restrictions regarding free movement within the Single Market are generated by differences between national tax systems, so that a degree of tax harmonization in the EU is necessary. Tax harmonization can be achieved either spontaneously (through market forces) or by active actions at EU level (the implementation of common policies, coordination, harmonization, etc.), or by passive actions of the European Court of Justice (the prohibition of certain types of behaviour by member states that do not comply with EU regulations). In the absence of tax harmonization, negative effects may occur, such as the erosion of national tax bases, the provision of services and public goods at a suboptimal level, undesirable changes in the structure of taxes and distortions in resource allocation across the Single Market.
- The adoption of the European system of VAT was the first step towards tax harmonization in the EU. During the last decades, significant progress has been made to align the member states' national VAT and excise duties legislation so that, to a large extent, the rules for the determination of the tax base and the collection and administration procedures of indirect taxes have been harmonized.
- In the field of direct taxes, the main tax harmonization measures were adopted to facilitate the activities of corporate groups within the EU. Thus, Directive 90/434/EEC on the common system of taxation applicable to mergers, divisions, transfers of assets and exchange of shares concerning companies of different member states tried to eliminate the fiscal difficulties caused by the restructuring and reorganization of multinational companies. Directive 90/435/EEC on the common system of taxation applicable in the case of parent companies and subsidiaries of different member states aimed to eliminate situations in which cooperation between companies from different member states was disadvantaged (through distribution of income tax issues) in relation to cooperation between companies within the same member state. The obstacles encountered in the case of interest and royalty payments made between associated companies of different member states were abolished by Directive 2003/49/EC. The EU Arbitration Convention (90/436/EEC) specifies the procedures for settling disputes arising from the application of transfer pricing and transfer of profits between the members of corporate groups.

The analysis of a wide range of specific items on corporate income taxes showed that different tax regimes operate in the EU. This situation can cause distortions in the location of FDI and optimal allocation of resources. Negative values of FDI net flows in some EU member states should not determine the assessment according to which these investments migrated to other countries that thus registered positive values of FDI net flows. Currently, the EU is a net investor from abroad, so it is clear that some outflux of FDI from member states is moving towards non-member countries. Several authors have tried, however, to demonstrate that the EU member states are involved in a competition to attract capital through taxation. Comparing the evolution of an effective corporate income tax rate with the evolution of FDI in certain member states, these authors have found that there is a direct link between tax competitiveness and the attraction of FDI.

Statistical data regarding the evolution of corporate tax revenues in member states are not certain proof of tax competition within the EU. Although the statutory corporate income tax rates in member states have been significantly reduced in recent decades, public authorities in many countries have expanded their tax bases in order to offset the losses in public revenue. However, increasing the gap between effective corporate income tax rates applied in EU member states could lead to distortions in the allocation of investments at the community level.

Fiscal relaxation measures taken to attract FDI are natural actions taken by some member states to counteract the competitive advantages held by the most developed member states. These measures are justified if gaps in economic development between member states are not diminished.

The absence of common corporate tax rules can generate the possibility of transferring the tax base from high tax countries to low tax countries. Companies with cross-border activities are able to avoid taxes using various instruments (including transfer pricing and intragroup loans). These forms of tax avoidance have generated significant efforts to regulate the international transfer of funds, so that corporate groups may face the risk of unilateral adjustment of the fiscal outcome as a result of investigation of suspicious intra-group transactions (commercial and/or financial).

Difficulties of compliance with the regulations in the field of transfer prices, the high costs of compliance with different tax laws and the general inability to offset losses against profits have generated complaints among representatives from the corporate sector within the EU. In this context, the European Commission's proposal to harmonize the corporate tax bases in the EU is supported by most business representatives at EU level. Systems of corporate income tax coordination within the EU, proposed by the European Commission, create mechanisms to solve problems arising from the existence of different national tax rules, such as: the distortion of competition in the Single Market by fiscal policy that stimulates corporate location decisions, transferring tax bases from high tax countries to low tax countries, administrative and compliance costs associated with corporate income taxation. Adopting these proposals will not, however, be easy.

Of the three systems of corporate income tax coordination proposed by the European Commission, the CCCTB has the best chance of application in the future. The proposal for a directive on the CCCTB, adopted on 16 March 2011, was based on numerous reports, analyses and evaluations published by the CCCTB WG, starting in 2004. A series of programmatic EU documents adopted in 2010 emphasized the need to increase competitiveness within the EU and to remove tax obstacles to the proper functioning of the Single Market and created favourable conditions for discussion of the project of harmonizing the corporate tax bases in the EU.

The need for a reform of corporate income taxes in the EU has become urgent, but the social preferences of each state should not be ignored, and this requires independent fiscal policy. On the other hand, corporate income tax harmonization is likely to cause different effects on member states in terms of changes in GDP and tax revenues. According to impact studies conducted at the request of the European Commission, some member states would suffer losses, although economic gains would be obvious in the EU as a whole.

Considering the unanimity rule for tax policy decisions in the EU, corporate income tax harmonization would probably be accepted only if the countries that appear to have winning positions compensated countries that appear to have losing positions. According to investigations on the effects of corporate income taxation harmonization, countries that would benefit from gains in GDP and welfare will register losses in tax revenue, so it seems unlikely that these countries would accept the granting of compensation to countries that register losses in GDP and welfare and gains in tax revenue. In this context, enhanced cooperation between a group of member states seems to be the solution used, ultimately, to introduce harmonized rules in the field of corporate taxation. An enhanced cooperation agreement between EU countries with a large corporate sector could significantly increase the volume of FDI in these countries because their specific location advantages would be accompanied by a more transparent tax environment.

The analysis of the effects of corporate income tax harmonization/coordination allows the conclusion that the introduction of a CCCTB will contribute to the creation of a new tax system, which will play a key role in improving competitiveness within the EU. Balancing the losses in corporate tax revenue (which have a low share of GDP in all member states) and the benefits from increased economic efficiency and the elimination of tax arbitrage opportunities, it is clear that member states should accept the introduction of the CCCTB. The intensification of cooperation relating to tax between member states will significantly improve the performance of national tax systems. Member states will be able to achieve policy objectives in the corporate tax field, while ensuring the removal of situations of discrimination and double taxation for corporate groups. National tax systems will thus contribute in a more efficient way to ensure a successful Single Market, in order to achieve particular objectives such as economic growth, employment, the competitiveness of EU companies in global markets, in accordance with the Europe 2020 Strategy.

It should be noted that, in the opinion of the European Commission, the tax fragmentation of the Single Market puts the EU at a disadvantage compared with other developed countries (the USA and Japan) in terms of attractiveness for foreign investors (European Commission, 2011b). According to information provided by The United Nations Conference on Trade and Development (UNCTAD) during 2007–2009, the EU experienced a trend towards disinvestment (UNCTAD, 2010, p. 7), affecting in particular the new member states (with the strongest growth of FDI flows before the onset of the global economic crisis). In the current international economic context, the EU must find solutions in order to attract FDI from non-member states. Even without the onset of the global economic crisis, the adoption of some measures to promote FDI in the EU had become urgent, in particular taking the following aspects into account:

- New member states (which attracted a significant volume of FDI due to the low cost of factors of production) were to gradually lose attractiveness, by increases in costs of factors of production (as a result of economic and social development).
- A number of countries located near the EU's frontier (Russia, Ukraine, Turkey, etc.) promote an active policy for the attraction of FDI, constituting an attractive location for investments in search of resources or markets.

The CCCTB system contains the necessary elements to make the Single Market a tax-friendly environment. Under the CCCTB, corporate groups operating in the EU will apply a single set of tax rules and will operate with a single tax administration (one stop shop). A company that opts for this system will not fall under the national provisions relating to corporate income tax in respect of all matters regulated by the common rules. Introducing the mandatory CCCTB in the EU (currently unlikely due to the opposition of some member states to corporate income tax coordination) would generate new challenges. Thus, in the absence of minimum limits on the corporate income tax rate, tax competition between the member states may intensify.

One should not forget that, at least so far, the administrative costs of introducing the CCCTB have not been evaluated exactly. It is obvious that public administration employees will need training in the application of future tax legislation; member states will be obliged to cooperate more in order to verify the documentation relating to the determination and allocation of the corporate income tax base. All these issues require more public spending. The European Commission considers that this shortcoming will be compensated for by a decrease in the tax arbitrage opportunities for group-organized companies. The number of disputes on issues regarding transfer pricing between tax administrations and companies should be reduced.

The CCCTB could contribute to the achievement of some important objectives of EU fiscal policy, including the following:

- Supporting the success and development of the Single Market by allowing all EU member states to compete in a loyal manner and extract the full benefits of the Single Market.
- The durable reduction of the overall tax burden in the EU, by ensuring a balance between cutting taxes, investing in public services and sustaining fiscal consolidation.

The main expected benefits of the introduction of this system include:

- A significant reduction in compliance costs. According to a study by Deloitte, at the request of the European Commission, companies' compliance costs will be reduced by over 60 per cent (Deloitte, 2009, p. 83).
- Solving the problem of double taxation for corporate groups in the EU.

- Removing a major obstacle to the free movement of capital and the unhindered exercise of the right of establishment, thanks to cross-border loss compensation.
- Removing tax avoidance practices through the use of transfer pricing, because intra-group transaction prices will not affect the distribution of the tax base in different tax jurisdictions.
- Facilitating the comparison of the effective tax burden in each tax jurisdiction (statutory tax rates become perfectly comparable when there is a single tax base), with the consequence of improving the quality of investment decisions and resource allocation across the EU.
- Suppressing the phenomenon of supra-taxation of some companies in the EU.

Thus, the CCCTB will contribute to the reduction of economic distortions caused by the many and varied types of tax incentives granted by EU governments. Also, the Single Market will become a more attractive economic space for companies with cross-border activities by simplifying the tax and accounting rules used to determine taxable income and reducing the effective corporate tax rate. According to estimates made at the request of the European Commission, on average, approximately 50 per cent of non-financial corporate groups and 17 per cent of financial corporate groups could benefit from cross-border loss offsetting (European Commission, 2011b, p. 10).

On the other hand, the negative aspects accompanying the European Commission's proposal must be highlighted:

- The CCCTB will increase the complexity of responsibilities of workers in tax administrations or will lead to the creation of new jobs, which means a rise in public spending.
- Achieving the tax audit will cause difficulties if the member states' competent authorities do not cooperate and coordinate their activities very well.
- Application of the EU apportionment formula can lead to disputes between member states (especially for specific sectors of activity).
- The introduction of the CCCTB does not eliminate the possibility of increasing tax competition, since national authorities will still be able to operate reductions in the tax rate as tax incentives for the attraction of FDI.
- The predictability of corporate tax revenues will be very difficult, because in order to estimate the taxable income of companies –

members of groups – national authorities will need to develop a comprehensive model that takes account of the economic, social and political conditions in all the member states where those groups operate.

Because Euroscepticism has registered an upward trend during the global economic crisis (many Europeans are disappointed that the entire European construct has failed to avoid the involvement of EU economies in the crisis started in the USA), the introduction of the CCCTB would be a clear signal of the member states' decision to continue and intensify efforts related to the furthering of economic integration. On the other hand, it has become clear that the lack of coordination between corporate income tax systems can generate the manipulation of taxation and therefore the erosion of tax revenues, interfering with the ability to determine efficient and balanced actions by national tax systems.

Considering the disadvantages of the introduction of the CCCTB for some member states, discussions on the draft directive should continue in order to harmonize the interests of all member states, so that common measures of corporate income tax may be accepted and applied throughout the EU.

Appendices

Appendix 1 The evolution of tax parameters that determined the corporate income tax rate (1998–2011)

Country	Period	Tax rate on profit (%)	Surcharge (%)	Local business tax rate (%)	Corporate income tax rate (%)
Austria	1998–2004	34	–	–	34
	2005–2011	25	–	–	25
Belgium	1998–2002	progressive rates	3	–	40.17
	2003–11	progressive rates (from 24.98 to 35.54)	3	–	33.99
Bulgaria	1998	progressive rates	–	10	37
	1999	progressive rates	–	10	34.3
	2000	progressive rates	–	10	32.5
	2001	progressive rates	–	10	28
	2002	progressive rates	–	10	23.5
	2003	23.50	–	–	23.5
	2004	19.50	–	–	19.5
	2005–06	15.00	–	–	15
	2007–11	10.00	–	–	10
Cyprus	1998–00	25	–	4	29
	2001–02	25	–	3	28
	2003–04	15	–	–	15
	2005–11	10	–	–	10
Czech Republic	1998–99	35	–	–	35
	2000–03	31	–	–	31
	2004	28	–	–	28

Appendix 1 (Continued)

Country	Period	Tax rate on profit (%)	Surcharge (%)	Local business tax rate (%)	Corporate income tax rate (%)
	2005	26	–	–	26
	2006–07	24	–	–	24
	2008	21	–	–	21
	2009	20	–	–	20
	2010–11	19	–	–	19
Denmark	1998	34	–	–	34
	1999–00	32	–	–	32
	2001–04	30	–	–	30
	2005–06	28	–	–	28
	2007–11	25	–	–	25
Estonia	1998–99	26	–	–	26
	2000–04	26	–	–	26
	2005	24	–	–	24
	2006	23	–	–	23
	2007	22	–	–	22
	2008–11	21	–	–	21
Finland	1998–99	28	–	–	28
	2000–04	29	–	–	29
	2005–11	26	–	–	26
France	1998	progressive rates	25	–	41.67
	1999	progressive rates	20	–	40
	2000	progressive rates	13.3	–	37.76
	2001	progressive rates	9.3	–	36.43
	2002–04	progressive rates	6.3	–	35.43
	2005	progressive rates	4.8	–	34.93
	2006–11	33.33 (15 for taxable income up to €38,120 + 1 for large companies)	3.3	–	34.43
Germany	1998	45	5.5		56
	1999–00	40	5.5	from 13.04% to 20%	51.6

	2001–02	25	5.5		38.3
	2003	26.5	5.5		39.6
	2004	25	5.5		38.3
	2005–07	25	5.5	from 7%	38.7
	2008–11	15	5.5	to 17.5%	29.8
Greece	1998–04	35	–	–	35
	2005	32	–	–	32
	2006	29	–	–	29
	2007–09	25	–	–	25
	2010–11	24	–	–	24
Hungary	1998–03	18	–		19.6
	2004	16	–		17.6
	2005–06	16	–		17.5
	2007–09	16	4	maxim 2%	21.3
	2010–11	19 (10 for taxable income up to 500 million HUF)	–		20.6
Ireland	1998–02	10	–	–	10
	2003–11	12.5	–	–	12.5
Italy	1998–00	37	–	4.3	41.3
	2001–02	36	–	4.3	40.3
	2003	34	–	4.3	38.3
	2004–07	33	–	4.3	37.3
	2008–11	27.5	–	3.9	31.4
Latvia	1998–01	25	–	–	25
	2002	22	–	–	22
	2003	19	–	–	19
	2004–11	15	–	–	15
Lithuania	1998–99	29	–	–	29
	2000–01	24	–	–	24
	2002–05	15	–	–	15
	2006	15	–	4	19
	2007	15	–	3	18
	2008	15	–	–	15
	2009	20	–	–	20
	2011	15	–	–	15
Luxembourg	1998–01	30	4	10	37.45
	2002–05	22	4	7.5	30.38
	2006–08	22	4	6.75	29.63
	2009–10	21	4	6.75	28.59

Appendix 1 (Continued)

Country	Period	Tax rate on profit (%)	Surcharge (%)	Local business tax rate (%)	Corporate income tax rate (%)
	2011	21 (20 for taxable income up to €15,000)	5	6.75 (this rate varies per municipality)	28.8
Malta	1998–11	35	–	–	35
Netherlands	1998–01	35	–	–	35
	2002–04	34.5	–	–	34.5
	2005	31.5	–	–	31.5
	2006	29.6	–	–	29.6
	2007–11	25.5	–	–	25.5
Poland	1998	36	–	–	36
	1999	34	–	–	34
	2000	30	–	–	30
	2001–02	28	–	–	28
	2003	27	–	–	27
	2004–11	19	–	–	19
Portugal	1998–99	34	10	–	37.4
	2000–01	32	10	–	35.2
	2002–03	30	10	–	33
	2004–06	25	10	–	27.5
	2007–11	25 (12.5 for taxable income up to €12,500 + 2.5 for large companies)	1.5	–	26.5
Romania	1998–99	38	–	–	38
	2000–04	25	–	–	25
	2005–11	16	–	–	16
Slovakia	1998–99	40	–	–	40
	2000–01	29	–	–	29
	2002–03	25	–	–	25
	2004–11	19	–	–	19
Slovenia	1998–06	25	–	–	25
	2007	23	–	–	23
	2008	22	–	–	22
	2009	21	–	–	21
	2010–11	20	–	–	20

Spain	1998–06	35	–	–	35
	2007	32.5	–	–	32.5
	2008–11	30	–	–	30
Sweden	1998–08	28	–	–	28
	2009–11	26.3	–	–	26.3
UK	1998	31	–	–	31
	1999–2007	30	–	–	30
	2008–2010	28	–	–	28
	2011	27	–	–	27

Appendix 2 Defining elements determining corporate taxable income in EU member states, available for 2011

	Austria	Belgium	Bulgaria	Cyprus
Taxable income	= (business/trading income + passive income + capital gains) – normal business expenses.	= annual worldwide income – allowable deductions.	= business profit adjusted for tax purposes.	= worldwide income – deductible expenses.
Depreciation	The straight-line depreciation method is permitted for machinery and equipments. Equipment costing €400 or less may be written off completely in the year of purchase.	The depreciation is usually based on historic cost. The straight-line depreciation method is normally used.	Tax-deductible depreciation is available on all assets costing over BGN 700. The applicable rate varies according to the type of asset from 4% (for buildings, equipment, etc.) up to 50% (for computers and software).	Depreciation rates vary depending on the nature of assets (3–4% for buildings, 20–25% for plant and equipment, 33.3% for software applications with higher value of €1709).
Taxation of dividends and with-holding tax on dividend payments	Dividends received by (1) an Austrian resident company; (2) a foreign company listed in the EC parent-subsidiary directive; or (3) a foreign company comparable to an Austrian company resident in certain EEA countries are exempt from corporate tax.	Dividends received by a company with a participation of at least 10% or an investment of at least €1.2 million in the distributing company, are 95% deductible from the fiscal profits of the recipient if the shares have been held for an uninterrupted period of at least 1 year.	Dividends received from companies resident in Bulgaria and other EEA states are exempt from taxable income. A 5% withholding tax is levied on dividends and distributions arising on the liquidation of resident companies to foreign legal entities, except where the dividends are realized by a permanent	Dividends received by a company located in Cyprus or abroad are exempt from corporation tax, under certain conditions. Dividends paid to a non-resident are not subject to withholding tax.

Dividends received from a foreign company that does not fulfil the above criteria are tax exempt if the following criteria are fulfilled (international participation exemption): (1) the foreign company is a company comparable to an Austrian company; (2) the parent company holds directly or indirectly at least 10% of the equity capital of the subsidiary; (3) the minimum 10% shareholding is held continuously for at least 1 year. Dividends paid to another Austrian company are exempt. Dividends paid to non-resident companies are subject to a 25% withholding tax unless the rate is reduced under an applicable tax treaty or exempt under the parent-subsidiary directive.	The 95% deduction is not available where the profits of the payer are subject to a tax regime which is substantially more advantageous than the Belgian tax regime. Belgium withholding tax on dividends is normally 25% or 15%. Full withholding tax exemption can be obtained for dividends paid by a Belgian resident company to a parent company resident in another EU member state, subject to certain minimum holding requirements, in accordance with the parent-subsidiary directive. An exemption from withholding tax is granted on dividend distributions, in accordance with bilateral tax treaties.	establishment in Bulgaria. Dividends and similar distributions are exempt from withholding tax where paid to companies and other legal entities resident in an EEA member state.

Appendix 2 (Continued)

Taxation of cross-border interest and royalty payments and with-holding tax on interest and royalty payments	No withholding tax is levied on interest unless the loan is secured against Austrian real estate or various other Austrian rights (the rate may be reduced or exempt under an applicable tax treaty). Royalties are subject to a 20% withholding tax, but may be reduced or exempt under an applicable tax treaty or the interest and royalties directive.	Full withholding tax exemption can be obtained for dividends paid by a Belgian resident company to a parent company resident in another EU member state, subject to certain minimum holding requirements, in accordance with the interest and royalties directive. Furthermore, an exemption from withholding tax is granted on dividend distributions on substantial participations held by foreign companies that reside in a country which has concluded a bilateral tax treaty with Belgium. Payments of royalties are normally subject to a withholding tax at the rate of 15%.	Interest paid to a non-resident is subject to a 10% withholding tax. The withholding tax rate of 5% on the interest and royalties accrued by permanent establishments to EU-based related parties is applied. As from 1 January 2015, Bulgaria must fully implement the interest and royalties directive.	Interest paid to non-residents is not taxed. Interest paid to residents is charged a special withholding contribution. Royalties may be exempt under an applicable tax treaty or the interest and royalties directive. Royalties paid to other non-resident companies are subject to a withholding tax with rates between 5% and 10%. These rates may be reduced under tax treaties between Cyprus and other countries.

Losses	Losses can be carried forward with no limit. There is no carry back for losses.	Losses can be carried forward indefinitely. However, this rule will no longer apply if there is a change in the control of a company which cannot be justified by financial or economic reasons other than the recapture of losses. Losses cannot be carried back.	The tax loss for the current year may be carried forward for the next 5 years. The amount utilized each year cannot exceed the tax profit for that year. Losses from foreign sources are deducted only from the profits arising from the same source with the exception of losses or sources of income from another EU member state. Losses may not be carried forward in the case of certain corporate reconstructions.	The tax loss incurred during a tax year, and which cannot be set off against other income, is carried forward and set off against future profits with no time restriction.
Foreign tax credit	Foreign tax paid may be credited against Austrian tax, but the credit is limited to the amount of Austrian tax payable on the foreign income.	A tax credit is available for foreign withholding tax levied on foreign-source interest and royalties.	A tax credit or exemption may apply under a tax treaty.	A tax credit is available for tax paid abroad.

Appendix 2 (Continued)

Consolidated tax returns	Companies can file consolidated tax returns when the holding of the parent company exceeds 50%.	Consolidated tax returns are not permitted.	Consolidated tax returns are not permitted.	The current year loss of one company can be set off against the profit of another provided the companies are Cyprus tax resident companies of a group. Losses from a permanent establishment abroad can be set off with profits of the company in Cyprus.
Incentives	Various incentive programmes are available, such as a 25–35% allowance for qualifying R&D expenditure. For the education and training of employees, employers can reclaim a tax allowance of 20%.	Incentives for industrial real estate investment, R&D, regional development, etc. are available.	Tax incentives for investments and the creation of new jobs in depressed regions are available.	Charitable contributions without any upper limit are fully deductible. Shipping companies are subject to a special tax regime.

	Czech Republic	**Denmark**	**Estonia**	**Finland**
Taxable income	= accounting profit, with adjustments for tax purposes.	= (business/trading income + passive income + capital gains) – normal business expenses.	= (business/trading income + passive income + capital gains) – normal business expenses, if there is an intention to share profits.	= (business/trading income + passive income + capital gains) – normal business expenses.

Depreciation	Straight-line or accelerated methods are available, but once selected, the method cannot be changed for the remaining life of the asset. Depreciation of intangible fixed assets is allowed where the acquisition cost exceeds CZK 60,000.	Tax deductible depreciation is available on all assets costing over DKK 12,300. Buildings for manufacturing, etc. are depreciated under the straight-line method.	Depreciation deduction based on normal accounting principles is not possible.	Buildings and other constructions are depreciated by using the declining balance method. The applicable rate varies according to the type of asset from 4% up to 30%.
Taxation of dividends and with-holding tax on dividend payments	Dividend distributions between Czech companies are exempt from tax if the parent company maintains a holding of at least 10% of the distributing company for an uninterrupted period of at least 12 months. Full withholding tax exemption can be obtained for dividends paid by a resident company to a parent company resident in another EU member state, subject to certain minimum holding requirements, in accordance with the parent-subsidiary directive.	Dividends received from a subsidiary resident within the EU or in a tax treaty country are basically exempt from tax if the parent company owns 10% or more of the share capital throughout a 12-month period in which the dividend is received. Danish outward dividends are generally subject to a 28% withholding tax.	There is no separate dividend withholding tax.	Dividends received from a subsidiary resident within the EU are exempt from tax. When dividends are paid to a non-resident, a withholding tax rate of 28% is applied unless a lower treaty rate applies. Dividends are exempt from withholding tax when paid to a company resident in an EU country if the company pays national corporate tax and holds at least 10% of the share capital in the distributing company.

Appendix 2 (Continued)

Taxation of cross-border interest and royalty payments and withholding tax on interest and royalty payments	Interest and royalties paid to non-residents are subject to a 15% withholding tax, unless the rate is reduced under a tax treaty or exempt under the interest and royalties directive. Taxpayers from EU/EEA member states are allowed to file a tax return at year end, where it will be possible to deduct costs related to interest payments.	Interest paid to non-residents are not taxed, but in some situations a withholding tax rate of 25% is applies. Royalties paid to non-residents are subject to a withholding tax of 25%. Royalties may be exempt under an applicable tax treaty or the interest and royalties directive. The rate may be reduced or exempt under an applicable tax treaty.	Interest paid to a non-resident company is subject to taxation at a rate of 21% if it significantly exceeds the market interest rate. The rate is applied on the difference between the actual interest rate charged and the market rate. A 10% withholding tax applies to royalties paid to non-residents. Royalties may be exempt under an applicable tax treaty or the interest and royalties directive.	Withholding tax is not imposed on interest and dividends paid to resident companies. Interest and dividends paid to non-resident companies are generally subject to a final withholding tax of 28% which may be reduced or eliminated under tax treaties or exempt under the interest and royalties directive.
Losses	Losses may be carried forward for 5 years. The carry back of losses is not permitted. Several anti-abuse provisions govern the utilization of tax losses.	Losses may normally be carried forward indefinitely. Losses may not be offset against interest and other capital income, if more than 50% of the shares in the company have changed ownership since the beginning of the previous year in which the loss was incurred.	The notion of tax loss does not appear in the tax legislation of Estonia.	Losses may be carried forward and set off in the subsequent 10 tax years. If more than 50% of the shares of the company are sold during a loss year or thereafter, losses from previous years cannot usually be deducted.

Foreign tax credit	The foreign tax credit is available under tax treaties. If the credit is not available under a treaty, income tax paid abroad may be deducted as an expense in the following year provided it is imposed on income included in Czech taxable income.	Foreign tax paid may be credited against Danish tax, but the credit is limited to the amount of Danish tax payable on the foreign income.	A tax credit is available for tax paid abroad.	Foreign tax paid may be credited against Finnish tax, but the credit is limited to the amount of Finnish tax payable on the foreign income.
Consolidated tax returns	Consolidated tax returns are not permitted.	Companies (resident and non-resident) can file consolidated tax returns.	Consolidated tax returns are not permitted.	Consolidated tax returns are not permitted. Profits may be transferred between certain Finnish companies.
Incentives	Tax exemptions are provided for new investments. There is a minimum investment with 60% or more invested in machinery. Expenses incurred on the implementation of R&D projects are fully deductible.	Expenses for patents and know-how can be fully deducted in the year of their acquisition.	Corporate income tax is levied when profits are distributed to the company's shareholders.	Business start-up may be awarded for stimulating economic development in certain areas.

Appendix 2 (Continued)

	France	Greece	Germany	Hungary
Taxable income	= profits of any business carried on in France, with adjustments for tax purposes.	= worldwide income + capital gains – normal business expenses.	= (business/trading income + passive income + capital gains) – normal business expenses.	= income (all sources) – normal business expenses.
Depreciation	The straight-line method is the most commonly used. Assets acquired for a cost of less than €500 excluding VAT can be totally written off in the first year.	The applicable rates are fixed and vary according to the type of asset.	Straight-line methods are available. Tax-deductible depreciation is available on all assets with a value of less than €410.	The straight-line method is normally adopted. The applicable rate varies according to the type of asset, from 2% up to 50%.
Taxation of dividends and withholding tax on dividend payments	Dividends received by resident companies are included in taxable income. If the parent held 5% of the subsidiary's capital for at least 2 years, dividends are 95% exempt. Dividends paid by a French company to a non-resident are subject to a 25% withholding tax. Full withholding tax exemption can be obtained for dividends paid by a resident company to a parent company resident in another EU member	For dividends distributed in 2011, the rate is 21% (25% for dividends distributed in 2012). No withholding tax will apply if the parent-subsidiary directive conditions are met.	Dividend income is subject to 25% withholding tax plus a surcharge, with a possible 40% refund for non-resident companies. The withholding tax rate may be reduced in accordance with tax treaties or the parent-subsidiary directive.	There is no withholding tax on dividends paid to non-resident companies. Dividends received by a Hungarian company are exempt.

	state, subject to certain minimum holding requirements, in accordance with the parent-subsidiary directive.			
Taxation of cross-border interest and royalty payments and withholding tax on interest and royalty payments	Interest paid to non-residents is, generally, not taxed. Royalties paid to non-residents are subject to a 33.33% withholding tax. The rate may be reduced or eliminated under tax treaties or exempt under the interest and royalties directive.	Interest and royalties are subject to a 40%, respectively 25% withholding tax. The rate may be reduced under tax treaties. If the interest and royalties directive conditions are met, interest and royalties are subject to a 5% withholding tax (until 30 June 2013).	With some exceptions, interest payments are not taxed. Interest is subject to a 15% withholding tax plus surcharge. The rate may be reduced or eliminated under tax treaties or exempt under the interest and royalties directive.	Interest and royalties paid to legal persons are not taxed.
Losses	Losses can be carried forward indefinitely, unless the company has changed its effective business activity or merged. Losses can be carried back against the undistributed taxable income of the 3 preceding years.	Losses may be carried forward for 5 years. The carry back of losses is not permitted.	In the year in which they are incurred, losses may, in principle, be deducted without restrictions.	Losses can be carried forward indefinitely.
Foreign tax credit	Foreign tax paid on dividends, royalties and interest may be allowed as a credit against the French tax.	A tax credit is available for tax paid abroad.	A tax credit is available for tax paid abroad.	A tax credit is available for tax paid abroad.

Appendix 2 (Continued)

Consolidated tax returns	A corporate group may opt to consolidate profits and losses. The parent company must be subject to French tax and must hold at least 95% of the share capital in the subsidiaries.	Consolidated tax returns are not permitted.	Companies may be taxed on a consolidated basis, if the parent company holds a majority share capital in subsidiaries and the managerial control.	Consolidated tax returns are not permitted.
Incentives	Tax incentives and tax credits are available for R&D, new enterprises facing financial difficulties, etc.	Certain R&D expenditure can be deducted at 150%. Tax incentives are available for certain investment.	Tax incentives are available for founders of new enterprises, acquisition of new movable assets, etc.	Tax incentives and tax credits are available for R&D, certain investment, etc.

	Ireland	**Italy**	**Latvia**	**Lithuania**
Taxable income	= income (all sources) – normal business expenses.	= net income (all sources) earned in a financial period.	= accounting profit, with adjustments for tax purposes.	= (business/trading income + passive income + capital gains + positive income) – normal business expenses.
Depreciation	The straight-line method is normally adopted. The applicable rate varies according to the type of asset, from 4% up to 12.5%.	Fixed assets are depreciated on the basis of rates established and regularly updated by the Ministry of Finance.	Fixed assets should be depreciated using the reduced balance method. Intangible assets should be depreciated on a straight-line basis.	The straight-line method is normally adopted. The applicable rate varies according to the type of asset.

Taxation of dividends and withholding tax on dividend payments	Dividends received/paid by resident companies are exempt. Dividends received by resident companies are subject to tax, but a tax credit is available for foreign tax paid. Dividends paid by a resident company to a non-resident company are subject to a 20% withholding tax. No withholding tax will apply if the parent-subsidiary directive conditions are met.	Dividends received by resident companies from their subsidiaries are 95% exempt, only if the subsidiaries are not located in low tax jurisdictions. Dividends paid to a non-resident company are subject to a 27% withholding tax (with a potential refund of the foreign tax paid). No withholding tax will apply if the parent-subsidiary directive conditions are met.	Dividends received/paid from/to resident companies in EEA countries are not taxed. Dividends received from other companies are exempt if the Latvian recipient holds more than 25% of the capital and voting power of payer company and this is not located in tax havens. In other situations, dividends are taxed at a 15% rate. Dividends paid to foreign shareholders are subject to a 10% withholding tax in Latvia unless a reduced rate is allowed under a particular double tax treaty.	Dividend received by resident companies from their subsidiaries are exempt from tax if the parent company maintains a holding of at least 10% of the distributing company for an uninterrupted period of at least 12 months. The same tax regime is applied for dividends received from companies located in EEA countries. Dividends paid to non-residents are subject to a 15% withholding tax. The rate may be reduced or eliminated under tax treaties or exempt under the parent-subsidiary directive.

Appendix 2 (Continued)

Taxation of cross-border interest and royalty payments and withholding tax on interest and royalty payments	Interest and royalties are subject to a 20% withholding tax. The rate may be reduced or eliminated under tax treaties or exempt under the interest and royalties directive.	Interest and royalties are subject to a 12.5% or 27%, respectively 30% withholding tax. These rates may be reduced or eliminated under tax treaties or exempt under the interest and royalties directive.	Interest paid to non-residents is subject to a 10% withholding tax (5% if the non-resident is a commercial bank). Royalties paid to non-residents are subject to a 5% or 15% withholding tax. If the interest and royalties directive conditions are met, interest and royalties are subject to a 5% withholding tax (until 1 July 2013).	Interest and royalties are subject to a 10% withholding tax. The rate may be reduced or eliminated under tax treaties or exempt under the interest and royalties directive.
Losses	Trading losses can be carried forward indefinitely. Losses incurred in a trade can be offset against other trading income in the same accounting period or the preceding accounting period.	Losses may be carried forward for five taxable periods. Losses incurred by a company during the first three taxable periods can be carried forward indefinitely.	Tax losses generally can be carried forward for eight years. The carry back of losses is not permitted.	Operational losses may be carried forward indefinitely if the entity continues carrying on the activity that resulted in the losses. The carry back of losses is not permitted.

Foreign tax credit	Foreign tax paid may be credited against Irish tax, but the credit is limited to the amount of Irish tax payable on the foreign income.	Foreign tax paid may be credited against Italian tax, but the credit is limited to the amount of Italian tax payable on the foreign income.	Foreign tax paid may be credited against Latvian tax, but the credit is limited to the lower tax attributable to foreign income.	Foreign tax paid may be credited against Lithuanian tax on the same profits, but the credit is limited to the amount of Lithuanian tax payable on the foreign income.
Consolidated tax returns	Consolidated tax returns are not permitted, but tax losses can be transferred within a group of companies resident in EU member states.	Consolidated tax returns are permitted for domestic corporate groups, if the parent company holds a majority share capital in subsidiaries and the managerial control.	Consolidated tax returns are not permitted, but tax losses can be transferred within a group of companies under certain conditions.	Consolidated tax returns are permitted.
Incentives	Tax credits are available for R&D, acquisition of certain assets, etc.	Incentives are available to support economic investment in depressed areas.	Tax reductions are available for entities located in certain economic zones.	Scientific research and experimental development costs may be deducted three times when calculating corporate income tax. Incentives are also provided for micro companies and companies in free economic zones.

Appendix 2 (Continued)

	Luxembourg	**Malta**	**Netherlands**	**Poland**
Taxable income	= profit (as stated in the commercial balance sheet) + certain adjustments provided for under the tax law.	= income (all sources) – normal business expenses.	= (business/trading income + passive income + capital gains) – normal business expenses.	= (business/trading income + passive income + capital gains) – normal business expenses.
Depreciation	Straight-line or reduced balance methods are available.	The straight-line method is normally adopted. The applicable rate varies according to the type of asset.	The applicable rate varies according to the type of asset. The tax written down value cannot be reduced below certain limits.	The straight-line method is normally adopted. The applicable rate varies according to the type of asset, from 1.5% up to 30%.
Taxation of dividends and withholding tax on dividend payments	Dividends received by resident companies from their subsidiaries are exempt from tax if the parent company maintains a holding of at least 10% of the distributing company for an uninterrupted period of at least 12 months. Dividends paid to a non-resident company are generally subject to a 15% withholding tax. The rate may be reduced or eliminated under tax treaties or exempt under the parent-subsidiary directive.	Resident companies may be subject to various tax and accounting regimes that generate different tax liabilities regarding dividends. Dividends received by resident companies from their subsidiaries are exempt from tax if the parent company maintains a holding of at least 10% of the distributing company for an uninterrupted period of at least 12 months.	Dividends received/paid by resident companies are exempt under certain conditions (related to the participation). Dividends paid to a non-resident company are generally subject to a 15% withholding tax. The rate may be reduced or eliminated under tax treaties.	Dividends received by resident companies from their subsidiaries are exempt from tax if the parent company holds 5% of the subsidiary's capital. Dividends paid to a non-resident company are generally subject to a 19% withholding tax. The rate may be reduced or eliminated under tax treaties or exempt under the parent-subsidiary directive.

Taxation of cross-border interest and royalty payments and withholding tax on interest and royalty payments	Luxembourg does not levy withholding tax on interest and royalties.	Usually, Malta does not levy withholding tax on interest and royalties.	The Netherlands does not levy withholding tax on interest and royalties.	Interest and royalties are subject to a 20% withholding tax. The rate may be reduced under tax treaties. If the interest and royalties directive conditions are met, interest and royalties are subject to a 5% withholding tax (until 30 June 2013).
Losses	Losses can be carried forward indefinitely.	Trading losses can be carried forward indefinitely. The carry back of losses is not permitted.	Losses may be offset against the taxable profits of the preceding year and carried forward for a period of 9 years.	Losses from a given tax year can be offset against the income in the 5 subsequent tax years, but the amount deducted in any one year cannot exceed 50% of the loss incurred in the previous 5 tax years. The carry back of losses is not permitted.
Foreign tax credit	Foreign tax paid may be credited against Luxembourgian tax, but the credit is limited to the amount of Luxembourgian tax payable on the foreign income.	A tax credit is available for tax paid abroad in certain circumstances.	A credit for foreign tax may be granted under various tax treaties.	A tax credit is available for tax paid abroad.

Appendix 2 (Continued)

Consolidated tax returns	Fiscal consolidation is allowed for corporate and business tax purposes. The fiscal unity may be formed only by a Luxembourgian company, or a Luxembourgian permanent establishment of a foreign company subject to tax corresponding to Luxembourg's corporate income tax rates.	Consolidated tax returns are not permitted.	If a parent company owns at least 95% of its subsidiaries, it may form a fiscal unity, under which the losses of one company may be offset against the profits of another.	Companies may form a tax capital group. The group is treated as a single taxpayer for corporate income tax purposes.
Incentives	Tax credits are available for certain investments. Tax incentives are available for shipping companies.	Tax incentives are available for R&D, SMEs, education and training programmes.	Tax incentives are available for R&D, shipping companies, etc.	Tax incentives are available for new enterprises, acquisition of performing technologies, etc.

	Portugal	**Romania**	**Slovakia**	**Slovenia**
Taxable income	= (business/trading income + passive income + capital gains) – normal business expenses.	= revenue from any source – the expenses incurred in order to achieve the income – non-taxable income + non-deductible expenses.	= accounting profit, with adjustments for tax purposes.	= income – expenses (recognized in the income statement according to accounting standards).
Depreciation	Straight-line or declining-balance methods are available.	Straight-line, accelerated or declining-balance methods are available.	Straight-line or declining-balance methods are available. Once the method is selected, it cannot be changed.	The straight-line method is normally adopted. The applicable rate varies according to the type of asset, from 3% up to 50%.

Taxation of dividends and withholding tax on dividend payments	Dividends received by a resident company from (1) resident subsidiaries in the EU if the parent company maintains a holding of at least 10% of the distributing company for an uninterrupted period of at least 12 months; (2) subsidiaries located in EEA countries under a tax treaties; or (3) subsidiaries located in African countries having Portuguese as their official languages or East Timor, if the parent company held 25% of the subsidiary's capital for an uninterrupted period of at least 2 years are exempt. Dividends paid to a non-resident company are generally subject to a 21.5% withholding tax. The rate may be reduced or eliminated under tax treaties or exempt under the parent-subsidiary directive.	Dividends received by resident companies from their subsidiaries are exempt from tax if the parent company maintains a holding of at least 10% of the distributing company for an uninterrupted period of at least 2 years. Otherwise, a 16% tax applies. Dividends paid to non-residents are subject to a 16% withholding tax. The rate may be reduced or eliminated under tax treaties or exempt under the parent-subsidiary directive.	Dividends received/paid by resident company are exempt from taxes.	Dividends received by resident companies are exempt from taxes. Dividends received by resident companies from companies located in tax havens are subject to tax. Dividends paid to non-residents are subject to a 15% withholding tax. The rate may be reduced or eliminated under tax treaties or exempt under the parent-subsidiary directive.

Appendix 2 (Continued)

Taxation of cross-border interest and royalty payments and withholding tax on interest and royalty payments	Interest and royalties are subject to a 21.5%, respectively 15% withholding tax. These rates may be reduced under tax treaties. The rate may be reduced under tax treaties. If the interest and royalties directive conditions are met, interest and royalties are subject to a 5% withholding tax (until 30 June 2013).	Interest and royalties are subject to a 16% withholding tax. The rate may be reduced or eliminated under tax treaties or exempt under the interest and royalties directive. Interest and royalties paid to subsidiaries located in EEA countries if the parent company holds 25% of the subsidiary's capital for an uninterrupted period of at least 2 years are exempt.	Interest and royalties are subject to a 19% withholding tax. The rate may be reduced or eliminated under tax treaties or exempt under the interest and royalties directive.	Interest and royalties are subject to a 15% withholding tax. The rate may be reduced or eliminated under tax treaties or exempt under the interest and royalties directive.
Losses	Losses may be carried forward for 4 years if the entity continues carrying on the activity that resulted in the losses and at least 50% of the shares in the company have not changed ownership.	Losses may be carried forward for 7 years.	Losses may be carried forward for 7 years.	Losses can be carried forward indefinitely.
Foreign tax credit	Foreign tax paid may be credited against Portuguese tax, but the credit is limited to the amount of Portuguese tax payable on the foreign income.	Foreign tax paid may be credited against Romanian tax, but the credit is limited to the amount of Romanian tax payable on the foreign income.	Foreign tax paid may be credited against Slovak tax, but the credit is limited to the amount of Slovak tax payable on the foreign income.	Foreign tax paid may be credited against Slovene tax, but the credit is limited to the amount of Slovene tax payable on the foreign income.

Consolidated tax returns	Consolidated tax returns are allowed for resident corporate groups under certain conditions.	Consolidated tax returns are not permitted.	Consolidated tax returns are not permitted.	Consolidated tax returns are not permitted.
Incentives	Tax incentives are available for R&D, certain investments, entities located in certain economic zones, etc.	Tax incentives are available for R&D. Reinvested profits are not subject to tax.	Tax incentives are available for certain investments.	Tax incentives are available for R&D, acquisition of certain assets, etc.

	Spain	**Sweden**	**United Kingdom**
Taxable income	= income – expenses (recognized in the income statement according to accounting standards).	= income (all sources) – normal business expenses.	= (business/trading income + certain non-trading income + capital gains) – normal business expenses.
Depreciation	Depreciation can be deducted on a straight-line basis, reducing-balance basis in the case of new tangible assets with a life of more than 3 years, or on an individual basis (if approved by the tax authorities).	Tax-deductible depreciation is available on all assets with a value of less than 21,400 Swedish krona.	The depreciation of land, buildings or other tangible fixed assets is not deductible for tax purpose. A tax relief is available for certain assets.

Appendix 2 (Continued)

Taxation of dividends and withholding tax on dividend payments	Dividends received by resident companies are subject to corporate income tax. Dividends paid to non-residents are subject to a 19% withholding tax. The rate may be reduced or eliminated under tax treaties or exempt under the parent-subsidiary directive.	Dividends received by a resident company from non-resident companies are subject to corporate income tax. Dividends received by a resident company from resident companies are exempt. Dividends paid to a non-resident company are generally subject to a 30% withholding tax. The rate may be reduced or eliminated under tax treaties or exempt under the parent-subsidiary directive.	Dividends received by resident companies are exempt from taxes, with some exceptions.
Taxation of cross-border interest and royalty payments and withholding tax on interest and royalty payments	Interest and royalties are subject to a 19%, respectively 24% withholding tax. These rates may be reduced or eliminated under tax treaties or exempt under the interest and royalties directive.	Sweden does not levy withholding tax on interest and royalty.	Interest and royalties are subject to a 20% withholding tax. The rate may be reduced or eliminated under tax treaties or exempt under the interest and royalties directive.

Losses	Losses may be carried forward for 15 years.	Losses may normally be carried forward indefinitely, if the ownership is not changed.	Trading losses can in general be offset in the current year against other income. Trading losses can only be carried forwards against the profits of the same trade, if the ownership is not changed within 3 years.
Foreign tax credit	A tax credit is available for tax paid abroad.	Foreign tax paid may be credited against Swedish tax, but the credit is limited to the amount of Swedish tax payable on the foreign income.	Foreign tax paid may be credited against UK tax, but the credit is limited to the amount of UK tax payable on the foreign income, when certain conditions are satisfied.
Consolidated tax returns	Consolidated tax returns are allowed for resident corporate groups under certain conditions.	Consolidated tax returns are not allowed but, under certain conditions, the consolidation of income through "group contributions" is allowed.	Consolidated tax returns are not allowed, but tax losses can be transferred within a UK group of companies under certain conditions.
Incentives	Tax incentives are available for R&D, environment investments, etc.	Tax incentives are available for certain enterprises.	Tax incentives are available for R&D.

Appendix 3 Direct investment flows as % of GDP[1] and intra-EU direct investment reported by EU member states (€ million)[2]

	2004	2005	2006	2007	2008	2009	2010
Belgium[1]	9.4	8.7	12.7	17.4	43.6	–3.8	0.8
Belgium[2]	:	15,635	28,893	35,093	–119,645	–10,053	711
Bulgaria[1]	–0.8	1.1	0.5	0.7	1.5	–0.2	0.5
Bulgaria[2]	–187	216	62	85	425	–150	81
Czech Republic[1]	0.9	0	1	0.9	1.9	0.5	0.9
Czech Republic[2]	554	–105	1,223	987	2860	196	1181
Denmark[1]	:	6.3	3	6.6	3.9	2	1.1
Denmark[2]	:	10,008	–700	3,627	10,0111	2,243	1,722
Germany[1]	0.8	2.7	4.1	5.1	2.1	2.4	3.3
Germany[2]	10,140	43,799	58,642	77,824	46,137	44,257	52,091
Estonia[1]	2.2	5	6.6	7.9	4.7	8.1	0.7
Estonia[2]	193	376	813	1,070	773	1,197	123
Ireland[1]	9.7	7	6.9	8.1	7.2	11.9	8.6
Ireland[2]	:	10,604	6,162	7,214	6,491	12,635	5,912
Greece[1]	0.4	0.6	1.5	1.7	0.7	0.6	0.3
Greece[2]	:	:	239	1,179	685	1,142	605
Spain[1]	5.8	3.7	8.4	9.5	4.7	0.7	1.6
Spain[2]	:	20,755	64,414	71,300	18,925	–1,322	7,763
France[1]	2.8	5.4	4.9	6.4	5.5	3.9	3.3
France[2]	40,367	65,121	46,768	93,174	63,403	58,784	44,418
Italy[1]	1.1	2.3	2.2	4.3	2.9	1	1.6
Italy[2]	:	27,577	18,582	66,069	30,862	10,872	7,612
Cyprus[1]	4.4	3.3	4.8	5.7	10.8	1.6	3
Cyprus[2]	:	212	81	640	63	518	–178
Latvia[1]	0.8	0.8	0.9	1.3	0.7	–0.2	0.1
Latvia[2]	15	42	27	124	83	26	–6

Lithuania[1]	1.2	1.3	1	1.5	0.7	0.6	0.2
Lithuania[2]	:	:	187	370	192	151	51
Luxembourg[1]	246.5	334.4	269	518.3	234.5	437.6	345.6
Luxembourg[2]	55,561	65,966	62,001	108,425	6,885	40,092	75,996
Hungary[1]	1.1	2	3.4	2.7	1.4	1.4	1
Hungary[2]	719	637	1,194	1,896	–804	68	–613
Malta[1]	0.1	–0.3	0.5	0.2	3.6	1.7	1.1
Malta[2]	–20	–29	18	28	168	92	73
Netherlands[1]	4.8	20.6	9.6	7.1	7.8	3.4	6.4
Netherlands[2]	15,236	89,652	:	:	:	:	:
Austria[1]	2.8	3.8	4.2	10.4	7.1	2.6	2.2
Austria[2]	:	6,044	7,299	11,585	11,224	2,753	–82
Poland[1]	0.4	1.1	2.6	1.3	0.8	1.2	1.2
Poland[2]	392	1,155	6,177	2,004	1,469	2,344	3,584
Portugal[1]	4	1.1	3.5	2.4	1.1	0.3	–3.7
Portugal[2]	4,969	1,410	3,724	2,481	1,626	2,033	–
Romania[1]	:	0	0.3	0.2	0.1	–0.1	0
Romania[2]	:	12	163	70	38	–146	28
Slovenia[1]	1.4	1.9	2.4	4.1	2.6	0.5	–0.2
Slovenia[2]	:	58	99	423	175	–113	–69
Slovakia[1]	–0.1	0.3	0.9	0.8	0.6	1	0.4
Slovakia[2]	–53	81	392	398	331	557	208
Finland[1]	–0.6	2.2	2.3	2.9	3.4	2	4.4
Finland[2]	–1,520	5,500	3,878	4,231	4,319	2,524	6,142
Sweden[1]	6.1	7.5	6.7	8.1	6.4	6.4	4.1
Sweden[2]	9,193	15,272	11,913	5,947	15,127	12,097	–1,291
United Kingdom[1]	4.1	3.5	3.5	11.3	6.9	1.8	1.6
United Kingdom[2]	:	19,493	5,923	102,053	59,399	–	19,493

Note: [1] Direct investment flows as % of GDP.
[2] Intra-EU direct investment reported by EU member state (million EUR).
Source: EUROSTAT, Statistics, Balance of payments – International transactions, date accessed 29 March 2012.

Notes

1 The Tax Harmonization in the European Union

1. OECD, Glossary of Tax Terms, available at www.oecd.org/document/29/0,3343,en_2649_34897_33933853_1_1_1_1,00.html.
2. Official Journal of the European Union, C115/47, Consolidated version of the Treaty on the functioning of the European Union, 9 May 2008.
3. The holding company term is used to describe an entity that holds shares in other entities and whose main activity is the management and control of these holdings.

2 The Evolution of Tax Harmonization in the European Union

1. Report from the Commission to the Council and the European Parliament, Application of Council regulation (EEC) no. 218/92 of 27 January 1992 on administrative cooperation in the field of indirect taxation (VAT), COM(96) 681 final, Brussels.
2. International Bureau of Fiscal Documentation, The Report of the Fiscal and Financial Committee and the Reports of the Sub-Groups A, B and C, an unofficial translation prepared by H. Thurston, Amsterdam, 1963.
3. European Commission memorandum of 26 June 1967, taken from B. Terra and P. Wattèl (2001) European tax law (Fiscale Studieserie: Deventer), pp. 174–175.
4. Official Journal of the European Communities C 2/1, Conclusions of the ECOFIN Council meeting on 1 December 1997 concerning taxation policy, Brussels.
5. The open method of coordination (OMC) is governance based on the voluntary cooperation of EU member states. The method rests on guidelines, indicators, benchmarking, sharing of best practices, etc. This means that there are no official sanctions for states that do not translate the guidelines of the European institutions into national and regional policies. Developments of the OMC are regularly monitored and evaluated and the results are published. There is considerable scope for it to help set the policy agenda and persuade reluctant member states to implement agreed policies.
6. European Parliament, Lisbon European Council 23 and 24 March 2000: Presidency conclusions, available at http://www.europarl.europa.eu/summits/lis1_en.htm.
7. Official Journal of the European Union, L 225/1, Council Directive 90/434/EEC of 23 July 1990 on the common system of taxation applicable to mergers, divisions, transfers of assets and exchanges of shares concerning companies of different member states, 20 August 1990.

8. Official Journal of the European Union, L 58/19, Council Directive 2005/19/EC of 17 February 2005 amending Directive 90/434/EEC 1990 on the common system of taxation applicable to mergers, divisions, transfers of assets and exchanges of shares concerning companies of different member states, 4 March 2005.
9. Official Journal of the European Union, L 225/6, Council Directive 90/435/EEC of 23 July 1990 on the common system of taxation applicable in the case of parent companies and subsidiaries of different member states, 20 August 1990.
10. Official Journal of the European Union, L 007/41, Council Directive 2003/123/EC of 22 December 2003 amending Directive 90/435/EEC on the common system of taxation applicable in the case of parent companies and subsidiaries of different member states, 13 January 2004.
11. Official Journal of the European Union, L 225/10, 90/436/EEC: Convention on the elimination of double taxation in connection with the adjustment of profits of associated enterprises – Final Act – Joint Declarations – Unilateral Declarations, 20 August 1990.
12. Official Journal of the European Union, L 157/38, Council Directive 2003/48/EC of 3 June 2003 on taxation of savings income in the form of interest payments, 26 June 2003.
13. Official Journal of the European Union, L 157/49, Council Directive 2003/49/EC of 3 June 2003 on a common system of taxation applicable to interest and royalty payments made between associated companies of different member states, 26 June 2003.

3 The Need for European Union Coordination of Corporate Income Taxes: Facts and Statistics

1. Official Journal of the European Union, C147/49, Resolution of the Council and of the representatives of the governments of the member states, meeting within the Council, of 27 June 2006 on a code of conduct on transfer pricing documentation for associated enterprises in the European Union, 28 July 2006.

5 Coordination Systems of Corporate Income Tax in the European Union

1. Panel Discussion, available at http://ec.europa.eu/taxation_customs/taxation/company_tax/conferences_events/article_1281_en.htm
2. Summary of the study conducted by Gammie M. and S.-O. Lodin (Home State Taxation, IBFD Publications, Amsterdam, 2001) is available at http://ec.europa.eu/taxation_customs/resources/documents/hst_book_summary.pdf.
3. Results of the questioning of 194 small and medium enterprises in 11 member states showed that almost half of the respondents were interested in participating in a five-year pilot scheme.
4. Information about the work of the CCCTB WG are available at http://ec.europa.eu/taxation_customs/taxation/company_tax/common_tax_base/index_en.htm.

5. Communication from the European Commission, Europe 2020 – A European strategy for smart, sustainable and inclusive growth, COM(2010) 2020, Brussels, 3 March 2010.
6. Workshop papers can be found at: http://ec.europa.eu/taxation_customs/taxation/company_tax/common_tax_base/ccctb_en.htm.
7. Commission Regulation (EC) no. 1725/2003 of 29 September 2003 adopting certain international accounting standards in accordance with Regulation (EC) no. 1606/2002 of the European Parliament and of the Council; Commission Regulation (EC) no. 707/2004 of 6 April 2004 amending Regulation (EC) no. 1725/2003 adopting certain international accounting standards in accordance with Regulation (EC) no. 1606/2002 of the European Parliament and of the Council.
8. Official average corporate tax rates applicable in the member states are published annually by the European Commission; they are calculated as an arithmetic average corporate tax rate applied in the member states.
9. Benefits granted to a shareholder who is an individual, his spouse, lineal ascendant or descendant or associated enterprises, holding a direct or indirect participation in the control, capital or management of the taxpayer shall not be treated as deductible expenses to the extent that such benefits would not be granted to an independent third party.
10. A body shall qualify as charitable where the following conditions are met: (a) it has legal personality and is a recognized charity under the law of the state in which it is established; (b) its sole or main purpose and activity is one of public benefit; an educational, social, medical, cultural, scientific, philanthropic, religious, environmental or sportive purpose shall be considered to be of public benefit provided that it is of general interest; (c) its assets are irrevocably dedicated to the furtherance of its purpose; (d) it is subject to requirements for the disclosure of information regarding its accounts and its activities; (e) it is not a political party as defined by the member state in which it is established.
11. Official Journal of the European Union, L 64/1, Council Directive 2011/16/EU of 15 February 2011 on administrative cooperation in the field of taxation and repealing Directive 77/799/EEC, 11 March 2011.
12. Improvement costs are any additional expenditures on a fixed asset that materially increases the capacity of the asset or materially improves its functioning or represents more than 10 per cent of the initial depreciation base of the asset.
13. A reliable estimate shall be the expected expenditure required to settle the present obligation at the end of the tax year, provided that the estimate is based on all relevant factors, including past experience of the company, group or industry. In measuring a provision, the following shall apply: (a) account shall be taken of all risks and uncertainties, however, uncertainty shall not justify the creation of excessive provisions; (b) if the term of the provision is 12 months or longer and there is no agreed discount rate, the provision shall be discounted at the yearly average of the Euro Interbank Offered Rate (Euribor) for obligations with a maturity of 12 months, as published by the European Central Bank, in the calendar year in the course of which the tax year ends; (c) future events shall be taken into

account where they can reasonably be expected to occur; (d) future benefits directly linked to the event giving rise to the provision shall be taken into account.

14. Examples were taken from the annex of the working document produced by the CCCTB WG – Possible elements of a technical outline, Brussels, 26 July 2007, available at http://ec.europa.eu/taxation_customs/resources/documents/taxation/company_tax/common_tax_base/ccctbwp057_en.pdf.
15. These conditions shall not apply where the third country is party to the European Economic Area Agreement and there is an agreement on the exchange of information comparable to the exchange of information on request provided for in Directive 2011/16/EU.
16. The following categories of income shall be taken into account for the purposes of point (c), in so far as more than 50 per cent of the category of the entity's income comes from transactions with the taxpayer or its associated enterprises: (a) interest or any other income generated by financial assets; (b) royalties or any other income generated by intellectual property; (c) dividends and income from the disposal of shares; (d) income from movable property; (e) income from immovable property, unless the member state of the taxpayer would not have been entitled to tax the income under an agreement concluded with a third country; (f) income from insurance, banking and other financial activities.
17. The tax system must be able to generate growth in all EU member states in proportion to the size of economic activity conducted on their territory.
18. The state budget must have tax receipts; each taxpayer is obliged to pay taxes according to their capacity to pay.
19. The collection of taxes should be considered as a compensation of expenses incurred by public authorities in the provision of public goods (infrastructure, education and training, justice, etc.).
20. The tax system should not create major distortions in the behaviour of consumers and producers. A tax should not alter the decisions of investors by favouring certain categories of investments and disadvantaging others.
21. Taxes levied by public authorities must be sufficient to finance the government's current needs and to ensure the continuity of a country's fiscal policy.
22. A tax system should be simple, so that taxpayers can comply with its rules easily and do not generate high costs of administration.
23. This rule shall only apply where the following conditions are met: (a) this employment lasts for an uninterrupted period of at least three months; (b) such employees represent at least 5 per cent of the overall number of employees of the group member from which they receive remuneration.
24. The following entities shall be regarded as financial institutions: (a) credit institutions authorized to operate in the EU in accordance with Directive 2006/48/EC of the European Parliament and of the Council; (b) entities, except for insurance undertakings, which hold financial assets amounting to 80 per cent or more of all their fixed assets.

6 Effects of Corporate Income Tax Harmonization/ Coordination in the European Union

1. Jesper, J. and Svensson, P., Economic effects of tax cooperation in an enlarged European Union. Simulations of corporate tax harmonisation and savings tax coordination, Copenhagen Economics, 2004.
2. Inputs targeted the data available for 2002.
3. The CORTAX model is a simplified version of the CETAX model. It is designed to simulate the economic implications of unilateral and multilateral corporate tax policies.

7 Impact Assessment of the Common Consolidated Corporate Tax Base

1. The authors used the Orbis data base edited by Bureau van Dijk Electronic Publishing.
2. The methodology used to estimate the impact of introducing the CCCTB on certain economic indicators was based on the elasticity coefficients of GDP, employment and volume of FDI to the cost of capital and effective tax rate.

8 Supporters and Opponents of Corporate Income Tax Coordination in the European Union

1. BUSINESS EUROPE represents small, medium and large companies. BUSINESS EUROPE's members are 40 leading industrial and employers' federations from 34 European countries.
2. UEAPME is the employers' organization representing crafts, trades and SMEs from the EU and accession countries at European level. UEAPME has 85 member organizations, which represent crafts and SMEs across Europe, covering over 12 million enterprises with 50 million employees.
3. ACCA is the global body for professional accountants with 71,000 members across Europe.
4. Under the principle of subsidiarity, in areas which do not fall within its exclusive competence, the Union shall act only if and in so far as the objectives of the proposed action cannot be sufficiently achieved by the member states, either at central level or at regional and local level, but can rather, by reason of the scale or effects of the proposed action, be better achieved at Union level (Article 5(2) – Treaty on European Union).
5. IPEX, the InterParliamentary EU information eXchange, is a platform for the mutual exchange of information between the national parliaments and the European Parliament concerning issues related to the European Union, especially in light of the provisions of the Treaty of Lisbon.

References

Agúndez-García, A. (2006) "The delineation and apportionment of an EU consolidated tax base for multi-jurisdictional corporate income taxation: a review of issues and options", *Taxation Papers*, Working paper no. 9, Directorate-General Taxation and Customs Union, European Commission, pp. 32–38.

Avi-Yonah, R. (2001) "Globalization and tax competition: implications for developing countries", *CEPAL Review*, 74, p. 61.

Association of Chartered Certified Accountants (25 May 2010) "Common Consolidated Corporate Tax Base (CCCTB)" – position statement, http://www2.accaglobal.com/pubs/about/public_affairs/unit/european_briefings/PAMR-PP-CCCTB.pdf, date accessed 1 December 2011.

Barrios, S., Huizinga, H., Laeven, L. and Nicodème, G. (2008) "International taxation and multinational firm location decisions", *CESifo Working Paper Series*, 2503, CESifo Group Munich, p. 26.

Becker, J., Fuest, C. and Hemmelgarn, T. (2006) "Corporate tax reform and foreign direct investment in Germany – Evidence from firm-level data", *CESifo Working Paper Series*, 1722, CESifo Group Munich, pp. 9–32.

Bellak, C. and Leibrecht, M. (2005) "Effective tax rates as a determinant of foreign direct investment in central- and east European countries: A panel analysis", *Discussion Papers SFB International Tax Coordination*, 7, WU Vienna University of Economics and Business, p. 21.

Bénassy-Quéré, A., Fontagné, L. and Lahrèche-Révil, A. (2003) "Tax competition and foreign direct investment", *CEEPII Research Center*, Working paper no. 17, p. 18.

Bettendorf, L., van der Horst, A., de Mooij, R. and Vrijburg, H. (2010) "Corporate tax consolidation and enhanced cooperation in the European Union?", *Centre for Business Taxation*, Working paper no. 1001, Oxford University, pp. 17–26.

Bettendorf, L., van der Horst, A., de Mooij, R., Devereux, M. and Loretz, S. (2009) "The economic effects of EU-reforms in corporate income tax systems", Study for the European Commission Directorate-General Taxation and Customs Union, *CPB Netherlands for Economic Policy Analysis*, pp. 32–59.

Bond, S., Chennells, L., Devereux, M.P., Gammie, M. and Troup, E. (2000) *Corporate Tax Harmonization in Europe: A Guide to the Debate* (The Institute for Fiscal Studies: London), p. 58.

Brøchner, J., Jensen, J., Svensson, P. and Sørensen, P.B. (2006) "The dilemmas of tax coordination in the enlarged European Union", *CESifo Working Paper Series*, 1859, CESifo Group Munich, pp. 6, 18–33.

BUSINESS EUROPE (16 March 2011) "Common Consolidated Corporate Tax Base to aim at global competitiveness for cross-border business" – Press Release, http://www.businesseurope.eu/content/default.asp?PageID= 609, dated accessed 1 December 2011.

Chen, D., Lee, F. and Mintz, J. (2002) "Taxation, SMEs and entrepreneurship", *OECD Science, Technology and Industry Working Papers*, 09, OECD Publishing, p. 4.
Christensen, J. and Kapoor, S. (2004) "Tax avoidance, tax competition and globalisation: making tax justice a focus for global activism", *Accountancy Business and the Public Interest*, 3(2), 6–9.
Cline, R., Neubig, T., Phillips, A., Sanger, C. and Walsh, A. (2010) *Study on the Economic and Budgetary Impact of the Introduction of a Common Consolidated Corporate Tax Base in the European Union* (Ernst and Young LLP: Washington DC), pp. 4, 65–77.
Cnossen, S. and Shoup, C.S. (1987) *Tax Coordination in the European Community* (Kluwer Law and Taxation Publishers: Deventer), pp. 59–84.
Coates, D. (1993) "Tax competition among jurisdiction with public and private employment", *National Tax Journal*, 46, p. 177.
Council/Commission of the European Communities (1970) "The establishment by stages of economic and monetary union in the Community (Werner Report)", Supplement to Bulletin 7 – 1970 of the European Communities, Brussels.
Council of the European Union (1999) "Report from Code of Conduct Group (Business Taxation) to ECOFIN Council on 29 November 1999", Brussels.
Dalibor, R. (2006) "Evidence and myths about tax competition", *New Perspectives on Political Economy*, 2(2), p. 88.
de Mooij, R. and Devereux, M.P. (2009) "Alternative systems of business tax in Europe an applied analysis of ACE and CBIT reforms", *Taxation Papers*, Working paper no. 17, Directorate-General Taxation and Customs Union, European Commission, p. 17.
de Mooij, R. and Ederveen, S. (2003) "Taxation and foreign direct investment: a synthesis of empirical research", *International Tax and Public Finance*, 10, p. 23.
Deloitte (2009) "EU project on corporate tax compliance cost", p. 83, available at http://ec.europa.eu/taxation_customs/resources/documents/common/publications/studies/ccctb/deloitte.pdf.
Deloitte (2011) *International Tax and Business Guides*, Deloitte Touche Tohmatsu.
Devereux, M.P. (2006) "Taxes in the EU new member states and the location of capital and profit", *Centre for Business Taxation*, Working paper no. 7, Oxford University, p. 5.
Devereux, M.P. and Griffith, R. (1999) "The taxation of discrete investment choices", *Institute for Fiscal Studies*, Working paper no. 16, pp. 40–46.
Devereux, M.P. and Loretz, S. (2008) "Increased efficiency through consolidation and formula apportionment in the European Union?", *Centre for Business Taxation*, Working paper no. 12, Oxford University, pp. 1, 14–29.
Devereux, M.P. and Sørensen, P.B. (2006) "The corporate income tax: international trends and options for fundamental reform", *Economic Papers*, 264, Directorate-General for Economic and Financial Affairs, European Commission, pp. 69–71.
Devereux, M.P., Elschner, C., Endres, D. and Spengel, C. (2009) *Effective Tax Levels* (Centre for European Economic Research: Mannheim and Oxford), p. 2.
Directorate-General Taxation and Customs Union (10.12.2004) "General tax principles", Working Document of CCCTB WG, Brussels, pp. 3–5.

Directorate-General Taxation and Customs Union (26.06.2006) "Personal scope of the CCCTB", Working Document of CCCTB WG, Brussels, p. 3.
Directorate-General Taxation and Customs Union (13.11.2007) "CCCTB: possible elements of the sharing mechanism", Working Document of CCCTB WG, Brussels, p. 13.
Directorate-General Taxation and Customs Union (27.03.2008) "Various detailed aspects of the CCCTB", Working Document of CCCTB WG, Brussels, p. 4.
Edwards, C. and Rugy, V. (2002) "International tax competition: A 21st-century restraint on government", *Policy Analysis*, no. 431, Cato Institute, pp. 21–22.
Elschner, C. and Vanborren, W. (2009) "Corporate effective tax rates in an enlarged European Union", *Taxation Papers*, Working paper no. 14, Directorate-General Taxation and Customs Union, European Commission, pp. 8–19.
Ernst and Young (2009) "Survey of the implementation of Council Directive 90/434/EEC", pp. 14–17, available at http://ec.europa.eu/taxation_customs/resources/documents/taxation/company_tax/mergers_directive/study_impl_direct.pdf.
Ernst and Young (2010) "Global transfer pricing survey: addressing the challenges of globalization", pp. 5–13, available at http://www.ey.com/Publication/vwLUAssets/2010-Global-Transfer-Pricing-Survey/$FILE/2010-Global-Transfer-Pricing-Survey.pdf.
EUROCHAMBRES (10.01.2007) "Company taxation – complement the freedoms of the Single Market to foster the growth of European businesses" – Position Paper, pp. 3–4, http://www.eurochambres.eu/DocShare/Common/GetFile.asp?PortalSource=692&DocID=661&mfd=off&pdoc=1, date accessed 1 December 2011.
European Commission (12.02.1969) "Commission memorandum to the Council on the co-ordination of economic policies and monetary co-operation within the Community", COM(69)150, Brussels.
European Commission (23.07.1975) "Proposal for a Council Directive concerning the harmonization of systems of company taxation and of withholding taxes on dividends", COM (75)392 final, Brussels.
European Commission (23.04.1980) "Proposal for a Council Directive on the common system of taxation applicable to mergers, divisions and contributions of assets occurring between companies of different member states", COM(80)203 final, Brussels.
European Commission (13.04.1988) "Europe 1992: The overall challenge (Summary of the Cecchini Report)", SEC(88)524 final, Brussels, p. 9.
European Commission (1992) "Report of the committee of independent experts on company taxation (Ruding Report)", Luxembourg, pp. 69–120.
European Commission (22.10.1996) "Taxation in the European Union: report on the development of tax systems", COM(96)546, Brussels, pp. 8–13.
European Commission (01.10.1997) "Towards tax co-ordination in the European Union – A package to tackle harmful tax competition", COM(97)495, Brussels, pp. 2–5.
European Commission (07.06.2000) "A strategy to improve the operation of the VAT system within the context of the internal market", COM(2000)348, Brussels.

European Commission (23.10.2001a) "Towards an Internal Market without tax obstacles. A strategy for providing companies with a consolidated corporate tax base for their EU-wide activities", COM(2001)582 final, Brussels, pp. 4–11.
European Commission (23.10.2001b) "Company taxation in the internal market" – Commission Staff Working Paper, SEC(2001)1681, Brussels, pp. 223–267.
European Commission (20.10.2003a) "Review and update of VAT strategy priorities", COM(2003)614, Brussels, p. 20.
European Commission (24.11.2003b) "An Internal Market without company tax: obstacles achievements, ongoing initiatives and remaining challenges", COM(2003)726 final, Brussels.
European Commission (18.01.2005a) "Questionnaire on corporate tax as a barrier to EU expansion of small and medium-sized enterprises", Brussels.
European Commission (07.11.2005b) "Proposal for a code of conduct on transfer pricing documentation for associated enterprises in the EU", COM(2005)543 final, Brussels, pp. 2–5 and 15–17.
European Commission (23.12.2005c) "Tackling the corporation tax obstacles of small and medium-sized enterprises in the Internal Market – outline of a possible Home State Taxation pilot scheme", COM(2005)702 final, Brussels, pp. 8–11, 13–24 and 39–63.
European Commission (19.12.2006a) "Coordinating member states' direct tax systems in the internal market", COM(2006)823 final, Brussels.
European Commission (19.12.2006b) "Tax treatment of losses in cross-border situations", COM(2006)824, Brussels pp. 8–10.
European Commission (02.05.2007a) "Implementing the community programme for improved growth and employment and the enhanced competitiveness of EU business: further progress during 2006 and next steps towards a proposal on the Common Consolidated Corporate Tax Base (CCCTB)", COM(2007)223 final, Brussels, pp. 10–11.
European Commission (26.02.2007b) "Communication from the Commission to the Council, the European Parliament and the European Economic and Social Committee on the work of the EU Joint Transfer Pricing Forum in the field of dispute avoidance and resolution procedures and on Guidelines for Advance Pricing Agreements within the EU", COM(2007)71, Brussels, pp. 5–7.
European Commission (15.09.2008) "Report from the Commission to the Council in accordance with Article 18 of Council Directive 2003/48/EC on taxation of savings income in the form of interest payments", COM(2008)552 final, Brussels.
European Commission (2009) "Report from the Commission to the Council in accordance with Article 8 of Council Directive 2003/49/EC on a common system of taxation applicable to interest and royalty payments made between associated companies of different Member States", COM(2009)179, Brussels, p. 10.
European Commission (2010) "Legislative proposal for a Common Consolidated Corporate Tax Base (CCCTB)" – Roadmap, version no. 2, Brussels, pp. 7–8.
European Commission (16.03.2011a) "Proposal for a Council Directive on a Common Consolidated Corporate Tax Base (CCCTB)", COM(2011)121/4, Brussels, pp. 15–16, 22, 35, 39–40, 46–47 and 64.

European Commission (16.3.2011b) "Summary of the impact assessment. Accompanying document to the Proposal for a Council directive on a Common Consolidated Corporate Tax Base (CCCTB)", Commission Staff Working Document, SEC(2011) 316 final, Brussels, pp. 4–7.

European Commission (16.3.2011c) "Impact assessment. Accompanying document to the Proposal for a Council directive on a Common Consolidated Corporate Tax Base (CCCTB)", Commission Staff Working Document, SEC(2011) 315/2, Brussels, p. 6.

European Commission – Taxation and Customs Union (2011) "Taxation trends in the European Union. Data for the EU Member States, Iceland and Norway", pp. 130, 300–301, 362, 398.

European Parliament (16.01.2008) "European Parliament resolution of 15 January 2008 on Tax treatment of losses in cross-border situations" (2007/2144(INI)), Strasbourg.

European Parliament (2011a) "Reasoned opinion by the House of Representatives of the Kingdom of the Netherlands on the proposal for a Council Directive on a Common Consolidated Corporate Tax Base (CCCTB)", Strasbourg.

European Parliament (2011b) "Reasoned opinion by the House of Commons of the United Kingdom of Great Britain and Northern Ireland on the proposal for a Council Directive on a Common Consolidated Corporate Tax Base (CCCTB)", Strasbourg.

European Parliament (2011c) "Reasoned opinion by Dáil Éireann of the Republic of Ireland on the proposal for a Council directive on a Common Consolidated Corporate Tax Base (CCCTB)", Strasbourg.

European Parliament (2011d) "Reasoned opinion by the House of Representatives of the Republic of Malta on the proposal for a Council Directive on a Common Consolidated Corporate Tax Base (CCCTB)", Strasbourg.

European Parliament (2011e) "Reasoned opinion by the Riksdag of the Kingdom of Sweden on the proposal for a Council Directive on a Common Consolidated Corporate Tax Base (CCCTB)", Strasbourg.

European Parliament (2011f) "Reasoned opinion by the Sejm of the Republic of Poland on the proposal for a Council directive on a Common Consolidated Corporate Tax Base (CCCTB)", Strasbourg.

European Parliament (2011g) "Reasoned opinion by the National Council of the Slovak Republic on the proposal for a Council Directive on a Common Consolidated Corporate Tax Base (CCCTB)", Strasbourg.

European Parliament (2011h) "Reasoned opinion by the Chamber of Deputies of Romania on the proposal for a Council Directive on a Common Consolidated Corporate Tax Base (CCCTB)", Strasbourg.

European Parliament (2011i) "Reasoned opinion by the National Assembly of the Republic of Bulgaria on the proposal for a Council Directive on a Common Consolidated Corporate Tax Base (CCCTB)", Strasbourg.

Faria, A. (1995) *Tax Policy Handbook. Tax Coordination and Harmonization* (International Monetary Fund: Washington), pp. 228–230.

Fuest, C., Hemmelgarn, T. and Ramb, F. (2006) "How would formula apportionment in the EU affect the distribution and the size of the corporate tax base? An analysis based on German multinationals", *Discussion Paper, Series 1: Economic Studies*, no. 20, Deutsche Bundesbank, pp. 19–20.

Gammie, M., Giannini, S., Klemm, A., Oestreicher, A., Parascandolo, P. and Spengel, C. (2005) *Achieving a Common Consolidated Corporate Tax Base in the EU* (Centre for European Policy Studies: Brussels), pp. 23–65.

Ghislain, J. (2002) "Transfer pricing: The EC arbitration convention as a dispute resolution mechanism", *International Tax Journal*, 28(2), p. 47

Grau, P. and Herrera, P.M. (2003) "The link between tax coordination and tax harmonization: limits and alternatives", *EC Tax Review*, 12(1), p. 30.

Griffith, R. and Klemm, A. (2004) "What has been the tax competition experience of the last 20 years?", *Institute for Fiscal Studies*, Working papers no. 4, pp. 14 and 28.

Hellerstein, W. and McLure, Ch. E. Jr. (2004) "The European commission's report on company income taxation: what the EU can learn from the experience of the US states", *International Tax and Public Finance*, 11, pp. 211–215.

Hemmelgarn, T. and Nicodème, G. (2009) "Tax co-ordination in Europe: assessing the first years of the EU-savings taxation directive", *Taxation Papers*, Working paper no. 18, Directorate-General Taxation and Customs Union, European Commission, p. 26.

Huizinga, H., Laeven, L. and Nicodème, G. (2007) "Capital structure and international debt-shifting", *IMF Working Paper*, 39, p. 4.

Infanti, A. (2002) "Spontaneous tax coordination: on adopting a comparative approach to reforming the U.S. international tax regime", *Vanderbilt Journal of Transnational Law*, 35, pp. 1128 and 1133.

IPEX (2011) "Information on parliamentary scrutiny", http://www.ipex.eu/IPEXL-WEB/dossier/dossier.do?code= CNS&year= 2011&number= 0058, date accessed on 3 December 2011.

International Bureau of Fiscal Documentation (1963), "The Neumark Report", Amsterdam, unofficial translation by Dr. H. Thurston.

James, S. (2000) "Can we harmonize our views on European tax harmonization?", *Bulletin for International Fiscal Documentation*, 54(6), p. 263.

James, S. and Oats, L. (1998) "Tax harmonization and the case of corporate taxation", *Revenue LJ*, 8, p. 9.

Janeba, E. and Schjelerup, G. (2002) "Why Europe should love tax competition – and the U.S. even more so", *NBER Working Paper*, 9334, p. 6.

Jesper, J. and Svensson, P. (2004) *Economic Effects of Tax Cooperation in an Enlarged European Union: Simulations of Corporate Tax Harmonization and Savings Tax Coordination* (Copenhagen Economics: Copenhagen), pp. 18–25, 39 and 62.

Kopits, G. (1992) "Overview", in *Tax Harmonization in the European Community: Policy Issues and Analysis* (International Monetary Fund: Washington), p. 3.

Lanno, K. and Levin, M. (2002) *An EU Company Without an EU Tax? A Corporate Tax Action Plan for Advancing the Lisbon Process* (Centre for European Policy Studies: Brussels), p. 3.

Matei, G. and Pirvu, D. (2010a) "Premises in implementing the common consolidated tax base system", *Theoretical and Applied Economics*, 2(543), p. 112.

Matei, G. and Pirvu, D. (2010b) "Controversies regarding the corporate tax harmonization trend in the European Union", *Theoretical and Applied Economics*, 8(549), p. 29.

Matei, G. and Pirvu, D. (2011) "Transfer pricing in the European Union", *Theoretical and Applied Economics*, 4(557), pp. 104–106.

Mitchell, J.A. (2001) "Tax competition primer: why tax harmonization and information exchange undermine America's competitive advantage in the global economy", *The Heritage Foundation Backgrounder*, 1460, p. 2.

Moore, P. and Ruane, F. (2005) "Taxation and the financial structure of foreign direct investment", *Institute for International Integration Studies Discussion Paper*, 88, Trinity College Dublin, p. 7.

Negrescu, D. and Comanescu, A. (2007) *Trends in EU Tax Harmonization: Challenges for Romania*, Project SPOS 2007 – Strategy and Policy Studies, Study no. 5 (European Institute of Romania: Bucharest), pp. 14, 46, 61–63 and 73.

Oates, W.E. (1993) "Fiscal decentralization and economic development", *National Tax Journal*, 46(2), pp. 237–243.

OECD (1998) "Harmful tax competition – an emerging global issue", available at http:// oecd.org/dataoecd/33/1/1904184.pdf.

OECD (2000) "Towards global tax co-operation", available at www.oecd.org/dataoecd/25/27/44430257.pdf.

OECD (2008) *Model Convention on Income and on Capital*, 2008, p. 47, available at http://www.oecd.org/dataoecd/14/32/41147804.pdf.

OECD (2009) "A progress report on the jurisdictions surveyed by the OECD global forum in implementing the internationally agreed tax standard", available at www.oecd.org/dataoecd/38/14/42497950.pdf.

OECD (2010a) *Transfer Pricing Guidelines for Multinational Enterprises and Tax Administrators* (OECD Publishing), pp. 59–105.

OECD (2010b) "Promoting transparency and exchange of information for tax purposes" (OECD Publishing), p. 2.

Oestreicher, A. and Spengel, C. (2007) "Tax harmonisation in Europe: the determination of corporate taxable income in the EU member dtates", *ZEW Discussion Paper*, 035, pp. 27–34.

Osterloh, S. and Heinemann, F. (2009) "The political economy of corporate tax harmonization – why do European politicians (dis)like minimum tax rates?", *Conference Papers: Reflections on Fiscal Federalism: Elaborating the Research Agenda*, 30–31 October 2009, pp. 16 and 31–32.

Patterson, B. and Martinez Serrano, A. (2000) "Tax coordination in the European Union", *Economic Affairs Series*, Working Paper no. 125, Directorate-General for Research, European Parliament, pp. 4–5.

Portugal, M. (5.07.2007) "Long-term fiscal sustainability: recent advances and future challenges" – opening speech at the seminar of IMF Office in Europe, Paris, http://www.imf.org/external/np/speeches/2007/070507.htm, date accessed 15 July 2011.

PricewaterhouseCoopers (2008) "Impact of corporate income tax reforms at the EU level on European business taxpayers. Report on the impact on taxable profits", pp. 7–27, available at http://ec.europa.eu/taxation_customs/resources/documents/common/publications/studies/ccctb/pwc_taxable.pdf.

PricewaterhouseCoopers (2010) "Transfer pricing perspectives", p. 71, available at http://www.pwc.com/en_GX/gx/transfer-pricing-management-strategy/pdf/pwc-tp-perspectives-resolutions-10-cee-offices.pdf.

Rounds, T. (1992) "Tax harmonization and tax competition: contrasting views and policy issues in three federal countries", *Journal of Public Administration Research and Theory*, 22, p. 24.

Schratzenstaller, M. (2005) "Company tax co-ordination in an Enlarged EU", paper submitted for the *Second Euroframe Conference on Economic Policy Issues in the European Union* "Trade, FDI and Relocation: Challenges for the EU?", Vienna, 3 June 2005, p. 36, available at http://www.euroframe.org/fileadmin/user_upload/euroframe/docs/2005/session5/eurof05_schratzenstaller.pdf.
Sørenson, P.B. (2006) "Can capital income taxes survive? And should they?", *CESifo Working Paper Series*, 1793, CESifo Group Munich, pp. 3–11.
Spengel, C., Oestreicher, A., Elschner, C., Reister, T., Ernst, C., Grünewald, M., Finke, K., Prassel, J. and Cui, L. (2008) *Study on the Impact of Reforms of Corporate Income Taxation Systems at the EU Level on the Size of the Tax Bases of the EU Companies, Using the Model "European Tax Analyzer"* (Centre for European Economic Research: Mannheim and Göttingen), pp. 36–37.
Talpos, I. and Crasneac, A. (2010) "The effects of tax competition", *Theoretical and Applied Economics*, 8(549), pp. 39–40.
Tiebout, C. (1956) "A pure theory of local expenditures", *The Journal of Political Economy*, 64(5), pp. 416–424.
Trovato, M. (2007) "The threat of fiscal harmonization", *Liberales Institut Paper*, p. 2, available at http://www.steuerwettbewerb.ch/papers/Massimiliano-Trovato-The-Threat-of-Fiscal-Harmonization.pdf.
Tulai, C. and Serbu, S. (2005) *Comparative Taxation and Tax Harmonization* (Publishing House of Science Book: Cluj-Napoca), p. 133.
UEAPME (8 April 2008) "Taxation rules a key barrier to cross-border trade for SMEs" – Press Release, http://www.ueapme.com/docs/press_releases/pr_2008/080407_tax_forum.pdf, date accessed 1 December 2011.
UEAPME (16 February 2011) "Common tax base good in principle but EU plans are too complex" – Press Release, http://www.ueapme.com/IMG/pdf/110316_pr_CCCTB.pdf, date accessed 1 December 2011.
UNCTAD (2010) *World Investment Report*, p. 7, available at http://www.unctad.org/templates/Download.asp?docid=13423&lang=1&intItemID=2068.
Ussher, K. (2000) *The Spectre of Tax Harmonization* (Centre for European Reform: London), pp. 9–10.
van den Tempel, A.J. (1970) *Impôt sur les sociétés et impôt sur le revenu dans les Communautés européennes* (EUR-OP: Luxembourg), pp. 11–30.
van der Horst, A., Bettendorf, L. and Rojas-Romagosa, H. (2007) "Will corporate tax consolidation improve efficiency in the EU?", *Tinbergen Institute Discussion Paper*, 76, p. 31.
Vanborren, W., Cattoir, P., Neale, T. and Pillet, P. (2004) "European tax survey", *Taxation Papers*, Working paper no. 3, Directorate-General Taxation and Customs Union, European Commission, pp. 5 and 23–37.
Vrijburg, H. and de Mooij, R. (2010) "Enhanced cooperation in an asymmetric model of tax competition", *CESifo Working Paper Series*, 2915, CESifo Group Munich, pp. 31–32.
Weichenrieder, A. (2007) "Profit shifting in the EU: evidence from Germany", *CESifo Working Paper*, 2043, CESifo Group Munich, p. 21.
Wilson, J.D. (1999) "Theories of tax competition", *National Tax Journal*, 52(2), pp. 289–291.
Zodrow, G. and Mieszkowski, P. (1986) "Pigou, Tiebout, property taxation, and the underprovision of local public goods", *Journal of Urban Economics*, 19(3), pp. 356–370.

Index